SOME
HIDDEN
THUNDER

Brenda Despontin

First published 2024
by Rowanvale Books Ltd
The Gate
Keppoch Street
Roath
Cardiff
CF24 3JW
www.rowanvalebooks.com

The abuse of convicts on the ships and in the penal colony might upset some readers.
The novel is probably best suited for adults and older teenagers. It has some references to violence, and implied sexual activity in the Van Diemen's Land section. John Frost wrote about these abuses so they should be referenced, albeit subtly.

A CIP catalogue record for this book is available from the British Library.
ISBN: 978-1-83584-027-6
Ebook ISBN: 978-1-83584-026-9

For the courageous men and women, in every age and country, who challenge tyranny and oppression in the quest for a better world.

Contents

"Is there not
Some hidden thunder in the stores of heaven,
Red with uncommon wrath, to blast the men
Who owe their greatness to their neighbour's ruin?"

—John Frost, *Letter to Prothero postscript,*
1821

Beginnings

"I am a part of all that I have met."

Tennyson, *Ulysses*

"What's that you're scribbling, lass?"

The old man had been watching his daughter for some time. She sat hunched over the yellowing paper, light fading outside and the fire dying. But she did not respond, not even when he tapped his pipe against the grate.

"You'll be needing some light," he said, more to himself than to her, and rose to shuffle across the room, returning to place the oil lamp near where she sat. It lit her pale face, and he noticed faint traces of grey along the parting in her hair. Once, she could have been pretty, but now her scowl was almost permanent, and she had an annoying, unattractive habit of chewing her lip as she was currently doing. She did not endear herself easily to strangers.

Silence. More scowling.

The smell of burning oil. The scratching of her pen.

The old man tried again. "What's so important, lass? You'll ruin your eyes if you don't stop soon. It's black as hell outside."

Startled, she looked up as if previously unaware of his presence.

"People should know, Father."

"Know what?" He heard his sharpness, but had lately lost patience with this tendency of hers to be evasive.

The woman hesitated a while, and the clock measured the awkwardness between them. She was so afraid he would disapprove or, worse still, laugh at her ambitions, but eventually, almost inaudibly, she whispered, "Your story. I want to tell your story."

This was Anne, his youngest. Barely out of childhood when they took him away and a woman when he returned, she had nursed his beloved Mary in those final years, and now was here, uncomplaining, his only companion.

And she wanted to record his life.

The old man raised himself slowly out of his chair. His last fall had left him with daily pain in his hip, but he preferred not to mention it. He had suffered far worse.

He placed a hand on her shoulder and she flinched. Why had he always found physical affection so difficult with his children? he wondered, and he quickly moved his hand away to wipe his forehead. "I'd do it myself, lass. God knows, I've wanted to since I came home… but these eyes of mine… even in daylight I struggle. And you're right. It's a story that needs a telling…"

He limped to his room and opened an old wooden chest. From it, he brought out bundles of letters, some tied carefully with silk ribbon, others with fine leather threads. He handed her piles of yellowing newspaper and several leather journals. She recognised his distinctive writing and, flicking through the entries, read, *"London 1805… Newport 1835… Van Diemen's Land 1845… San Francisco 1854… New York 1855."* They were stuffed with documents, pamphlets, tickets, letters.

A patchwork of his life.

He was disappointed when she showed no response. "You'll find much of what you need somewhere in all this," he said, sweeping an arm over the documents. "And the rest is still here." Smiling, he tapped his forehead. "It may not be long before I meet my maker, Anne, but this old memory's not gone yet."

She still looked sour.

"I don't want to write a history book, Father," she said suddenly, "nor a political treatise. Left to you, I fear that is what would happen. A good story, even one such as yours based on fact, has to trap a reader so he never wants to put it down. It must absorb you so that it becomes your world, should keep you from your work, your food, your family and hold you in thrall late into the night. Silently, insidiously, it makes escape impossible, and the reader is soon like this little chap." She used her pen to point at an insect caught in the fine web spanning the corner of the grate, and flicked it away with her shawl. Then, her confidence growing, she added, "Too many dull facts will soon bore a reader… and besides, memory – yours included, Father – can be a fickle mistress…"

Her outburst surprised him, but he suspected she was right, and was relieved she had chosen to take on such a challenge, before it was too late. "I suspect there will be gaps where neither my memory nor my journals can give you the answers you seek, so then you will have to use… what shall we call it… some credible creativity? What I'm doing, Anne, is giving you the canvas and the brushes," he said softly, placing the last pile of letters on her desk. "But you must paint the picture for yourself." He paused, then added with a smile, "And I won't object to a little colour in places."

Of the material before her, one sheet in particular caught her eye. It was a set of notes scribbled in New York by her sister Catharine. Anne ran her fingers over the familiar signature. Catharine, the clever one, the pretty one, always confident and razor-like in her arguments when their father's radical friends came to smoke in the parlour, charismatic men with dangerous ideas, men like Henry Vincent. Catharine, the courageous one, who sailed alone to be with their father in Van Diemen's Land, then on with him to America. Catharine, the favourite.

But they had not heard from her in many months, and then only a brief note to tell them she was well. Always an integral part in this man's tale, always the one whose name made him smile, his favourite would not be the one to tell it.

This, finally, was Anne's time.

NEWPORT
May 1784

It was cold for May. The last few stragglers huddled over the bar in the taproom of The Royal Oak, reluctant to face the night air. When the baby's cry broke their silence, the publican paused briefly as he wiped the bar, looked upwards towards the room above, and shook his head.

"We celebrating?" A toothless old sailor shook his empty pot expectantly.

"Piss off!" grunted the landlord. "And clear out. Go home… all of you."

As the men shuffled towards the door, the woman who helped behind the bar came downstairs. She had gone to assist the landlady, whose labour had started during the evening's busy hours, but had barely had time to wipe beery hands on a filthy apron before the baby was there, small but breathing.

"It's a boy," she said, and proceeded to sweep up the sawdust as she did every night.

"And my wife?" the landlord muttered, still gathering pots from the tables.

"Tired… but she'll live," the woman replied. "You need to let her rest though." She hesitated by the bar as he emptied the cash box. "Any chance of a little extra something for my services tonight?" His look was answer enough. "What about a nip against the cold then?"

He poured her a small brandy which she devoured in one gulp, then she wrapped a ragged shawl around her scrawny shoulders and bade the landlord goodnight.

It was another hour before he climbed the bare wooden staircase to his rooms. He found his wife sitting up in their bed, her newborn at her breast. In the dark corners of the room, acrid now from the stale smell of blood and sweat, the ghosts of other babies, long dead.

"I've brought you some ale," he said, placing the jug by her bed. She looked pale, he thought, and her grey hair belied her years. "We'll call him John," he added, then returned to the bar below to spend the night on a bench and let his wife rest.

He had not once looked at the child.

***

When he tried in old age to recall those early years, John Frost struggled to separate memories he thought were real from the truths he was told later. He remembered the smells: stale beer, urine, the chickens he was sent to feed in the yard behind the bar, the pungent sweat of working men with blackened fingernails who frequented the taproom. He remembered the feel of straw under his bare feet, and the brass spittoons from which he was expected to clean the blood-flecked phlegm of wheezy sailors, dock men and miners. He recalled card games with hard-drinking boys just a few years older, already worn down by relentless labour around the docks, and how the taproom would fall silent when Tomos Hughes, the undertaker's son, brought in a newspaper, often a few days old. Revered because he knew his letters, Tomos never needed to pay for his ale, but would read haltingly column after column as the men crowded round him and sipped in silence. Tales of a newly rebuilt theatre at Covent Garden for plays by Shakespeare, of Nelson losing an eye in Corsica, of trials for treason, and of a man called Tom Paine. Tales from another world.

Of his father, John held no clear memories at all, but had heard he was a sickly, angry man who drank too willingly to run a public house and who seemed to hold a permanent grudge with life. "Strong drink is the wine of wickedness" were the earliest words John recognised, looming large on the sign above the bar. As an old man, closing his eyes, he could still see it, and hear his evangelical mother warning some drunken soul to mend his ways. She did so without the slightest breath of irony.

But he did recall vividly the day his mother, dressed in borrowed black, wept inconsolably as strangers came to the darkened bar to tap him on the head and say they were sorry. He remembered it particularly because, shortly afterwards, his mother took him in his Sunday best to visit his grandparents. He recalled his mother telling him to be a good boy and do what he was told, then hugging him close before disappearing across the yard. He sat outside for an hour before he realised she was not coming back.

"Come and sit over by here, John my love." He would never forget: the old cameo brooch holding the lace at her neck, the fine white hair plaited in a crown around her head, the rise and fall of the heavily accented English which she would insist they speak. His grandmother, kind and portly, offering him soup and a warm smile. By contrast, his grandfather eyed him suspiciously, grunted, and said, "I want no noise in this house, mind. You can come to watch me work tomorrow, but don't you dare disturb the customers, or I'll tan your backside."

John liked his little room under the roof. It was his refuge, his place to dream. If he stood tiptoe on the bed, he could see out of the tiny window, down to the busy docks, and could fall asleep to the rhythm of the ships' rigging at night when the wind was strong. He often dreamed of distant ports waiting for those ships now in dock. He was an imaginative child for whom the world stretched far beyond the shabby town in which he lived.

Days were spent in his grandfather's shop. There, the old man took the finest leather and shaped bespoke shoes for the gentry and their ladies. The boy glimpsed for the first time a world far from The Royal Oak, and witnessed the difference woven by wealth. He had previously seen the rough shoes and spiked boots of Newport's workers. Now he saw how the richest residents of his town treated his skilled grandfather with disdain, quibbling over every penny spent on his craftsmanship.

One day, John remembered hiding in the den he made under his grandfather's workshop table when a rich alderman entered. "My shoes ready?" the man demanded with all the arrogance of his status. Seeing the fine leather shoes on which John's grandfather had laboured for many hours, he scoffed. "These aren't anywhere near good enough. I will pay half of what you were asking, no more. Don't try to argue, mind… I'll make sure your reputation is ruined if you do. Here." And he threw some coins on to the table, slamming the door as he left.

John was furious. "The bastard!" he yelled loudly, kicking the table leg in frustration.

But his grandfather was firm: "Mind your tongue, lad. Your grandmother won't want you swearing in her house. Besides, folk like him are keeping food on our table. Never forget that."

His grandmother was more understanding, keen to help the boy accept the order of things. "There are those born rich, with fine houses and clothes," she told him one night after supper, "and there are those who are poor. It may not seem Christian or right, but people have to be careful not to stir up trouble. It wouldn't take much to encourage folk to build a guillotine on these shores too."

She taught him his letters and saw how fast he learned. He was often in deep thought, questioning her about the people in his town and how things were decided. He had a grasp of injustice way beyond his years and she knew he was destined for more than a life making shoes. She worried he had so few friends, and one day, after visiting her brother who farmed further up the valley, she returned with a puppy.

It was an unruly mongrel, and John tried for days to train it to sit, lie down or beg for leftovers. Finally in frustration he shouted,

"I'll show you who's master here," and started to hit the terrified animal with a large stick. His grandmother caught his hand before it could strike again.

"No!" He had never before heard her raise her voice. She took the stick, still shaking. "That is not the way, bachgen. Fear never breeds loyalty or obedience. Never. Let's try something else." And for the next few days, she spoke softly to the animal, massaging the top of its head. She issued great praise when it did as she desired, rewarding it with food and affection, encouraging John to do the same, until before long he had the most devoted of companions.

Years later, catching a glimpse of his reflection in the broken piece of glass which served as his mirror in Van Diemen's Land, he would touch the scars on his face and remember her fond care that time she nursed him through the boyhood illness which had left its telltale reminders.

He always believed she had taught him how to love.

***

One night, John's grandfather came in from his workshop, smelling of the leather and oils which seeped into his skin. He was clearly angry.

"That damned boy!" he spat. "I try to teach him a trade, but he refuses to listen. His head is in the clouds somewhere. Doesn't he see how lucky he is? Many's the lad who'd bite his arm off to be here, learning a proper trade."

His wife was darning, and as always, she waited before responding to her husband's outburst. "John is clever, is all," she replied without lifting her eyes to the man. "He thinks deeply about things." Then, some time later, when he was calmer and had consumed his nightly porter, she added, "I think we should send him to Bristol to school. He can board there in the week and come home at weekends to help here. What say you?"

He knew better than to argue with his wife, and besides, the local schools were of little worth. Newport was an ugly, dirty place, the rancid armpit of Wales, and the lad would be better suited in Bristol if he were ever to improve himself. Perhaps they'd instil some discipline in him there; John's view of the world was becoming dangerous.

***

A stormy channel made for an uncomfortable crossing from Newport, but when he stepped down from the cart which took him and his belongings from the quayside to the school, John could barely believe that what greeted him was a school. He had only ever seen tiny schoolrooms run by well-meaning widows, but before him now was a carved stone edifice with sombre turrets and a great oak door. It was more like a church than anything else, and just as unwelcoming. He was terrified, uprooted from all that was familiar, cast adrift. Suddenly sensing a profound loneliness, he steadied himself and tried to be strong. Didn't he love books and learning new things? Well, here at least he would find an abundance of both.

The long dormitory where he was transferring his belongings into a set of drawers by his iron bed was not empty for long. A group of loud boys, all clearly known to each other, surrounded the newcomer, bombarding him with questions.

"I say, new boy, where was your prep?"

"Does your family hunt?"

"What does your father do?"

John answered honestly, unashamedly, his naivety a magnet for their inevitable ridicule. Their laughter dissolved him.

Once again he felt the dissonance between people. From the start, he was never accepted. They called him names, laughed at his accent, ridiculed him in every way they could, with that indefinable confidence privilege buys. He would rise each day and close his eyes each night to angry frustration and isolation.

His vocabulary soared way beyond those around him, but he would hold all his life the memory of a particular English master who made him stand before the class and repeat, over and over, "Put it *here*. Put it *here!*" until any trace of Newport and a sound closer to "year" were lost. It was as if they wanted to erase his soul.

We carry the past like a shadow we cannot see but which follows us everywhere, and for John, speaking in public would remain a lifelong torment. But in his studies he was unmatched. He loved the Classics, and could write with a passion and fluency his masters admired. Grudgingly, the other boys recognised his academic superiority, and he was eventually left alone, spending hours in the solace of the silent library with its high windows and oak tables. He read voraciously, nourished by new ideas, ever more interested in law and politics.

Holidays he spent in Newport. He pottered disinterestedly around his grandfather's workshop and borrowed books from anyone likely to have something of interest. Sometimes, he would run up to St Woolos' Church at the top of Stow Hill and wait there to see the *Tredegar* sail in from Bristol, then race down to the dock to wait for his parcel of books.

"What's that about?" his grandfather asked in bewilderment after John had spent a whole day lost in the pages of one such delivery.

"This one's a favourite." John stroked the pages with reverence. "It's Blackstone's *Laws of England*."

"England! Laws of England, eh? Why would you want to read that? You need to be thinking about work, lad, and an apprenticeship, not filling your head with rubbish."

STAPLETON, BRISTOL
1876

Anne preferred to write in the morning before her father rose, before the interminable chores could interrupt her thoughts, so she often settled by the window as dawn broke, having first tickled the fire to life. Besides, it irritated her if he hovered behind her, struggling to read what she wrote. Sometimes she heard him sigh. Sometimes he would laugh quietly.

"Are you sure, Anne? Are you sure you want to write about me as a lad?" He had just finished reading the last page she had completed. "Who'll want to read about my school? And my grandmother? Isn't it better to start with the march on Newport, or the trial?"

She chewed her lip for a minute or so, then, turning to glare at him, slammed her hand on the table. "Absolutely not!"

She surprised herself. It was not in her nature to contradict her father, but this time she was adamant. "Lives don't start in the middle," she retorted, her heart pounding. "We are what we have seen, how people have treated us, what cards we have been dealt. For anyone to understand, they need background. Where it began, what shaped your path…" She softened her tone then, aware of the frail old man before her. "And I need your memories of that time."

She thought of her own life: the youngest in a house full of bigger people with older voices, struggling to be heard, always trailing behind, never consulted. Then, later, at thirteen or so, snatching half-understood snippets from the others about her father's fate. It had made her timid, afraid of her opinions, considering them of no consequence. She found argument difficult, even now when her father was so old, even when it was so important to be heard. It was easier to say nothing, to accept the views of others, so that her own became dough shaped by a stranger's hands.

But John recognised a stubborn streak when he saw one, and smiled. "Right then, lass. Let's get to it."

His memory served him well still, and he described for her with clarity the people and places from decades before, indelible tableaux that had shaped a life. He spat out venomously the names he had never forgotten of those Bristol schoolboys, their faces as clear in his mind as they were in that schoolroom a lifetime before, but he was much quieter when Anne wrote about his grandmother. Touching again the faint scars on his wrinkled face, he simply reminded his daughter to add a detail,

"My grandfather," he said. "I remember… she used to call him cariad."

CARDIFF
1800

Leaving the Bristol school for the last time, John dreaded the dull reality of apprenticeship with his grandfather, so was surprised to be called to the parlour shortly after his return. Sitting at the table with a letter open before him, his grandfather looked stern.

"Sit down, lad. I have something of importance to suggest." He took off his half spectacles and rubbed his eyes wearily before saying, "We cordwainers in Wales have a craft guild based in Cardiff. They meet in a fancy old hall. Have done for centuries, but I don't go often. Cardiff's too far, and I can't bear some of the members... pompous farts really... think they're the crach. But I do have an old friend there. We were apprenticed together, and he lives in Cardiff now. Turns out his son's a tailor, pretty good at it too. Trade's busy, so he's looking for an apprentice. What say you to that, John? Cardiff's not a grand place, but it's a start, since you don't fancy making boots here with me. You'd be on your own, mind, but somehow I think you'll enjoy that."

Two weeks later, after visiting his mother, married for some years now to a man he scarcely knew, John was seated uncomfortably on the back of a cart bound for Cardiff. Parting from his grandmother had been difficult. She waited until he was about to leave before shuffling up, shawl pulled tight.

"Stay safe, John, and promise me you'll be true to yourself. Follow your heart, because I know it's a good one. You'll find the right path, and don't ever waver from that. Pob lwc." Before hurrying away, she thrust into his hands a small parcel covered with rough cloth and secured with a single thread of his grandfather's cast-off leather.

Leaving Newport behind him, he unwrapped her gift, and smiled. It was Tom Paine's *The Rights of Man*.

***

First impressions. High expectations. But for John, nothing but disappointment. This was to be the start of his adult adventure, yet the town which greeted him was little more than a dirty, noisy smattering of cottages surrounding a few larger, ugly buildings. And water everywhere, foul-smelling rivers which served as floating dumps for carcases of dead animals, offal and detritus. He arrived as the evening mist was filtering the streets, swept in from the sea in the distance. Workers building the new harbour trudged their way home to their cottages or to the many public houses to drink away the day's wages.

He found his lodgings, a draughty room above the tailor's shop, left his meagre belongings on the bed and decided to explore a little before night fell. In a reasonable-looking hostelry near St John's Church, he ordered some bread, cheese and ale and sank into a corner. John had been used to men in drink, but this was different. The customers spoke in a dozen different tongues and were rougher, coarser than The Royal Oak regulars. Many were seafarers, swapping tales of the "raging tigers" they met in the bay next to the new harbour before their ships sailed off into the Channel. But at the next table a group of men caught his attention.

"Sentenced to death, they were," said one. "That bastard judge wanted the poor buggers dead. It ain't right, I say. A man works all his life and still can't feed his family. Bloody scandal."

"I been to Merthyr once," his companion added. "Hell itself can't be that bad, I tell you. Twenty people in one tiny house. Shit everywhere… and the stench. Christ! So many dead babies. So many sick widows. I guess those poor sods felt enough is enough."

"They won't die though." This was the third drinker. "At least not on these shores. They're off to the Colonies, which some say is an even worse sentence."

John had heard talk of the trouble in Merthyr before he left home, and suddenly felt himself clenching his fists in anger, consumed by an almost physical need to do something, devastated to feel such a sense of powerlessness.

"Treat men worse than dogs, and they will one day bite," he heard himself say aloud. "The English bastards who own the mines think they own the men too, body and soul. They deserve all they get, and get it they will, one day."

His anger surprised him, but silenced the men at the next table. One got up to go.

"I'm off. Missus'll kill me if I'm late again tonight."

"And I have a card game to win," said the second, grabbing his cap.

The third, an Irishman from his accent, finished his drink, then turned to John and whispered, "Watch your words, son. We live in dangerous times. Careful who you trust, or you'll be on a sea voyage sooner than you think."

***

The Cardiff tailor was a jovial, kind fellow who enjoyed a chance to share his trade and his passion with an intelligent, willing learner. And learn John did – everything he could about fabrics and cut, fashion and sales. The Bristol schoolroom had provided John with an ease of phrase and manner, making him popular with the customers. He could flatter the gentlemen, the clergy and the aldermen seeking to display their importance in the growing town. He could charm the ladies, the doctors' wives and daughters, the wealthy widows, into choosing a more expensive fabric or enough for two new dresses not one. His grandfather was quietly proud to receive a letter from his friend some months after John left home, with news that the tailor was delighted with his new protégé.

The tailor had a son, Charlie, a few years older than John, good-humoured like his father and destined soon to join the navy. He took John to see the new Custom House in the bay, and showed him the leviathan coal barges on the Churchill Way canal, their cargo heading far beyond Wales.

"Trust me, John." Charlie said after one such visit. "This place is about to become famous all over the world. Couple of years and you won't recognise it."

John laughed, but saw for himself the offices being built of a new printing press, the first bank opening and the novelty of the town's first coffee shop. Maybe there was something in his friend's prophecy, but it was mightily difficult to believe.

Once, after an evening when they both lost badly at the town's cockpit, Charlie took John to a public house near the quay, down an alley where they were forced to step over ragged figures in the darkness, gagging against the putrid smell of rotting meat and faeces.

"Let's have some fun," his friend urged.

Her name was Rose, and she couldn't have been much older than John's sixteen years but looked weary with life already. She took him to a sad little room above the bar and whispered affection as she took control, experienced beyond her years. It was quick, primitive and barely human, but he appreciated her kindness as he stumbled into manhood.

Throwing some coins on her bed after it was over, he stepped on a crude wooden toy he hadn't spotted before. Outside, John almost fell over an old woman seated on the stairs, wrapped in a coarse blanket and nursing a baby. He walked back to his lodgings unable to rid his mind of the girl's dull eyes and the old woman's knowing grin.

Waiting for him was a brief note from his grandmother. The familiar smell of lavender from her writing desk.

"Come quick, John. Tadcu is very ill."

STAPLETON, BRISTOL
1876

It was as if she was being judged. Sometimes he would sit in the old, high-backed wooden chair by the fire, using its curved arms to lift his weight if he rose. Most days he would listen to what she had written, but not tonight. He wanted to read for himself.

Anne chewed her lip as he read her pages slowly, squinting whilst holding the paper to the light. A long silence followed before he said, "He died at Trafalgar, you know... Charlie, the tailor's son. Saving someone else, or so I heard. Met a friend of his father's when I lived in London, and he told me. Loved a wager, did Charlie – cockfighting and the like. Guess he took one risk too many. But I did like him, and his father was always kind to me. It was the town I couldn't bear. They say it's better now, with fancy houses and parks. But I never went back."

Later, over supper, he said, "I remembered Rose when I was in Van Diemen's Land. There were lots like her there. Girls sent away for stealing bread to feed their little ones. Some were barely out of childhood, but they made a living in the only way they could, in a place with so many lonely, desperate men. But that's for later in the tale, lass. I'm off to bed." He kissed her roughly on her cheek, and she smiled. Such gestures were rare.

So many times she doubted. After her day's chores, Anne would sit and read again the pages from the day before, altering a word here, a phrase there. She could not tell if it read well; she was too close. Oftentimes, she would tell herself it was all too much. The tale needed a cleverer mind, a better scribe. But there were no siblings to help; she doubted she would ever see Catharine again.

Each time, she would return to the waiting pages, challenged by their blank stare.

Each time, she would pick up again the threads of this man's remarkable life.

NEWPORT
1803

The cold November rain was unforgiving, horizontal, relentless. He held his grandmother close and noticed her pale skin and trembling, spotted hands. He couldn't cry, but his teeth chattered uncontrollably from an unfamiliar numbness inside him. For the first time, he saw how each death changes other lives for ever.

Mourners at the graveside in St Woolos' did not linger in the deluge but headed swiftly to The Royal Oak for something warming. John's mother had blacked out the windows and was unusually subdued, but she could never miss an opportunity, so played the perfect hostess, filling the cash box as her father's friends toasted his farewell. John remembered her anger once – he would have been eight or nine perhaps – when, on one of his visits to her, he had left a solitary customer alone in the taproom. "You keep him talking, lad!" she had scolded him, with a slap.

"What about?" John had asked.

"Whatever is his passion. Horses, ships, pigeons, dogs… you keep him talking, and buying ale."

Now, years later, as the drink flowed and people got louder, John found it all too much and turned to leave.

"John, isn't it?"

The man behind him was holding out a hand in greeting.

"My God, you've changed! Haven't seen you since you were running around here barefoot. Been an apprentice in Cardiff I hear?'

Still John couldn't quite place him. His eye was now trained to recognise expensive cloth cut well, and he saw this portly individual with balding head and large whiskers was a man of means, not one of the regulars in the place.

"William," he said by way of introduction. "William Foster. You used to call me Uncle Will."

Then John remembered, his mother's distant cousin, or so she claimed, a man of influence, property and money. John recalled the visits when he was a child, usually when no one else was around. Choice cuts of meat would appear, or fruit never seen elsewhere in Newport. And his mother giggling as "Uncle" William leant a little too close to her, running a hand up her back.

"Your mother says you've done well," the man added. "But Cardiff's no place for a young man to get on in life. Better a place in Bristol, then perhaps London, eh?"

"Well, that can't happen," replied John, suddenly cross that his newly departed grandfather's efforts were being summarily dismissed in this way. "I can't just leave, even if I wanted to. I am bound to a tailor for some time yet."

William's smile had no warmth. "You leave that to me, lad. I know people." John followed the other man's gaze to the opposite side of the room, where the tailor's father was in conversation with a few other cordwainers who had come to pay their respects to a fellow guildsman. "And some of them owe me…"

John had no reason to disbelieve him, and sat in a quiet corner listening as his future took shape.

STAPLETON, BRISTOL
1876

Her father was sitting in the dark, and she jumped when she saw him there.

"Sorry, lass. Didn't mean to scare you. Lost in my thoughts is all."

He was holding something in his hands, weaving it through his fingers, round and round. She turned up the lamp and saw it was a long, thin piece of rough leather, one of those which he had used to tie some of his notes together. Like the thread he had worn around his wrist for the twenty years since his return.

"It's from my grandfather's workshop," he said, reading her thoughts." It's all I have left of the miserable old bugger."

"I think you're wrong about him," she said after a while. "In his way, I'm sure he loved you."

He snorted. "And where in all this," he asked, gesturing to the papers around the chair, "did you get that impression?"

"He saw who you were, and he let you go." She turned on her way out to the kitchen. "He set you free."

BRISTOL
1804

John was never quite sure how the deal had been done but, freed from Cardiff and the tailor, he was once again in Bristol, this time to take up employment with a woollen-draper in Bridge Street.

He noticed the difference in the place immediately. The dock itself was bigger and noisier. There was an air of prosperity and an exotic mix of people and language. He would watch the ships arrive from Spain and Portugal carrying the fortified wines for sale at William Parry's in Denmark Street. He came to know that place well, since the merchant and his partner Thomas Urch were regular customers of the draper. As an old man, he remembered often seeing a small boy running around the warehouse there: the young John Harvey, who would later give the famous Bristol sherry its name.

He heard in the hostelries the local tales of press-ganged men who had been sent off to fight "Old Boney" when Bristol was threatened with invasion, and once, when he was sent to deliver wool to the warden at Stapleton Gaol, he glimpsed in the yard the few remaining French prisoners, a raggle-taggle bunch with dead eyes and a dejected mien.

Older now, John settled quickly to the new surroundings, worked hard and was well regarded by his new employer, another of his "uncle's" many contacts. Several months after his arrival, he was surprised by a visit from William Foster himself.

"Aren't you going to congratulate me, John?" he asked. "You're looking at the new Mayor of Newport." And sneering with pride, he dusted some of the journey's debris from his fine outer coat. They were dining at an inn John could never normally afford.

"I'm here today in the city on business, John," he explained. "But I told your mother I'd stop by. I have another proposition you might like…" He stopped to swig from the wine he had poured liberally into his cup. "There's a merchant tailor friend of mine in London… growing concern… all sorts of rich customers. He's interested in you. It's the place to be, John – London. You'll never look back."

What the older man could not have known was that sitting on the small table in John's lodgings was a copy of Cobbett's *Political Register*, picked up quite by chance the previous Saturday. Someone had left it in a local hostelry and it was a few weeks old, but John was transfixed by the newspaper's radical ideas. They stirred something, articulating the disconnect and hurt he had carried for years, born in his grandfather's shop and honed in a schoolroom in this city.

He had learnt that London housed groups of such radicals, keen to change the way of things. This offer from Foster seemed to be the signpost he was seeking, and by the meal's end, the next stage of his journey was decided.

STAPLETON, BRISTOL
1876

The winter was bitter that year, and a chill sent John to his bed. In the autumn, because she knew he always loved the smell, Anne had collected the pale husks of lavender from their garden and nestled them gently into linen bags made from one of her mother's petticoats. She placed one or two under her father's pillow and tenderly wiped his clammy forehead with cool water. "I've made you this," she whispered, offering him warm honey and lemon dissolved with cloves and cinnamon. He thought once, when the fever raged, that he was back in Newport with his grandmother nursing him, and he held his daughter's hand, each of them weeping silently.

Whenever he slept, she continued to write, untying the bundles of documents and reading the newspapers and journals, stepping back to his life, to a father she had never really known. And she began to understand him now – what had driven him to endanger them all, to lose his liberty for so long. She began to glimpse what it was that Catharine had found to be so compelling that it took her to the other side of the world.

She was here now in his London years, few in number perhaps but transformational. Amongst the papers she found a bundle tied meticulously and bearing names she had not encountered before. Records from the past clearly not in her father's hand. She waited till he woke and, seeing he was brighter than he had been for several days, asked, "Who was Francis Place? I've never heard you speak of him, father. These papers seem to be from him."

John's grey eyes smiled in recognition of the name. "I haven't thought of Francis in years," he replied. "Ah, now he was a *real* character... a hoarder who kept everything from those radical days in London – letters, papers, pamphlets. You might think I hoarded stuff, but he was a true fanatic. Drafted the first Charter, you know… some forty years ago now. When he died his family sent that bundle to your mother for safekeeping, and she kept them with my own journals and all the letters I wrote to her across the years, hoping I would one day come back to write my story." He paused to hold again some of the pieces of his past, and said, "His was the biggest private library I had ever seen, behind his shop in Charing Cross… all the dreamers of the day – Bentham, Mill, Owen – they all met there in a maelstrom of hope and ideology. What a time that was…" And he slipped back onto his pillow.

She dipped her nib into the inkwell and began again.

LONDON
1805

The unbearable smell of excrement everywhere. A canvas of grey, dank smog which choked every living creature. This was London, home to one million souls: the overcrowded, disease-ridden, largest city in Europe. As his carriage passed through the turnpike at Hyde Park Corner and he dismounted into his new life, John felt his senses had been assaulted. There were riders on horseback, wagons, landaus and carriages in all directions. The noise was extraordinary, the streets underfoot clogged with horse dung and urine, the crowds of people loud, indifferent, overpowering.

His carriage had passed through the affluent West End with its mansions and leafy squares and he now found himself in a very different part of the city in the east, near his place of work. His lodgings, however, were clean and adequate, and his landlady affable, offering to prepare his meals. Sitting on his bed on the night he arrived, Bristol and Newport were worlds away, but in his bag he had, still wrapped in its old cloth and tied with the leather thread, his grandmother's gift, and he fell asleep reading once again the familiar words of the radical writer.

Out in the city, just as he had once done as that young boy in Cardiff, John observed what this new world presented. Old soldiers from the Napoleonic Wars rubbed shoulders with Chinese, Africans, Indians and returned colonists from North America. The expansive West India Docks, recently opened, attracted ships and sailors from across the globe, and casual manual labourers jostled for daily employment building the new East India Quay.

A city of contrasts. Wealthy merchants and city gents kept their families securely apart from the people on whose labour they depended. Elsewhere, a desperate poverty crouched unaided in poorly constructed hovels. Cattle were driven through the streets, their suffocating earthy odour mingling with the sweat of the masses. Rain would fall as liquid soot, and the gutters would overflow with floating horse dung.

Just a week after he arrived, a house near his lodgings collapsed, burying eight children and their mother. He saw working men forced to wash in the Thames, itself an open sewer, after a day's labour in the docks, because the pump at their tenement could only be turned on by the landlord for three or four hours per week. And he had never before seen "night-soil men", often labourers by day, whose task after dark was to remove excess excrement from the cesspits beneath the privy of each house. Hawkers, pickpockets, beggars and thieves everywhere: at times he wondered if he had entered a circle of Hell.

"Where are the rights of these poor souls?" he would ask himself when he witnessed the sad stratum of humanity which kept the city wheels turning.

The other young apprentices in the shop were local East London boys, coarse and loud. He went once or twice to drink with them after work, but they had their own lives. John sensed he was different, and though they were not as interminably cruel as those Bristol boys from years before, he heard them mock his accent sometimes and joke about his ideas. They would never be his friends.

His wages were slightly better now, but everything here was costly, and he sometimes spent more than he knew he should on books. He could not live without them. Smiling as he purchased some new tome, he could hear again his grandmother's voice across the miles: "If John only had a shilling left in the world, he would spend it on a book!" Never fiction, of course. He had no time for nonsense. History, philosophy, politics and law would keep him awake in his draughty room, squinting as the candle flickered.

But this was a lonely life. Sometimes he longed for the taste of his grandmother's cawl or to hear again the sound of the wind in the trees at the top of Stow Hill. Occasionally he would cross to Vauxhall Gardens to see the jugglers and bawdy singers, and once spent a week's wage on a painted companion waiting in the shadowy bushes in a lonely corner of the park.

Many times he lay at night and stared at the London sky, wondering if this was all there was. At twenty-one he had the job and independent life many back home in Newport would envy. And yet… He would scan the room in the fading light and consider his few possessions, his cherished books, and would fall asleep wondering if this was how his life would be measured. Never particularly zealous in his nonconformist views, John nevertheless questioned if there was any sort of plan he was supposed to follow, and if so, how would he know it?

The merchant tailor known to his "uncle" and for whom John worked as a shopman was Daniel Mason. Tall, wiry, balding and ambitious, he was keen to make a profit wherever he could, but he saw that John was a hard worker who knew how to exercise discretion and deference when wealthy clients called, and he soon came to trust his new employee.

"I need you to take this across town," he announced one morning to John. "It's for a tailor shop in Charing Cross. Mind you don't stay too long. There are rumours about some meetings there after hours… people of dubious ideas. Don't you be getting caught up in all that."

The shop was bigger than Mason's, and crowded when John arrived.

"Package for Mr Place," he announced to the nearest shopman.

"Put it in the back," muttered the man, scurrying off to his next customer.

John opened the oak door and stepped into an enormous library. Books wall to wall, floor to ceiling. Books on chairs, on tables, on sideboards. Newspapers piled everywhere, documents and pamphlets. He put down the parcel and glanced at the paper open on the table. He slumped into the nearest chair and started to read. It criticised a recent parliamentary decision, advocated revolt and better representation in the House.

"Anything interesting in there?"

John was startled and embarrassed. He stood and placed the pages back on the table.

"Sorry," he stuttered. "I've just come from Mason's with a parcel for Mr Place, and there was no one in the room, so I—"

"You may keep it if you like," the man interrupted, handing the paper back to John. "But you're not from London, are you? Where's home?"

John told the stranger, who sighed and shook his head. "The land of the Merthyr Rising, eh? My God, things go so badly for the poor souls struggling to live there, enslaved as they are by coal and iron while their masters get fatter and richer. It's a travesty. And something's got to change or we'll see on these shores what happened in France. Those Merthyr lads were just the start.

"I'm Francis," he added, offering his hand, "Francis Place, and this is my shop… and my library. Welcome."

John could hardly believe he was facing a London merchant not only au fait with but actually supportive of the Merthyr martyrs. "I'm John, John Frost," he replied, "currently shopman to Daniel Mason. I'm grateful for this." And he waved the paper in the older man's direction. "I've read Cobbett, but I've not seen this before." He paused. "You seem well informed about Welsh affairs."

"Look," he said. "I have a shop full of customers and can't talk now. Come back tonight around seven. I've a feeling you might enjoy yourself." And he was gone.

When John returned later, the library was full, voices competing with the smoke from pipes and the raging fire. Francis spotted him across the room and welcomed him warmly.

"There's someone you must meet," he announced, leading John through the groups of men engaged in animated discussions. "He's a John too… John Gale Jones, a Welshman like you. We call him 'Gaol Jones' because he flirts with trouble whenever he opens his mouth. But he's always got something interesting to say, even if those in power don't agree with him. He's made sure we know about what's happening in your homeland, though. You'll get on well!"

And so it was that new friendships were formed, founded on shared beliefs and a common hunger for justice, fairness and enfranchisement. John would meet them whenever he could, energised by their passion, deeply affected by the confidence and certainty of these men, by the radical nature of their ideas. Sometimes, he was so inspired, he was almost unable to breathe. During meetings they would argue whether violence was ever justified, whether revolution was possible here as it had been in France and America. And they read aloud from letters sent clandestinely from radicals abroad. Often afterwards he found he could not sleep, but would imagine a vastly different world, one in which he hoped he would find his place.

STAPLETON, BRISTOL
1876

"Your mother, she kept it all those years while I was gone," he said.

He was holding a yellowing, torn paper from sixty years before, bound carefully with his journal from those London years. "She knew about Francis Place, and the men who met behind his shop. She understood their part in my story. They changed me, Anne. It was the first time I knew who I was… and that I was not alone."

"So why not stay? Why return to Newport? If you wanted to change the way of things, it was surely better to be with the other men who thought like you, closer to Parliament and the national press? I don't understand and I can find nothing in all the documents here."

John shivered and coughed. She had noticed how frail he had become since the last chill, and she rose to wrap a warm shawl around his shoulders.

"There were two reasons," he answered after a while. "Mason wanted to move us. He'd suddenly come into a lot of money, and found a shop closer to his West End clients. It would have been impossible to get there every day from my lodgings, and I couldn't afford to pay for anything further west. Besides, I had good reason to believe Mason's money came from trading with the slave ships… Something I overheard one of the other apprentices say. Oh, he knew how to position himself, did Mason. He'd swagger off to Merchant Taylors' Hall in Threadneedle Street and ingratiate himself there with the wardens and livery men. He knew how to flatter them, to secure their confidence, but then, like the leech he was, he'd suck out the latest gossip and money-making ruses. Such a sudden increase in his wealth could only have come from one source, and it sickened me to be part of that, Anne."

"And the second reason?" She was chewing her lip again, trying to retain these details to record them later.

"A letter, out of the blue, from my mother. I'd been a year in London and she'd never written, so I knew this was important. The Royal Oak had been mine since father's death, but I had no interest. It was hers in all but name."

He rummaged through the papers lying on the footstool before him and handed her a thin piece of parchment. "I thought I still had it."

Anne read the brief missive, struggling to decipher the crude and faded handwriting:

"Dearest John,

Forgive my writing but I must urge you to come home. Your stepfather is gravely ill, and can no longer help me with the heavy lifting. Your Uncle William suggests you come back to Newport. He promises he will make it right with Mr Mason.

Do not forsake me, John.

Your loving mother."

"Loving mother indeed!" John threw down the letter as if it was infected. "I always believed afterwards that Mason had written to William Foster telling him about my supposedly 'dangerous' contacts and that it was all a ploy to get me away from that Charing Cross shop. And she..." He jabbed the letter viciously. "She was complicit in that. I never forgave her."

He looked across at his daughter. The habit she had, securing behind her ear the stray curls as she leant forward, reminded him always of Mary. His face softened, and he continued: "But it suited me, I suppose. At least I did not have to stay with Mason. Besides, things have a strange habit of working out well sometimes. At the time, it felt like a step backwards, but now I see there was a purpose to my return..."

"Not least to meet my mother," Anne added with a smile.

NEWPORT
1806

Not long after John's return to The Royal Oak his stepfather died, and John spent several months helping to manage the busy alehouse. Newport was thriving, central to the transport of the coal and iron roaring incessantly down the canals from the valleys beyond the town. The dock was expanding and local landowners were increasing in wealth and influence.

His grandmother had lived with her daughter for some years, and spending time with her made John's return to Newport a little more bearable. She wanted to hear all about London and the radical thinkers he had befriended there. She relished their nightly arguments about enfranchisement and parliamentary representation.

Then, on a grey November morning, when she failed to appear at the breakfast table, John found her as if asleep, peaceful at the last. He had never been one for outward demonstrations of emotion, but he wept now, shattered by the cold reality of her absence. They buried her with his grandfather at St Woolos' and often afterwards, John would walk up to the hilltop grave to be near her again.

John found no pleasure in this new path he was on. He hated the publican's life, and was disgusted watching his mother flirting with the men who ogled her over their beer. It was no time before she had a new suitor, and John was relieved when they announced they would wed and that the man was willing to take on the duties of landlord.

Besides, he had money now. His grandmother had made sure when she sold the cordwainer's shop that he would inherit. He had spotted a vacant store on the town's main commercial street, and made it his. There were opportunities in this town now, with its new wharf and bridge making trade and transport easy, and he'd seen in Bristol and London how moneyed people always needed fine cloth. He would use the skills learnt elsewhere to make something of himself. And so it was that "Frost, J: Provider of fine cloth and tailoring" opened in High Street.

Some weeks after the opening, he spotted a young woman eyeing a fine red cotton. He took in her dark curls, and the curve of her back. "May I help you?" he stuttered.

She turned and her dark eyes met his for just a moment too long.

"Do you have this in blue?"

He could barely speak. Years later he would say that he knew from that first moment she would be his. He barely managed a reply. "Ship's bringing some from Bristol next week... I'll put some aside if you want."

"You've met Mary, I see." A familiar voice. His "Uncle" William, taking the young woman's arm.

John hadn't seen much of William Foster since his return, just a brief greeting at his grandmother's funeral. He was a wealthy man now, with a large house in Newport and a mansion in a smart garden suburb of Cardiff. His business tentacles infiltrated every corner of commercial life, and John suspected some were less legitimate than others.

"Just popped by to see how it's all going. Splendidly by the look of things! Good for you, I say. Always knew you'd do well – and your time as an apprentice paid off, eh?"

He introduced the young woman. "Mary's my sister's girl... and these two scallywags are her offspring."

John was aware for the first time of two small children peeping at him from behind the corpulent frame in front of him. She was married! How did he not think of that? What an idiot he was!

"I'll call next week, Mr Frost," she said. "For the blue, if you'll keep some for me." Her voice was soft and she had a gentle smile. He felt such a strong connection to this stranger, and as she left the shop and turned to smile again, he knew without the slightest doubt that she felt the same.

"She's a fine filly, that one!" This was Rhys, the young clerk who helped John with the shop's finances, staring after Mary as she left.

"What's her husband do?" John tried to sound casual.

"Dead," Rhys announced. "A year or more ago, leaving her with two littluns to raise. Her uncle's been good to them, mind. He's not short of a bob or two."

She was back the next week, unchaperoned, and spent longer than was required examining the cloth John had put aside.

"I'll take it," she whispered, and for the briefest of moments, their hands touched.

"May I call on you sometime?" he asked, and she blushed.

"I'd like that very much."

He would wander with her along the riverbank to Caerleon, or into the fields around the town. Sometimes they were joined by her children, who had taken a liking to John. He in turn was surprised by how much he enjoyed having them around. When spring came, he walked with Mary up to Bettws Woods and he lay with her on a bed of bluebells, hidden from the main path.

Everywhere there were signs of new life, birdsong in the high branches and lambs on distant farms. Mary gathered some of the flowers, her hair falling forward in the sunlight, and he knew.

"I love you," he whispered, holding her close, surprised to hear himself confess into her dark curls. He had never thought himself capable of such joy.

They made love slowly and passionately, the light patterning their skin through the trees, and afterwards, as she lay with her head on his shoulder, she sang some old Welsh ballad.

"Marry me," he said and she laughed.

"What do you want with a widow and two small children? There are many fine young women with their eye on a successful businessman like you, John."

"I'm not one to take no for an answer," he replied. "And your children would be mine, you know that. Besides, I'm planning on us having lots more…"

And, laughing together, they held each other close, the scent of bluebells all around, until the evening breezes hastened them home.

STAPLETON, BRISTOL
1876

This part of the story was a revelation to her. Anne had never seen her father as a romantic. Gruff, blunt, brave, pragmatic, opinionated even, but never romantic. Yet his love for her mother had been consuming and instant. It made her realise how hard those years apart must have been for them, her mother moving away from all the political noise in Newport to be here in Stapleton with her children. She'd had to protect them, and yet somehow preserve his legacy, so had chosen not to join him on the other side of the world. Catharine had gone instead. Now, Anne regretted she and her mother had never talked about all this. Instead, they had just got on with living.

After the trial, the authorities had searched her home for any sign of sedition, to confirm John's guilt, but Mary had hidden every document so well: some with the linen, some in the chimney breast, some even in a bedpan, anywhere she could. She later wrapped up all his books and papers and tied them securely with her ribbons until she was able to unpack them safely in her new home across the Bristol Channel.

"You'd think that would have been enough for me, wouldn't you?" John had been reminiscing all afternoon, and the daylight was fading. "On that long sea journey, and many times in Van Diemen's Land, I wondered why I had risked it all. She was my only love, Anne. We were happy, blessed soon with your brothers and sisters. I had a thriving business and money in the bank... a burgess within a couple of years. People looked up to me... I knew things. I could recite the law, had read more than they and had mixed with political thinkers in London. Newport was growing and trade was good." He paused, chewed his pipe a while, then added, "But I just couldn't turn a blind eye to what I saw was wrong around me, Anne. And so much was wrong in those days."

She saw he was tired. "You need to rest," she said, "but I wanted to show you something I found in one of the bundles Mother kept."

She handed him a small green book of poems, the cover fading and the gold lettering on the front barely legible. He smiled reading the frontispiece: *Tennyson: Poems.*

"I gave her that when she agreed to marry me. She did so love all those silly verses," he laughed. "I used to tease her about them… could never see the appeal myself. But she said she'd found comfort in a particular favourite… 'Ulysses'. Do you know it?"

Anne shook her head. Her life had not held much poetry.

"You should read it. Yet another patient wife waiting for the return of an errant husband lost in some 'untraveled world'. How did it go now?" And he tried to recall Mary's voice reading the line to him…

"Ah yes I remember… *'To strive, to seek, to find and not to yield.'*"

"Look inside," said Anne.

And there, accompanying the words of Tennyson's hero, John found the flowers, pressed into the pages, shrivelled by time but still an unmistakeable blue.

***

Anne waited until he was in bed before she returned to the small table where she usually wrote. This was a difficult stage of the telling. She looked at the piles of documents in front of her, the papers, the letters and pamphlets. Here was the local announcement of the wedding in 1812, some minutes of a meeting in 1837 where he was elected town mayor. There was a newspaper detailing the attack on the Westgate. There was a cutting from *The Times* covering John's trial, and there were letters, dozens of letters, written to John by supporters from across Europe.

So much information. Too much by far for a reader coming new to this tale. She was facing a series of choices now, with no one to tell her which were the best. Knowing what to include would be critical if any future reader was to stay interested, but she could not afford to exclude details either, because somewhere in all this were the answers to her own questions: How exactly did the successful draper with a young family become a rebel charged with treason? What and who sent him spiralling to the condemned cell, then transportation?

She suddenly felt overwhelmed by the enormity of the task ahead. It was all so many years ago, and the characters were long dead. Yet she needed to search the sources carefully so as to discover who these people were – Cobbett, Henry Vincent and others. How should she include them, if at all? Besides, who would care about any of this? In reality, few knew her father still lived, and no one talked about Chartism anymore. She wondered if the task she had undertaken was beyond her. Was it worth her effort? It would be so easy to abandon it all, but her eyes rested on the little book her mother had kept all those years. It was Anne now who needed to strive, to seek and to find a way. She would not yield.

She needed a structure, a time line, a thread.

That night, Anne worked without pause, and only when she had finished did she realise how cold she was, and that the fire had long died. A pale dawn sent her to bed but she could not sleep. All these years, yet she had known so little, had not realised her father had already been to prison once *before* the riot, in Monmouth then London; that he could write so passionately; that there were so many men who saw him as their leader and saviour; that the authorities had tried hard to destroy him. That he had almost died, and more than once.

But she believed she had identified the source of John's personal grievance, one that had turned an erstwhile general discontent with authority into a deeply personal vendetta. One that was to provide the lens through which John saw every future interaction, not just with local politics but also with the wider struggle for social justice. It centred on a letter to a powerful, deeply unpopular local solicitor but started with a will. She had found fading copies of both.

Just whose will it was had initially surprised her until she saw the deep irony of it all. Yet again, the one shaping John's destiny was none other than "Uncle" William Foster.

Actions and Consequences

*"I am become a name
For always roaming with a hungry heart."*

Tennyson, *Ulysses*

NEWPORT
1820

Iron and coal had made Sir Charles Morgan a very wealthy man. The railroad crossed his estate at Tredegar Park and the levy added an annual £3000 to his already substantial coffers. He could afford the services of the best agent in the area, and Thomas Prothero, local attorney and clerk of the peace, was undoubtedly good at his job. Known locally for "sharp practices" and a ruthless pragmatism, his was a domineering presence everywhere in the area, a man who knew his own worth, who could intimidate without mercy when the need arose. As Morgan's agent, he was made. It gave him unlimited power over the landowner's tenants, who were all required to engage his service, and his alone, for all legal matters. He had many enemies, but even more very powerful friends.

It sickened John to witness the unchallenged, unelected power held by a handful of gentry and mine owners in Monmouthshire. Merthyr, Dowlais and the "top towns" of the far valleys were like feudal estates to men such as Crawshay, who owned their workers' homes, their only food store and even the public houses where pay would be handed to thirsty workers. "It's no better than the slave trade," John used to tell Mary. "They've got seven year olds down the damn mines, same age as our eldest." And he'd hold his young son close. In his hometown, ruled by the likes of Morgan and Prothero, he saw injustice at every turn. Deals were sealed over port and cigars in a gentlemen's club somewhere, and major decisions were often made far away in London by a group of unelected men no one knew or respected, and who had no one's interest at heart but their own.

And John was not alone in how he felt: in recent years the local burgesses had begun to assert themselves against those who controlled all aspects of their lives. It was that frustrated sense of powerlessness again, and they needed a voice to spread their discontent and unite them. John provided that, active on their committees, impressing them with his intelligence, clarity of vision and courage. They believed that if anyone could change things, John could.

John's fight with Prothero took a different, much more personal turn. William Foster had died, having remarried some years before to a much younger woman. There was no love lost between John and the new bride. She saw John as beneath her husband socially and John detected her influence when William Forster called his former protégé a "bumptious young radical" in public. He was quietly relieved when his "uncle" stopped calling at the shop.

But Mary had a fondness for the man, who had long promised her an inheritance after his demise. The will, however, was a complete revelation.

"She'll keep it all," Mary said, almost in disbelief. "She'll be sure not to remarry, and she'll play the merry widow, keeping us out of it. Even if she dies, it's all for my eldest two children, and in trust for me. There's nothing for your children, John, and Uncle William did everything to keep you personally away from his wealth. I am truly sorry."

"I cannot believe the man who fixed so much for me when I was a lad would be so vindictive," he admitted. "This is her doing. I'm going to see Prothero. He would have drafted the original will, because I think this is nothing but a complete fabrication."

Prothero was a short, corpulent man with a red face and a permanent sneer. He had a habit of wiping his forehead with his pocket handkerchief in an ostentatious manner to punctuate his statements.

"Why, Mr Frost!" He greeted John with a limp handshake and a sour grin. "To what do I owe this greatest of pleasures?"

"I'll come straight to it," John asserted, refusing the offer of a seat. "William Foster's will. I cannot believe it was the man's genuine wish to exclude my family and I in such a manner. He had promised my wife much, but it's his new bride who benefits. What say you, Prothero? Is this a fabrication as I suspect?"

"Leave it with me," Prothero replied. "I'll do some checking. You can trust me on this."

Weeks passed without a word from the attorney, each day fuelling John's anger and disappointment. It was as if all he had long suspected about those with power and money had now conspired against him personally. A letter written to the solicitor went unanswered, angering John even further, so, following a sleepless night, he made his way across town.

"John, my friend. Good to see you... but to what do I owe this visit? I'll not be needing a new coat just yet!" It was Sam Etheridge, Newport's printer, known locally for his radical ideas and as a scourge of the landowners.

"I want you to print this," John said. "It includes a letter to Prothero that he never had the courtesy to answer – and a few additional thoughts I have about the man!" He handed some handwritten sheets to Sam, who sat in silence whilst he read, occasionally shaking his head and sighing.

"Are you sure you know what you're starting here, my friend?" the older man asked. "This is slander, and will stir the vipers' nest if printed. You could face court... a fine... gaol."

"Won't happen," John replied with confidence. "We'll send it to Prothero first. He'll react sharpish, you'll see. He won't want any bad publicity. Wider publication won't be necessary. Besides, how can the truth be slanderous?"

"All you write here about the will and Prothero pocketing large parts of Foster's estate may indeed be true," Sam continued.

"But you need proof. And some of this is incendiary, John." He proceeded to read aloud from the letter:

"'*Beware how you rouse the lion... sleep is nearly departing from him.*' Prothero may be loathed by burgesses like you, John, but he has powerful friends hereabouts, and your threats will worry the landed folk who are only too aware of events across the Channel. Think carefully, my friend." And he read again: "'*A great part of what you've done and what you do in future shall be laid before the public... the pen is my only weapon, and I will make use of it.*'"

John had been staring out of the printer's window onto the rain-swept hills which rose above his town. He turned now to face his friend. "Print it."

But Prothero still did not respond, and the pamphlet Etheridge subsequently printed for distribution, which included John's letter, stretched to forty pages. It sold four thousand copies in days, necessitating a second printing. Prothero raged, smarting from the humiliation, but John felt invincible. Further damaging publications followed, some also critical of Sir Charles Morgan himself. A legal case looked inevitable now, with John refusing to express any regrets.

"The bastard Prothero attacked me," Sam told John two days before the trial. "In broad daylight. Said he wanted to kill me, and here's the joke... He was fined a mere shilling! They won't be so gentle with you, John, you mark my words."

Sam was taken aback by John's calm acceptance of what lay ahead. "I've been sorting my affairs," John reassured his friend, "making sure my family will be cared for, and I'm happy to serve my time in gaol – but as an insolvent debtor. It won't be too irksome, and I'm damn sure I won't apologise or retract anything. The support I've had makes me stronger, Sam. Every day voices of rebellion are getting louder across this land." He reached across to his bookcase, overflowing with all manner of volumes. "I have been reading this again. Do you know it?" And he handed Sam a copy of Burke's *Thoughts on the Cause of the Present Discontents*. It was bookmarked and a passage had been underlined by John:

"When bad men combine, the good must associate; else they will fall, one by one, an unpitied sacrifice in a contemptible struggle."

STAPLETON, BRISTOL
1876

Anne had been to the weekly market, seeking the foods her father particularly liked: fresh vegetables, eggs and soft fish. He needed coaxing to eat most days, she found, and the years in Van Diemen's Land had long left him unable to digest much beyond the blandest dishes.

When she entered the house, she found him at her desk, reading her latest pages. He was holding the copy of Etheridge's publication of that letter to Prothero, and smiled when he saw her return.

"Funny how a shabby little pamphlet from half a century ago can bring it all back," he said. "But Sam was right and I should have listened. He realised what would happen once he published this, but I was such a stubborn bugger. Thought I could outwit them, didn't I? Thought I had all the answers, when truth be told, I hadn't even worked out the damn questions!"

John sat on the settle near the fire and stared at the coals. "I was so sure I would be out of Monmouth Gaol in no time, using that 'insolvent debtor' ruse. Thought I was so clever to plan it all before the trial, but Prothero wanted none of it. There I sat cockily in my cell reading, learning French – French! – playing the confident rebel. All such pompous nonsense! I even went on spouting my vitriol about them from there... and Sam went on publishing it all. It strikes me now as sheer arrogance to write to 'The radicals of Newport', inviting them to select a local property they'd like to have as their own because the day of reckoning was coming! What was I thinking, lass? That those in power would just leave me be? What a bloody fool I was."

"You were doing what you thought was right, I suppose... seeking a fairer world." She placed a hand on his shoulder and felt the bones beneath his old jacket.

"Yes, well, that's as may be," he replied, moving his shoulder away. "But I soon learned who was in charge. Instead of releasing me, Anne, they sent me to gaol in London for six months." Then he added, more softly, "God, that place! An anteroom of hell, as bad as anything I faced later. Many times I thought I wouldn't survive. But in there, Anne, deprived of what made me human, I faced an uncomfortable truth. There was little in fact to separate me from Prothero."

Anne looked puzzled by this.

"How many times had I accused that man of pride, of being arrogant and stubborn, of sacrificing whoever or whatever was necessary to achieve his own ambitions? But how was I any different? Look what I was doing to your mother… Our babes were all so young then, and your mother… Duw mawr… She deserved a better man than I…" He was shaking now, still angry with his younger self.

"I swore to myself in that London cesspit that if I survived I would step back, out from the political circus, and try to be a better husband and father. I owed it to the woman waiting for me, dealing – God knows how – with all the bitter repercussions of what I had done.

"When I came home they lined the streets you know, Anne. A band played and crowds with banners marched through Newport, deliberately past Prothero's house, of course." He smiled at the memory. "Who couldn't be affected deeply by such warmth? Flattered even, tempted to continue the fight? Pride blinkers you, lass, and it is easy to plough on like those old horses up in the fields above Bettws. But I had made a decision, determined to live more anonymously if I could. Prothero gloated publicly that he'd stopped my mouth for ever and I'd be heard of no more. For a while I thought he might be right."

"Now," he said, suddenly looking brighter. "Let's see what you've found in the market for us."

NEWPORT
1823

He tried. God knows he tried. He wanted to live his life in the shadows, quietly enjoying his family and home. At least, he thought he did. The business had just about survived during his absence, due in no small part to the efforts of friends and supporters. Even his mother had helped, softening with the years and with her grandchildren. But his money had gone, and he had to focus now on what mattered, he told himself.

He was glad to be back with Mary, but he noticed the fine lines which had appeared around her eyes whilst he was away. Their love-making on his return was passionate and fierce, and they often held each other silently, long into the night. Six infants of their own, all still under ten, had joined Mary's two eldest. The latest babe, Henry Hunt, had been born whist John was in gaol. The children accepted John's return without question, and he loved his newborn dearly. But it pained him to find John, his eldest, so changed. The boisterous, loud and carefree boy was now serious, taciturn, sullen even. He smiled rarely. It was as if he had shouldered the family woes, and it all but broke his father's heart.

"Are you back with us to stay now, John my love?" Mary was sitting with him after supper soon after his return. The children were all in bed, and a fire crackled in their hearth.

"Aye, that I am," he replied. "You should know how much I regret the misery I caused you… I marvel at how patient you have been." He tried to lighten the atmosphere between them. "I'm not planning on stirring any hornets' nests again," he joked.

"Then what is this?" she asked, and he saw she was holding one of Sam's printed pamphlets. He held her gaze, and he saw for the first time an unfamiliar hardness. "You think they'll ignore this too?"

It was the wish list he had compiled in Monmouth gaol, his template for a better, fairer world. In the pamphlet she waved at him he had described Whigs and Tories alike as "plunderous factions who have robbed the people without mercy". He pleaded for Parliament to be reformed, that every county should be represented by an MP in proportion to the population. He advocated a vote for every man over twenty-one, with candidates' names posted publicly and voting papers collected in churches, in sealed boxes.

A creed as much a part of him as his own breath.

"Burn it," he said. "All that's behind me now. Nothing matters except you, the children and the business. Trust me, Mary. I have no hunger to challenge the likes of Morgan and Prothero again." He leant over to kiss her but she moved her face so that his lips grazed the side of her cheek. He gently tucked one of her dark curls behind her ear. "I love you, Mary. Never doubt that… and I do not want us to be apart again." When she did not reply, he went up in the darkness to kiss his children goodnight.

Mary sat for some time re-reading the pamphlet. She held it over the dying flames, anxious to remove it from her life, but something stopped her. Instead, she crossed the room and opened a drawer in the old wooden dresser they had brought from his grandmother's house when they married. She lifted the volume of poetry she kept there, folded the pamphlet carefully and slipped it safely under the book.

***

And so he tried. He worked hard to restore financial security for his growing family. Mary was pregnant again, in poor health and struggling to manage the infants and the home. After supper, John would send her to rest whilst he read to the children and taught the eldest their letters. They all knew Catharine was his favourite. She was the quickest to read, she made him laugh with her constant questions, and she had the sweetest singing voice. He gave them little daily tasks: Elizabeth and Ellie collected the eggs from the two chickens, Sarah washed the dishes, Catharine swept the hearth, and John walked the puppy his father bought soon after his return.

"Treat him gently, lad," he told his eldest, remembering his own grandmother's words. "Fear is no way to gain loyalty from any creature."

James was born barely a year after John's return from prison. It was a difficult birth on an unbearably hot August afternoon, and for a terrifying few days, John thought he might lose both Mary and the baby. He was surprised by the kindness of his mother, who came from The Royal Oak, without being asked, to care for the children while he kept vigil at Mary's bedside. As the days stretched into weeks, fear became hope and then relief.

By Christmas, John's business was reasonably stable again, and he was determined the family would enjoy the best he could afford as they celebrated together. He had small gifts for them all, and on Christmas Day, he rose early to be sure the little parcels were distributed around the fireplace before everyone came down to breakfast.

He was putting more wood on the fire when he heard the scream, primal like that of a wounded boar he once heard in the woods above his home.

Upstairs, he found his wife bent over the baby James, rocking him wildly and choking back deep, incoherent sobs. "He's gone," she whispered eventually. "Our beautiful angel James has gone."

They buried him on a bitter day when the ground was almost too hard to dig, at St Woolos' alongside John's grandparents. But their growing family demanded they get on with the mundane ordinariness of living, and their home was again filled with the irrepressible noise and laugher of the young. Grief waited slyly, in shadowy corners, for the quieter times. They would need no words, but would simply stand and hold each other close, permitting the tears.

For months Mary resisted his more intimate caresses. "No more children, John. I barely survived last time, and James was a sickly babe from the start. Besides, we can ill afford more mouths to feed. The little ones grow so fast…"

He tried to respect her, and would wait until she was asleep before joining her in their bed. He would work late, and attended some local meetings, always careful to resist inflammatory discussions. They would take the children to see the ships in the burgeoning dock below the town, or up to the woods where they had once walked as sweethearts, and slowly, patiently, he waited for his Mary of old to come back to him.

In the October following James' death, on a day of glorious sunshine, he gathered for her some late autumn roses, and she took him to their bed, where they made love with an intensity he had not felt for many years. By Christmas, she knew she was pregnant again.

STAPLETON, BRISTOL
1876

"That was you, Anne," her father said, after reading her latest pages. "You were our last, a precious gift after our grief. Your brother John had already joined me in the shop by the time you were born – a good lad, always a wise head on young shoulders. But you are wrong about Catharine being my favourite, you know."

Anne shook her head, unconvinced. "Perhaps you just didn't see what was so obvious to the rest of us!"

"What I do know is that those eight or nine years in our home in Newport, happy with your mother and all of you, surrounded by children's laughter every day, and love, so much love… those years were as dear as life itself. The memories brought me great solace in the dark times to come. You cannot imagine how much."

Some hours later, he came over to where she was writing and, standing behind her, hesitating at first, placed his hands on her shoulders. "There is one other thing I remember," he said. "And I doubt you'll find it in these documents. Every Christmas your mother lit a special candle and laid an extra place at the table for the son we lost. She mourned him till the end."

***

He would spend hours watching Anne write, her brow wrinkled as she chewed on her lip. She was weaving the strands of his life with such gentle dexterity, working with a tenderness he felt he hardly deserved. She would stop to check dates and names in the documents, sometimes asking him for clarity. The task engrossed her, so that at times she forgot to eat. He was humbled by her interest in his past, by the love with which she created this for him, his legacy, her inheritance.

"You have such skill," he told her one day after reading her account of James' death. "You might have been a writer. Did you ever think of that for yourself?

"It was never an option for the likes of me." She shrugged. "And well you know it. Mine was another path… Mother needed me… and some things in life are beyond our control."

He knew she was thinking of the shy young clerk who used to visit her in the year before his own mother's death. Mary had told him she had never seen Anne so alive as after those visits, nor so happy. But a cholera outbreak which started at the docks where he worked took him and their future. There had been no others.

"Perhaps I was meant to do this for you," she mused. "We think we make the choices in life, but I wonder oftentimes if that is so. Do you think you were free to choose? To determine what happened next? Or were you just following your destiny?"

He was shaking his head. "Too easy to think that way, Anne. I blame none but myself. Heraclitus was right: a man's character is his fate."

NEWPORT
1830

He had tried. God knows he had tried. There were those in the town who admired him and envied his growing wealth, successful business and happy family. But once again he felt it, that old creeping disconnect. He needed more than cloth and children in his life. He didn't belong behind a counter, and at times, when he reread Cobbett's *English Grammar* with its excoriating honesty about the rich and entitled, or if he revisited Ward's *Black Book* with its details of the abject poverty and depravity still found in the industrialised valleys above his home, he felt muzzled, like a wild animal, suffocating in the comfortable life he had created.

One afternoon in late May, he was staring vacantly at a new delivery of cloth lying on his counter when the shop door opened.

"Sam!" The distraction pleased him. Here at least was a kindred spirit. "What brings you here?"

"I have a proposition. I want to sell the printing shop. It's a good business, and the townsfolk keep us busy with their needs, but I want it to go on publishing political pamphlets too. I can't think of anyone better than you, John, to take it on. Might you be interested?"

John looked across the shop to where his eldest, now nineteen, was serving. He had learnt all his father could teach him, had ideas of his own now, and would make a fine businessman.

It was time for change.

Two weeks later, Cobbett himself was in Monmouth, giving a speech in The King's Head. John was there early, determined to speak personally to the man who had influenced him so much and whose dreams he shared. It was quite an event. People poured out onto the cobbles between the inn and the Shire Hall, and Cobbett spoke to the crowd for two hours. John was transfixed.

"Friends," the visitor cried. "We have all seen how wealth has been accumulated by a few on the backs of these who labour, and I ask you here tonight, how is respect shown to the wealthy? Why, through fear and compulsion, nothing more."

His grandmother's lesson. The faithful puppy.

"And we are taxed so that those already rich can have more: the church expands its unfettered assets; we have financed wars nor fought in our interests; we continue to provide handouts to rich men in Parliament whom we have neither selected nor elected. Taxation causes poverty," Cobbett continued, expressing a sentiment which could easily have been John's own. "Poverty causes misery. Misery causes crime. The Tories rule us with rods... the Whigs scourge us with scorpions."

John rode home from Monmouth with a renewed self-belief and a determination to use his new printing press to bring the ideas of Cobbett and others to a wider audience. He saw the way forward, and he would not yield again.

For John, it was more than modest reform that was needed: society was owed a radical overhaul. For so many to live in misery just to serve a privileged minority was for him an injustice and contrary to the laws of nature. He remembered the words from his cherished Blackstone, that "the law of nature existed from the very beginning of mankind and was dictated by God himself". He now knew that if an intrinsically unjust situation could not be remedied by Parliamentary reform, then force would be necessary.

"What use is reform," he had asked Cobbett, not expecting an answer, "if it won't feed the hungry and clothe the naked?"

And so once more he dabbled with local politics. He joined a Patriotic Society, and then, in October, seven months after it was put before them, the Lords in London rejected the Reform Bill.

John was ferociously angry at the meeting subsequently held in Newport, articulating what the crowd was feeling, and what they needed to hear.

"Those applewomen in Parliament need to be kicked out!" he yelled. "The interests in this country between the governed and the governors are world apart. They want power, we demand freedom. Now, brothers and sisters, I'm not saying we need a revolution, though it's easy for those of us with food in the belly and a shilling in the pocket to be patient. Less so if you have nothing to lose. The Reform Bill promised us so much, but all was hollow. We must stay strong in our aims. We will prevail."

In November, John founded Newport's "Political Union of the Working Class". It was a London-based movement, and Francis Place had sent John its powerful manifesto, based on the belief that all men were born free with certain natural, inalienable rights, rights which a government had a duty to protect. At their meetings, members would share the news from elsewhere across the country: of an uprising in Tolpuddle, or of cries for reform in Manchester. Closer to home, Merthyr men had rebelled and their leader, Dic Penderyn, had been executed. Each incident fuelled a growing, irrepressible rage.

Local members saw John as their branch's natural leader, much to his own surprise. His frustration around the lack of reform was palpable and was shared by many similar minds in the town, but John it was who could articulate best their anger and impatience, weaponising powerful words to publicise their cause. It amazed him how his passion and conviction empowered him to overcome a natural reticence. He saw how his words could affect people… and now he also had the means to print them.

No small wonder that the union's rapidly growing popularity unsettled local men of authority. Chief amongst these was John's old enemy Thomas Prothero, and his young articled clerk, Thomas

Phillips. Pompous and exceptionally short, the younger man tried desperately to appear taller by bellowing when he talked. Nothing gave him greater pleasure than hearing himself speak in public. "He thinks he's the Lord Chief Justice!" John told Mary after witnessing one outpouring.

Prothero and this young clerk had in recent years orchestrated improvements to Newport's roads and railway, but there was significant opposition – not least from John – as to how these changes had been funded. The old mutual animosity was stirring in its lair again. Confrontation, albeit not immediate, would come. It was inevitable, inexorable, like the thunder hidden in those slate-grey rain clouds which swept up the Bristol Channel from Swansea. You could stand on the dockside to watch them coming from afar, but you could do nothing to change their course, and before you knew it the thunder was upon you.

By the following January, John was printing openly critical exposures of Sir Charles Morgan again.

"A new light is beaming in Europe," he warned the family that had dominated his town for so long. "Be mindful that formerly great French landowners are now shoemakers since the revolution there."

This was rebellious talk. Consequences were just biding their time.

One evening when he returned from a meeting, he found Mary waiting for him in the dark. Without comment, she had witnessed her husband change in recent months. The rebel was back, some strange fire burning in him. He seemed younger, more alive.

"Good meeting?" she asked.

He barely responded and she knew his thoughts were elsewhere. She poured ale, and waited until he sat near her.

"Look, John. I am no fool, and I can see where you are heading. I am afraid for you, afraid of what will happen to us… but I know you too. Nothing I say will stop this. Nothing I do will hinder your journey. I want you to know that I am ready for the storm when it comes." She looked up, and he saw tears in her eyes. "And come it surely will." She wiped the tears away, and tried to smile. "I thought perhaps you might want this again." And she handed him the pamphlet he had written in his prison cell. It had been hidden beneath her poetry book for the last seven happy years.

He had never loved her more.

STAPLETON, BRISTOL
1876

They were walking in the garden, John's arm through his daughter's, sharing memories of Mary. Unseasonably warm sunshine filtered through bare branches, giving a solitary thrush reason to celebrate the approach of Christmas. Anne was beginning to understand, beginning to find answers to the enigma of her father's life.

"She must have been very frightened for you," Anne said. "Men like Prothero and Morgan would never take such public criticism without retaliation."

"At the time I thought I was invincible… My pride again, I suppose. But I made myself a sitting target, didn't I?" John added. "Secure in the deluded belief that I was fulfilling some sort of destiny, defending those too timid to do so."

He shivered, so she guided him gently back inside to the fire.

"Have you seen this?" he asked. It was a copy of *The Welchman* dated 1832. The periodical had been born out of *his* press, this copy folded for so long it was difficult to read, but Anne could just make out his words written as if from another life: he promised his readers he would attend court cases as an observer, assess churchmen's integrity and monitor MPs' activities. Change was coming, he assured them, and if they remained strong, they would surely benefit.

"Worst of all," he sighed, struggling to read the print, "I also suggest here that I might stand as MP for Monmouth. Was I really that naive…?"

He sighed. "But they were special years, Anne. Our cause had support. People trusted me, a sacred trust I carried as their Justice of the Peace and town councillor, and then mayor and, truth be told, I did gain some authority. I gave that bastard Prothero and his obsequious clerk a run for their money more than once!" He smiled as he remembered something. "There were some in the town who called me the people's friend, and I admit I was proud of that. I had a duty as guardian of the Poor Law amendment to oversee care of the impoverished in Newport. God knows there were enough of them! So many desperate people, Anne, cast out to rot in those hellish workhouses. Someone needed to be their advocate."

Anne was searching for a document she had seen earlier. "Do you remember this?" she asked. "Let me find the words… It's something Cobbett wrote. Ah, here they are: 'What is a "pauper"? …Only a very poor man.'"

"He was right. It's too damn easy to label folk. That Poor Law system which demonised paupers was vicious," John said. "Poverty was punished as a crime. Families separated in workhouses unfit for pigs, food barely adequate… so many died." He shook his head before adding, "And the real problem? Nothing new, Anne. Those making and implementing the law to deal with the poor would themselves *never* be on its receiving end. It was alien to their experience. They simply didn't care."

"But you did – and so did he, from what I read," she replied, pushing across the table to John a faded print of a handsome young man. "Tell me about him."

"Why, that's Henry." He smiled. "Henry Vincent. I sometimes think that the next chapter of my life might have been very different were it not for him. His arrival triggered events which found me in the condemned cell. I shall tell you all, but not tonight. I need my bed, child. Talk of the past makes me weary!"

"Tomorrow is Christmas Eve," she said. "I'll make us a good supper, but if you are well enough in the afternoon, I'd like us to take a holly wreath to Mother's grave. She made sure we all prayed for you at Christmastime every year you were away."

John remembered all the Christmases in Van Diemen's Land, when he feared he would never again see those he had left behind, feared that they would forget him. "Aye, lass. We'll go together."

He did not tell her, could not have explained it anyway, but he somehow knew this visit to Mary's grave would be his last.

NEWPORT
1838–9

During his years in exile, through endless, empty hours of reflection and regret, John concluded that the advent of Henry Vincent to Monmouth was the catalyst to the Chartist attack on the Westgate, and ultimately his own trial for treason. But reality saw it differently. A virulent political fever had spread amongst the working men and women of South Wales long before Vincent's arrival. There was no cure, and there would be fatalities before it ran its course.

The Reform Bill passed through Parliament in 1832, and John was sceptical from the start. *"They make speeches in favour of reform,"* he wrote, *"but have their hands in your pockets."* Reform as outlined in this bill would be to the advantage of those already in control: still only eighteen per cent of the male population could vote; still the poorest remained voiceless. *"Let us depend on ourselves,"* he urged. *"Let the merchant, the farmer, the tradesman, the working man look to no one but himself... for if he depends on those who are in superior situations he will always be disappointed."* Little changed in Monmouthshire, and John later admitted, *"It is clear as the sun at noon day that the Reform Bill was humbug."*

In London, William Lovett launched the Working Men's Association and, with Francis Place, drafted *The People's Charter*, centralising ideals which had been debated in radical circles since before the days John worked in the city. In May of 1838 it was made public, in Glasgow, before a meeting of some 150,000. When John received a copy from his old friend Francis, he was overjoyed. Dreams he had articulated over ten years earlier were spelt out clearly in six demands: universal suffrage; MPs should not need to own property to be elected, and should be paid; annual elections; three hundred national districts of equal size, with a representative each; vote by secret ballot.

His friend sent a letter with the copy, telling John that not all "Chartists" were united in their strategies.

"I know you share with me the desire for peaceful reform, my friend. But there are other powerful voices advocating not moral but physical force. They are persuasive too. Feargus O'Connor is one such. He has many supporting him in the North, and even seeks to establish a community in his name in the countryside, populated by poor working men from the cities!

"Take care who you trust, John, because this Charter will unleash strange bedfellows." History tells us that oppression and injustice are natural harbingers of rebellion. A captive beast, it rages and prowls in its confinement, but release leaves an inexorably bloody wake. Sometimes, it takes just a single act or a charismatic speaker to free the monster. John Frost and a few other radicals such as the wealthy geologist Zephaniah Williams led with passionate enough conviction, and their many meetings to promote the cause attracted huge gatherings. Initially it was the artisans and tradesmen who supported the Charter – the corn merchants and the saddlers, carpenters, butchers – but then the dockmen and colliers followed. The six demands resonated across the country's workforce.

And then, along came this man Vincent, a printer from Yorkshire elected by the National Convention of Working Men to promote the People's Charter across Britain. Ah now, this man, he had it all! At twenty-two, he was handsome, eloquent and intelligent. He knew just how to win a crowd of men, how to woo their wives. He was fearless, passionate, defiant and for the vast crowds of desperate men and women listening to him in their beerhouses, on the streets or at the mountaintop gatherings, he was messianic. The tens of thousands who subsequently signed the People's Charter would follow the likes of Vincent into hell itself.

Francis Place wrote to John beforehand, asking his friend to host the fellow radical when he visited South Wales:

"You will like this fellow," Francis wrote. *"You have much in common, being both hot-headed, passionate about the Charter… and both of you printers. Just be wary for your daughters: he is devilishly handsome!"*

Vincent arrived accompanied by the wintry dregs of 1838. Mary had ale and warm soup waiting, and fresh sheets on the most comfortable bed. She wasn't sure about this showy young man, anxious about how he might influence John.

"This is wonderful," Vincent said, tasting her soup. "And I am honoured to stay here. I have admired your husband for so long." He watched as his flattery melted any reservations she harboured. "John is a lucky man to have such a loving family." He had a seductive, boyish habit of running a hand through his long curls, eyes that laughed when he spoke, and an infectious, dimpled smile. John's children were fascinated by the stranger's accent, devouring his every word, and Catharine, aged twenty now, was besotted. The normally confident, articulate young woman would stutter and blush whenever he glanced her way.

But he had a gift with words, that was certain. On the first day of the new year, they were at a public house in Pontnewydd. Smoke filled the taproom. Men and women jostled for space, seeking refuge from the bitter cold, but many listened out in the streets beyond, a thousand at least. John spoke first to reiterate the importance of the Charter. He had never completely overcome his nervousness when facing a crowd, but those present were fiercely loyal to him. They listened carefully and respectfully, applauding when he stepped down. But then Vincent rose to speak, and the crowd was instantly mesmerised.

"My friends," he said. "Working men and women just like you in Lancashire, Devon, Birmingham and London are united behind the Charter. It is time for Wales to join them. Enough is enough! We must bring down this government, challenge the crown and the lawmakers. Don't fear what the military might do, for soldiers support this charter too. We will win this fight, I tell you. Your readiness for action is all I ask! Are you with us, my friends?"

His fervour was raw, compelling, addictive and dangerous. A deafening cheer rose in the taproom, spread along the streets outside and soared upwards to the gathering storm clouds hanging low over the Welsh hills.

The two men toured South Wales throughout that month, telling rapt audiences how the Charter could change lives whereas the Poor Law did nothing to address their hardships. Word spread of this English radical in their midst, attracting thousands to hear his revolutionary talk. Whole families signed up for what they felt could offer freedom from subservient tyranny, the lure of an alternative life. Occasionally, the two men ventured to the coalfields of the upper valleys, where John would translate into Welsh the Englishman's passionate outpourings. Membership of the Chartist lodges increased exponentially, and twenty new branches with some fifteen to twenty thousand members were in place by February.

"We'll hold meetings of the Newport lodge in The Royal Oak," John told Vincent. "It's still mine. Catharine wants to start a women's group of fundraisers for the cause." John smiled. "Even Henry wants to help. He's starting a Junior Chartist group!"

John was proud of his family's response. Proud too of the overwhelming local support for the Charter. Years later he could see how easily he had been drawn into the intoxicating aura of Vincent's immense popularity. Who would not revel in such admiration and fame, which waited everywhere they went? There was no place for doubt. No thought of possible repercussions. No memory of what had led John to that London gaol cell fifteen years before this.

By the time both men attended the London National Convention in February, they were brazenly calling it "the authentic parliament of the people". Unsurprisingly, Parliament proper was not amused.

STAPLETON, BRISTOL
1877

She remembered now.

The stranger who stayed with them when she was thirteen or so. She remembered being cross with Catharine and Ellen when they snubbed her, spending hours on their curls and choosing which ribbons to wear at supper, arguing over the place nearest to the handsome visitor.

She also recalled how much extra work there was in the weeks when their father was absent. He had come home for Sarah's wedding, but had not stayed. They all had more chores, and she'd hated being sent to sweep the floor of the shop, which her brother now managed.

Decades had passed, yet she could still recall the loneliness of that time. Anne had been too young to attend with her mother and sisters those meetings of radical women in The Bush Inn, where Vincent would use his beautiful singing voice to entertain them before his address, and she was certainly too old to join Henry at the young Chartist group. The house would be filled with their excited chatter when they returned, their shared jokes and the names of people she did not know. It was all a foreign language for her, home an alien place where she was an intruder.

"You are quiet this evening." John had been watching Anne for some time.

"Not all memories are welcome," she said, frowning. She was holding that draft copy of the Charter which Francis Place had sent to John, and the letters he had written.

"I think Catharine was quite impressed by Vincent," she said, choosing her words carefully. "She rarely left his side when he called."

John was smiling. "She read everything about the Charter, all the papers and pamphlets on my desk. But Catharine has always been her own person. No one tells her what to think. I saw it again and again while we were overseas together. Even then, back in '39, she would face Henry, Zephaniah, William and the rest, not in the least intimidated, standing before them in our parlour. 'Don't you think women struggling to feed their babes know better than anyone what hardship means?' she would ask, challenging us like this." And John wagged a finger at Anne, remembering his other daughter. "She would ask us, 'How can you argue for enfranchisement but exclude half of the population?'

"We would explain to her that it was too much to ask at that time – democracy is a slow, lumbering beast, Anne – but she would hear none of it. For her, equality for all should mean just that." He shook his head before adding, "I admired her resolve even though I disagreed."

"No one ever asked me what I thought," Anne mumbled, but he did not hear. He was gazing out of the window.

"Look," he said. Outside, in silence, whilst they had been talking, a mantle of snow had covered the garden, and a solitary robin left his tiny prints in the fresh white world.

NEWPORT
1839

Another spin of the wheel.

Vitriolic in his criticisms of the government's ineptitude, John's menacing outpourings angered the Home Secretary so deeply it cost him the position as a JP in Newport. News of this demotion caused outrage in his hometown, stirring strong feelings even further. He wrote powerfully and at length to complain, challenging the authority of the Home Secretary himself:

"Your lordship receives a very large sum of money for holding the office of Secretary of State," he wrote. *"Paid, in part out of taxes raised by the inhabitants of the borough. Does your lordship owe them no duty? ... they, not your lordship, ought to decide whether I be struck off the commission of the peace."*

The newspapers printed the correspondence and a scandal ensued, with the Home Secretary labelled "frost-bitten". Never before had a JP dared to challenge a Secretary of State in such a manner.

The wheel was moving again.

By April, Vincent was back in Newport attracting flag-waving crowds and persuading scores more to sign the petition. The man was visibly exhausted. He had been touring for over a year, gathering signatures in Herefordshire, Gloucestershire, Somerset, speaking for hours every day, covering some six thousand miles. Articles by him appeared weekly in the *Western Vindicator* disguised as "The Life and Rambles of Henry Vincent", alongside John's own pieces vilifying the enormous sums paid out to royalty and the Privy Council.

"There is now more political feeling in this country," he told John, "than ever existed, perhaps in any nation in the world. It would seem that every man has become a politician. We shall be linked together as one."

"We have networks of committed Chartists everywhere," John agreed. "Strong threads bind our members through the minefields, the ironwork foundries, the work gangs, the trades, the families. We are unassailable and mighty. Twenty-five thousand signed up in the coalfields alone. We have sympathetic fellow printers distributing our words in Bristol, in Newcastle, in Birmingham, and then there is O'Connor with his hordes of Northern followers. I tell you, Henry, we cannot fail. We just need to be strong and patient, for a little while more."

But patience was far from paramount in the minds of the local men of means. Thomas Phillips, now Mayor of Newport, together with the Lord Lieutenant of Glamorgan each sent a warning to London that the local radicals were militant and threatening action. Once again, Vincent expressed public contempt for Phillips, inciting a large crowd with: "My friends, Chartism will crush the oppressors. As the barons learned with the Magna Carta… that's how the Charter will be obtained. Death to the aristocracy, I say! Up with the people!" Such seditious language forced the town mayor to seek help from the Home Secretary.

It was at that point the local magistrates declared all large assemblies illegal.

Vincent responded with derision, and his followers, in defiance, marched together through Newport, yelling, "Britons never will be slaves!" Leaning out of John's bedroom window to address a rowdy group, Vincent dared the magistrates to arrest him. "I have no fear," he claimed. "If your magistrates will not keep the peace, lay hold of them, and put them in the coal hole."

Again, the wheel turned.

On 6th May, the Chartists' petition with over a million signatures was rejected by a dismissive Parliament, and the government resigned a day later. Vincent was irrepressible, announcing that "every hill and valley of Wales should send forth its army". An equally incensed crowd responded, "We will, we will."

Pointing behind him on the street crammed with followers, he shouted, "I wish to see Prothero and Phillips hanging from this lamppost!"

For Henry Vincent, this was an ill-advised public challenge. It was the crucible in his fortune – and John's. Their fate was shifting now, like some slow, unstoppable juggernaut.

And further retaliation was promised: Chartists would be refused employment, reading a radical paper would lead to instant dismissal, tradesmen and landlords would be forbidden to trade with Chartists. John wrote that the magistrates' ruling against their meetings was "a declaration of war" against rights and liberty, and he would argue all his life that it was the final catalyst to the real violence which followed. More confident now, Prothero and Phillips were vocal in their contempt, relieved at last by the presence of armed special constables billeted in Newport.

Phillips had heard rumours that guns and muskets had been sent from Birmingham, then stored in remote mountain caves. He claimed that pikes were being made in the foundries and smithies of the valleys' ironworks and dockyards. He acted quickly, and his proposed legal proceedings against Vincent were approved without delay by the Home Office. By 9th May, the Yorkshire radical was arrested and incarcerated in the fortress that was Monmouth Gaol, charged with illegal assembling and conspiracy. Policemen from London and 159 "specials" surrounded the gaol.

"Stupid bugger!" It was Sam Etheridge, supping ale with John a few nights after the arrest. "It was always *when*, never *if* with that man, I reckon… Couldn't keep his mouth shut for a bit, could he? Reminds me of you in '22, John. But there'll be hell to pay now, mark my words."

"Already happening, Sam. They were fighting in the streets of Newport and outside Monmouth Gaol yesterday," John replied, his head in his hands. "I told them to go home, Sam. I tried to calm the waters. Christ, I tried. But there is just so much anger everywhere, and who knows where it will lead? Ordinary working men and women are turning into violent beasts… Saw it with my own eyes…. Remember John Richard from the Gelligaer lodge? Arrested, and after him his wife Martha, for assaulting the special constable who was struggling with her husband. Until now, a nicer couple you couldn't hope to meet."

He drained his ale, looked at Sam and said, "What have I done, my friend? This is a monster I can no longer tame. A wildfire I cannot control. Dear God, what have I done?"

STAPLETON, BRISTOL
1877

The blizzard continued through the night and the next morning, leaving an unrecognisable landscape around their home. The bright light hurt John's eyes, so Anne closed the curtains in the parlour where he sat, and moved to write in her own room. She was relieved to see the neighbour's lad Joe clearing their path to the gate, and later bringing fresh milk and vegetables. She would reward him generously, but now she had to focus.

Anne read and read again all the newspaper articles from that time, all the letters, and her father's own account of his trial. She spent time putting the events in a chronological order, attributing names and places. So much had happened so fast. This was 1839 – a critical period in her father's life; she dare not make mistakes. Men had died. Men had been tried for treason. Men had been sent a world away never to return. She owed them her honesty, her accuracy and diligence.

"Did they really have those weapons, the men who marched from the valleys?" She was checking the facts as she always tried to do, but she could see he found this almost too painful to discuss. It was darker outside now, but he had not opened the curtains. It was easier to face the memories that way.

"I fear they did," he told her. "But you must understand. It wasn't always easy to know what was happening in those remote valley meetings, and men differed in their values. I never wanted violence, never, but others were less squeamish. There were hotheads amongst them, convincing talkers, wild, reckless men like Jack the Fifer, who had fought at the Alamo. So it's possible…" He stopped, remembering the smell of gun smoke, the screams in the chaos, the bloodied bodies in a Newport street, the fear and the failure.

He rummaged amongst his papers and pulled out a well-thumbed pamphlet.

"This is Thomas Carlyle, Anne, writing about the movement a year after my trial. He called it a 'bitter discontent grown fierce and mad'. But that was not how it started. Our movement was supposed to be about liberty, a struggle for rights, a new dawn for the working men and women of this country. I ask myself over and over, how did that all get so lost, sucked into the whirlpool around Vincent's arrest? How did our hard work lead to nowhere but a massacre in a public bar?"

Anne moved across the shadows to adjust the old woollen shawl around his shoulders, her mother's favourite, and she saw he had been crying.

NEWPORT
1839

The wheel was spinning out of control.

In late May, John addressed a crowd of some thirty thousand at Blackwood, with magistrates in the crowd, making notes. Vincent's arrest had fuelled an already raging fire, and there was talk now of the members taking financial action, of a national strike, of their dealing only with tradesmen sympathetic to the Charter. In June, John was in Glasgow, this time facing a crowd of one hundred and fifty thousand, all eager to hear his vision for a better world.

Always he advocated action within legal boundaries, but acknowledged, progressively, that if their treatment continued as it had then many would seek less legal retaliation. "If our leading men be imprisoned, no violence having been committed," he proposed, "then we shall consider that a coal pit is quite as safe a place for a tyrannical persecutor as a gaol for an innocent Chartist." He urged them to "be firm, be peaceable, and our righteous cause will succeed." But his words nevertheless angered the Attorney General: it was an incentive to violence in his view, and John faced a trial of his own, to be held sometime in the months ahead, with possibly another prison sentence.

Mary was barely speaking to him. "This time they'll lock you up for good," she told him one night, lying at his side, neither touching the other. It was a warm night, and both were staring at the ceiling in the dark, unable to sleep. "Or worse," she added, and turned to face the wall.

In August, he wrote to his old friend Francis Place:

"They have sentenced Henry to a year in gaol, even though his defence lawyer got that bastard Phillips to admit there had been no riot, that he had himself heard us tell people to keep the peace. Now we are told our National Convention is illegal too.

My friend, I have a spirit in me difficult to repress. If power were placed in my hands... I should be afraid of myself, for revenge would triumph. I am sending you a copy of the Western Vindicator. You'll find my words to Wales' working men in its pages. I have urged them to stay firm and steady, but I share with you my private fears for what is to come. Those in power are citing 'high treason' now... it cannot end well."

By mid-September, Frost despaired of ever improving things for Vincent in spite of his letters to influential men in authority. The Convention itself was disbanded, and he knew that many Chartists now believed peaceful methods were ineffectual.

One evening in early October, John was sitting smoking his pipe, listening to Sam. "They're a wild rabble now, John. They've lost all hope. They need you to lead them, perhaps more than ever. Give them structure and purpose. You can do that, even with Henry in gaol. Let them see the cause still lives and breathes."

John was preoccupied, drafting a rough diagram on some paper in Sam's study.

"The men will organise themselves into groups of ten, Sam, each group with its leader, then larger groups forming a company, and companies a brigade. See, like this." And he passed the document to Sam. Later, it would be seized in the raid, and Sam would lie that it represented the troops for the Irish rebellion years before.

They were still discussing this plan when John's son Henry burst in. "Father, you must go to Blaina. There's a crowd gathering at Zephaniah's beerhouse – there's talk of a march already underway to free Vincent. They'll be slaughtered if they try to attack that gaol now. You must do something."

"Jesus, no!" John was already putting on his coat. "Tell your mother I may not be back till tomorrow. Let's hope Zephaniah keeps them calm till I get there."

John rode his horse hard across to Blaina, and was confronted by a sizeable rabble, noisy, febrile, all clamouring to get inside. A fug of cheap tobacco filled the taproom, laced with sweat and stale beer. In the confusion, John spotted Zephaniah at the bar, watchful as ever, dapper, a dignified intellectual.

"Are they marching?" John stuttered, breathlessly.

"Not yet," his friend replied, "but they're baying for blood tonight, John. And *he* doesn't help." Zephaniah was pointing at a figure standing on a table, holding court.

This was Jack the Fifer, whose exploits at the Alamo lent him legendary status in the surrounding hills and valleys. His was the raw, undisguised aggression of a man who was once a killer. Now, he judged exactly the mood of the men and voiced what they wanted to hear. "Are you ready, boys? Are you willing to show the bastards we mean business?" After each question, a resounding roar encouraged him to continue. He paced his words, pausing between each sentence.

"They have Vincent in gaol. Starving the poor bugger. They dismiss our petition. Laughed at it, they did. They're arresting Chartists across England. They call our meetings illegal. And still we suffer. We are trapped by our English masters, making them richer by our own sweat and blood." The atmosphere around him intensified his rhetoric, and he felt his power. "We must rise up and fight! There is no other way. We start by freeing Vincent. Who's with me?"

John felt the mood change in the room. He had to act to stop this folly, and as he stepped forward, those present fell silent.

"My dear friends," he began, trying to control the tremor in his voice. "Recent events have been disappointing, I know, a setback in our plans for enfranchisement and equality. But do not risk all now for a moment of irrational vengeance. The time is not right for an uprising. We would not get the support we need from outside Wales because they are not yet as organised as we are. Besides, there are armed militia in Newport and Monmouth, and they will not hesitate to protect the gaol. You must be patient."

"Go back to your comfortable house and your pamphlets!"

It was a drunken cry from a dark corner of the bar, but others murmured their agreement. John was not holding the crowd as he had done in the past. For the first time he felt a disconnect with his own people, and it was a thing of terror.

"I share your frustration, believe me, I do." He tried to stay calm, but he saw how they were avoiding his eyes. "Henry Vincent is my friend," he said, his tone desperate now, his pulse racing, "but we will have a greater chance of success using legal means. If I can only fix it so that I am chosen as your Member of Parliament in the election coming soon, I can try to orchestrate change from within. So let us march peaceably, I implore you, unified, in our thousands, a show of strength to ensure I am elected to serve you. Violence will never solve this. How could we match military might?"

They were not listening. They were facing the door, where another familiar face had appeared, that of William Jones. Men cheered his arrival, and the popular former actor greeted his audience amicably, shaking hands, placing an arm around the shoulder of one, then another, knowing every name. John was ignored now: here was a showman in a different league, also adept at reading the mood of the room.

"I agree with Jack," he announced, his voice booming into the dingy corners. "We are not cowards." Then, turning to John, he added, "And we have lost faith in Parliament and the promises of hollow words. Another peaceful march such as you favour will achieve little more than angering further the men in power. You're putting swords in our hands and ropes around our necks at the same time."

Jack felt the tension between John and the newcomer and heard the rumblings in the room. He shouted animatedly, "No more half measures eh, boys? Let's see a show of hands. Who's with us?"

John would remember until his dotage the arms waving before him, unanimous in their defiance. He had to do something to calm this storm.

"Then I ask you to rise only at my bidding when I think the time is right. Will you agree to that at least?" He was desperate now. "Are you ready at any time to meet me when called upon?"

"We are!" they roared as one.

"Then I will head the ranks to anything that will take place." As he uttered the words, he knew he was sealing his fate. There was no going back.

From a bench near the fire, an old man rose to speak. John recognised David Davis, delegate from the Abersychan lodge, an old soldier who had fought at Waterloo. His words were clear, and heard in complete silence. "We'll do as you wish, Mr Frost, but there's a condition. My lodge has one thousand six hundred members, and well over a thousand of them of them are old soldiers. The rest have never held a weapon, but we can turn them into fighting men in no time. I'm instructed to tell you that they'll rise with you only if you give them a list of exactly who we have to remove – that is, to kill."

The cheering could be heard throughout Blaina.

When the rabble finally left, John sat with just Zephaniah and William, and the three men talked late into the night, each acutely aware of his role in what might be a turning point in British history. Their arguments differed and wavered as they finalised plans for the weeks ahead, but beneath their elation was another emotion, common to all. Abject terror.

John rode home in the early hours of the next morning in a daze. He could not answer Mary's queries but sat staring at the dead coals in his grate, his pipe cold in his hands, until the dawn found him there, still in his riding coat.

STAPLETON, BRISTOL
1877

"That was a turning point, Anne. They were beyond any reasoning. All I could do was play for some time so we were better organised."

Anne had so many questions. She had searched through the piles of documents, the journals, but could find little written information about those critical weeks prior to the rising.

"You'll find nothing," he said. "Zephaniah, William and I deliberately kept secret all our plans. Weren't sure who else we could trust. It worked, you know. It convinced the authorities we had abandoned our cause. The Attorney General even announced 'the extinction of Chartism', much to our amusement. Nothing could have been less true, of course."

He moved in his chair, gripping the arm. The pain in his hip was always worse in cold weather, but he wanted to continue, to tell her what he remembered. "Stopping the movement was impossible now – Blaina had taught me that – so October '39 was a frantic month. I travelled up and down this land, whilst Zephaniah and William visited all the local lodges, keeping alive the cause. They brought back tales of weapons being made in caves above Tredegar... I always hoped they were just rumours, but my rational self knew otherwise."

"Where are the plans for the march on Newport?" she asked. "I've got newspapers with reports from your trial, but much of that was hearsay, or 'evidence' from men paid to say certain things. I do not fully trust any of that as truth." She swept her arm over the piles of books and papers around her, and added, "There is so much here which traces your life, but I find no details of that Newport rising anywhere."

"They're here," he said, tapping his head. "Some things are best kept unseen."

She started to scribble again, concentrating hard, chewing her lip as he continued to unravel his memories. On the table between them, a small vase of snowdrops, collected that morning in the weak February sunshine. Winter was almost done.

"The plan was that at some point between the end of October and early November, thousands of men would march, tens of thousands, from every valley. It would be three-pronged, the men in organised groups, and with Zephaniah, William and I each overseeing a particular route down to Newport.

"Some would take Brecon, others march on Newport. There would be little if any opposition – most soldiers supported us anyway. At Stow Hill, in Newport, the noise of the marchers would signal to local Chartists to seize the workhouse where the soldiers had been billeted. I was sure there'd be no bloodshed, Anne. Those soldiers not supportive of our charter would be asleep anyway."

John began speaking animatedly. He was back directing the rising again. "I told Zephaniah and William we could count on at least two thousand men marching on Newport alone. We would take it, and I believed with all my heart that the Charter would then be ours within weeks. Why? Well, just as soon as Cardiff and Monmouth succumbed, a signal would be sent across Britain to other cities and Chartist lodges, which would rise up in support."

He shook his head and sighed. "Strange how straightforward it all sounds now, but I told you before, Anne, it was so very difficult to keep in touch with those distant lodges with their belligerent delegates. We didn't want to tell them too much until the last possible moment, just that they were to be ready, but I fear that only made for confusion and mixed messages. William's men never made it to Newport in time…" He paused before adding wryly, "And we had not given any thought to the impact of the elements, nor to the lure of the alehouses on their route for men who had just been paid."

She stopped writing. She needed space, and stepped out into the crisp evening air, her breath clouding before her. Her father was looking back now, down a kaleidoscope of memory where hindsight makes failure easier to understand. At the time, as events unfurled rapidly around him, there was nothing to be done but follow his fate.

NEWPORT
1839

It rained all weekend. Relentless, unforgiving, cold-to-the-bone rain. It drenched the farmyards of the high valleys, turning the cart tracks between villages into mud. It hammered on the machinery of the ironworks and coalfields, silhouetted against the granite sky, angry giants menacing the rows of cottages at their feet. Fields flooded, and scraggy sheep huddled together against the hedgerows. Perhaps things might have gone differently had they marched in summer. Perhaps.

As it was, any hope of contacting neighbouring lodges to coordinate the men from those remote villages was fading. Those who marched were soon drenched and frozen, boots caked in mud, seeking the warm solace of the many alehouses along the route. Few knew the purpose of their march anyway, just rumours, and a belief it was their last chance to see the Charter made law.

In the days immediately before 4th November, things had turned ugly in some places. Men terrified of the repercussions on their families if they marched were forced to become card-carrying lodge members, intimidated by followers of Jack the Fifer and the like. Word had spread that something big was afoot, and those with the means had fled: clerks, bankers, shopkeepers, landowners. In the corners of wash houses, of taprooms and pit shafts, men and women spoke in whispers, uncertain of the plan. Lodges burned any record of their meetings and members, and the heightened atmosphere in every dwelling, in every valley, was one of anxious fear.

Not everyone in those valleys was as committed as those at the Blaina meeting. Passing through small villages as they trudged towards Newport, the marchers met resistance too. Women screamed at them as they dragged husbands and sons from under their beds to join the march. Others hid in farm buildings, mines, woods, caves.

Stories based on half-truths and drunken memories from that night later became the stuff of legend. Argoed folk remembered some three hundred men marching noisily down the tram road, panic spreading through the village. Women ran from house to house, drenched by the rain, screaming and gathering up small, tearful children.

The crowd soon reached the home of John Walters, a known Chartist opposer. "Bugger off!" he shouted as they demanded he and his sons join the march.

His shabby door provided little defence, and they barged in yelling, "Walters, you must come out! Your life is no better than ours!"

The barrel of a gun was against his chest, and he could see before him more muskets, a bill hook, a cleaver and a sword. He had no choice but to join them.

"Where are we heading?" he asked.

"They'll tell us later. Frost's meeting us at Newbridge," someone muttered, but it was clear none of the motley crowd leading him away had the faintest idea of what was about to happen. By the time they reached Newbridge, the Chartist leader had already left.

Around the same time, another story from that night. Two friends called at the home of William Ferriday, a Blackwood man. Illiterate, and wild in his youth, William was uncharacteristically quiet as he kissed his children goodbye.

"Where are you going, Will?" his wife asked, suddenly afraid.

"Don't know for sure," he admitted. "Nor how long I'll be gone, but don't you fret. Keep the kettle on."

Hours later, he was dead.

***

John had spent the night before the march at Job Tovey's cottage in Blackwood, reading letters which Mary had sent across to him from Newport. He threw them immediately afterwards into Tovey's fire. "Best that way," he explained to his host. "Nobody can point a finger."

As evening fell, they heard horses outside. John's son Henry was accompanied by a stranger with an English accent. He was soaked through and shivered near the fire. "I have an urgent message for you, Mr Frost. I've ridden from Bradford, from the weavers' lodge there." And he handed over yet another letter.

John read in silence, smiled, then watched it burn with the rest. "Take some food, lad, rest your horse, but then it's best you leave for home at dawn, whilst you can still get out of Wales. There'll be militia everywhere after that. And thank your fellow members for their support. We will not let them down."

Before they left, John held Henry close and whispered, "Tell your mother she is in my thoughts, always. Be strong for her, son."

By midnight he was in the hills above Risca as arranged. Riding was difficult: the roads rough, the mud deep and his horse fractious. He could hear distant thunder, which rolled ever closer as he reached the top, the lightning illuminating the slag heaps above Llancaiach, black monuments indifferent to the ways of men.

He dismounted to join the large crowd already gathered on the mountain, and noted their dispirited mood. There was no shelter on that wild upland, and it was difficult to keep lamps ablaze in such weather. In the dark he was not recognised.

"Halt there!" A toothless miner, pike in hand, yellowing eyes lit by a barely flickering lamp, stale beer on his breath.

"Beans," said John, to which the man replied, "Well." It was the agreed password to detect infiltrators, Beanswell being an area of Newport, but here, in the damp reality of a windswept mountain, it felt infantile as if part of a childhood game.

Except this was no game.

He wrapped his already saturated greatcoat closer around him and used his red cravat, a gift from Catharine, to wipe the icy rainwater dripping from his hair into his eyes. "We wait here, men… just a little while, then we take Newport!"

The cheer was lacklustre, cut by a mocking wind.

Meanwhile, Zephaniah was also waiting, pacing restlessly, on another bleak mountain near Ebbw Vale. He cursed himself for agreeing to William's idea. The latter had persuaded his two comrades to wait at these mountain venues, so that cohorts of marchers from Dowlais, Merthyr and elsewhere could rally with them. Three hours he waited, and the storm raged. These were hardened miners and ironworkers around him, but they were all struggling now to combat a howling wind and bitter rain. It was impenetrably dark, but he could hear their muttering and swearing, in both languages. Some, he knew, had already slunk away for the alehouses still open. He too had heard the rumours of free ale.

In the gloom, an old man he recognised as a former soldier shuffled up. "Talk to them, sir. They could use some comfort now. It worked in the army when we was low, like, and the officers wanted to cheer our spirits."

Zephaniah stood on a raised tump of muddy grass, and shouted against the wind. "This is our moment, my friends. Have courage now. We will soon join our comrades marching with John Frost and William Jones and we will take Newport, without shedding a drop of blood. The Charter will soon be ours. A better future for you and your children "

Much of what he said was lost to the rain, and the old soldier, who had draped the red, green and white Chartist flag over his shoulders against the elements, started to sing a Welsh hymn, its refrain picked up by those around him. Harmonies in the minor key. On the sea journey to Van Diemen's Land, Zephaniah told John he could hear that singing in his dreams, and it was a sound he was to remember all his life.

***

Eventually, by 7 a.m., convinced no one else was coming to join them, and chilled through, the two leaders each led a huge crowd of hungry, wet, half-drunk men towards Newport. There, Zephaniah's men settled in the rear behind John's.

Several thousand brothers bound by history.

John was now focused and resolute. "Men with guns, assemble at the front," he ordered. "Those with pikes, behind."

Jack the Fifer was with him, and volunteered to pass the order down through the crowds. "Let's take Newport!" he screamed, his eyes blazing now with anticipated violence. "With the bridge ours and no mail getting out, our brothers in Birmingham will be quick to follow our example!"

But where was William Jones? He had definitely been seen in Pontypool rallying Chartist support the night before, but for all his bluster about having the Chartist flag "on Newport church by 10 a.m. tomorrow" he could never command authority, and many who set off towards Newport with him were soon lured by the warmth of the public houses along the route.

He later tried to justify his late arrival, blaming the weather, the darkness, the men's drinking, the decision by some to go to Monmouth instead. John had never trusted William and was convinced the failed actor had deliberately held back, lacking the courage of his convictions. Whatever the truth, William and those left marching with him only reached the outskirts of Newport by 9 a.m. At Malpas Court, just outside the town, they were diverted further, breaking into the home of the judiciously absent Thomas Prothero. Then, as they left, they were approached by a miner carrying a pike, who recognised William. He was clearly distressed and in a hurry to get home.

"Best go no further," he warned, tears in his eyes. "There's war down there." And he pointed towards the town centre. "Soldiers armed in the Westgate… Dozens dead… Save yourselves now, and go home. Quick, like…" And he hurried off.

"Damn me, we are done for, men." William turned to face his followers. The weather had turned, and dawn brought a bright sunny day. Before him stretched his erstwhile revolutionary army, now just a sad gathering of mud-splattered, dispirited souls. "Get yourselves home, lads," he shouted. "And mind you say nothing of your part in all this."

STAPLETON, BRISTOL
1877

Anne did not find this part of the telling easy. She saw how it distressed her father to recall the events of the weekend which had so petrified his fate. Yet she needed his input. It was as close to truth as she would get.

"Zephaniah and I asked William many times afterwards why his men were not with us at the Westgate," he said. "I don't think the lying bugger ever gave us the truth… he'd probably started to believe his own fabrication, anyway. He was an actor after all. Learning a script was no problem.

"There's something else." John was puffing on his pipe, and had been silently watching her write for some time. "It concerns a brewer from Pontypool… name of Brough. He'd been to Cardiff, and on his way home that night he came upon a rowdy mob of Chartist marchers. He tried to escape but fell in the slippery mud, and they held the poor sod captive, wet, cold and terrified. They were threatening him, all of them fired up to punish anyone they felt like. I knew Brough – used to buy cloth from me – so he pleaded with them to fetch me. By then I was so tired, Anne, but I went. I feared what they would do to him. Prothero and Phillips had spies everywhere, you know, and once those men had a drink inside them… So I rode there myself, and told the men to let Brough go. They grumbled a bit, but they did as I asked."

"Why are you telling me this, father? It was the right thing to do."

"Maybe, but it did me no good, did it?"

She looked puzzled, so he added, "They used it at my trial… as proof that I was the one in command of the violent mob."

***

The next day, after breakfast, Anne suggested a walk in the fields around the house. Beyond a few feet, John saw little but white cloud now, but the birdsong told him spring was coming. She laughed as he recalled their sounds in another hemisphere, trying unsuccessfully to imitate those reminders of a different life.

He ate heartily afterwards, and seemed more cheerful.

"If you are ready," she said, sitting with her pen and ink before her, "it is time to tell me all you recall about the Westgate." Anne was holding old copies of newspapers from that day almost forty years before. "I know the truth matters to you, and that there is a bigger story than what's here."

She secured a loose curl behind an ear, and started to write.

NEWPORT
4th November 1839

At the turnpike above the town, John, irritated by William's absence, was trying to assemble the crowd into units. "Rank yourselves, tidy like," he shouted, hoarse now from battling all night to be heard against the storm.

The few who were on horseback rode down the lines of men with orders to arrange themselves as agreed in their lodges. But morale was missing. The men were miserable, their muddy clothes cold and damp, stuck to their shivering frames. John had been aware for some time of a boy stumbling along at his side. Trembling, sodden, his ragged clothes too thin to ward off the early morning chill, tears in his eyes, he would have been no older than fourteen. John beckoned to the lad, and recognised Dai Bevan, son of the Llancaiach delegate.

"Here," John said, and passed the boy his greatcoat. "Warm yourself, lad. We've quite a day ahead."

The boy smiled and saluted John. "Diolch, sir. I'll see you get it back."

Just after 8.30, Jack the Fifer came running up Stow Hill from the town.

"The bastards have arrested our brothers from the Newport lodge!" he screamed. "Just to stop them joining our march." He was on fire now, and John could see instantly the impact on the men around him. They needed this: a solid reason to move on. Jack was breathing life back into the march. "The mayor read the Riot Act at dawn. He's banned any gatherings in Newport, and he's got the poor buggers held prisoners in the Westgate!" he yelled. "What are we going to do, lads? Let's set them free, I say!"

Men waved muskets and pikes, roaring their assent, and John knew he was losing control. "Let's go towards the town, then," he bellowed, trying to retain authority and use this new momentum. "Let's show them who we are."

***

The shouting continued as they marched, terrifying locals emerging into the morning sunshine. A raging, ragged army marching fearlessly on the town. In the square before the Westgate, John told them, "Turn round, men, and show your appearance." And the crowd surged forward. In the lead, Jack the Fifer, wielding a sword high above his head, with those just behind him pushed relentlessly by the seething mass of men pouring into the square from behind.

Someone shouted, "Give us the prisoners!" and others joined the chant, advancing to within a breath of the constables guarding the Westgate doors.

"Never!" This one grabbed a pike from an old miner glaring into his face, so close he could smell his rotting teeth.

Truth is an elusive mistress, and what followed at the Westgate was later subject to many versions of telling. That windows were smashed is fact. That the lieutenant in charge ordered soldiers inside the hotel to load their weapons is fact. That some of the marchers pushed into the hotel hallway to be met by soldiers is also fact, but it was to be many years, and many miles, before John finally learned from Jack the Fifer the truth about who fired the first shot.

The gunshot echoed around the square, and there was absolute silence for ten seconds. Pigeons sought sanctuary on the bakery roof, and a woman buying her morning loaf screamed. The draper across the street came to his door.

Then hell itself found a corner of a Welsh town.

Events happened quickly, like the flickering images in a child's magic picture machine, but afterwards John recalled watching Prothero's man, Phillips, now town mayor, remove the shutters from inside. He heard clearly the lieutenant shout "Fire!"

A volley hit the crowd, and was followed by ten minutes of mayhem. Phillips screamed as a bullet struck his arm, and John remembered seeing one of the miners who had charged into the hotel fall backwards out of a window onto the damp cobbles, blood oozing from a gaping hole in his chest. Thick, bitter smoke blinded the Chartist marchers, all now turning to run, disoriented, falling over their friends who lay wounded and slain. Gunfire deafened them, and drowned out in the confusion any orders to retreat. The dying were trampled underfoot, or left begging, unheeded, for help.

Some of Zephaniah's men pushed into the hotel from the rear and stumbled over dead bodies in the hallway, its slate floor slippery with blood. They emerged at the front into a battlefield, choking on the smoke and rubbing their eyes. "Save yourselves!" Zephaniah coughed. "Run for your lives."

Screaming and coughing, they dropped their weapons in panic and headed back up Stow Hill, pushing against men still descending. Or they disappeared through the town's alleyways to safety, sometimes into the homes of known sympathisers.

John, however, could not move. He watched this nightmare unfold in dismay and disbelief. A cruel, incongruous sunshine pushed through the smoke, its rays caressing lifeless corpses and abandoned hope. It was probably minutes, but felt like hours, before he too staggered towards the exit of the square. Something beneath his feet caused him to stumble. He cursed what he thought was a bundle of old rags.

Sunlight on a button through the smoke.

His greatcoat.

Bending to retrieve it, John saw him. The small body twisted grotesquely, eyes open, accusatory. Blood trickled lazily from Dai's mouth, tainting the rainwater between the cobbles. Quietly, as with a sacred thing, John laid the coat back over the body, and wept.

***

Somehow he reached Tredegar Park, eyes smarting still from the smoke. He used Catharine's scarf to wipe his face and, holding it close to him, started to weep again, surprised by his tears. He passed a few men who were using the trees for shelter as they headed home. Each one avoided his gaze. Instinct drove him to find a place to hide, at least until darkness fell, and before long he came across an empty coal wagon and climbed inside, covering himself with a piece of torn hessian. Exhausted, he slept.

Hours later, as darkness fell, he climbed out, cold, stiff and hungry. He had to get home, collect some money, then head to London where he still had friends. Perhaps on to France.

They'd be looking for him now, for sure.

At the first crossroad he saw the hastily produced posters with sketches of Zephaniah, William, Jack and himself, offering £100 per man for the capture of "these traitors to the Crown". He would need to be especially careful. Loyalty was sometimes cheap to buy.

It was dark when he reached his home, and John could see a light in the parlour. Looking down, he realised how his clothes were torn, his shirt spotted with blood and filth. Mary must not see him like this. She would have heard by now of the deaths, of the failed march, and would be worried. John saw a light on in his neighbour's home and decided to call there first: he could wash, and perhaps borrow a change of clothes.

"John, my friend, you look like a dead man walking. Come in to the fire." James Partridge was a kind, simple man, also a printer, not especially political but a good neighbour. "Mary knows you are alive, John. Missus went in to see her around three. Some of your men heading home from the march had called by. Missus said she was busy hiding all your papers, like, and your Catharine was helping her. The clever lass left one or two lying around so to fool anyone who came looking."

John did what he could to wash away the residue of the previous day. After putting on clean clothes, he felt calmer, and ready to say his farewells to Mary and the children. After that, he would submit to the whims of good fortune and fair winds.

"Thank you, James," he said, "you are…"

He never finished his thanks. The front door burst open, and constables barged in followed by T. Jones Phillips, town clerk and toady to Prothero. At first he did not recognise John sitting in the shadows on the wooden settle, dressed in the other man's clothes. Besides, it was the last place he expected to find the fugitive, so close to his own home.

"We're here to search your premises, Partridge!" he announced. "Mrs Frost couldn't help us much, but we think Frost might have hidden some of his…" He stopped short, stared at John in disbelief, and marched up to him. "You bastard!" He was so close to John's face, his spittle landed on the forehead of the fugitive seated before him. "You dare to show your face after what happened yesterday? You are under arrest for endangering the good people of Newport, and for plotting against our noble queen. It's the end of the road for you, Frost… may you rot in hell."

Arms grabbed John roughly, pulling his limbs and hair so violently he screamed. Outside, the noise of his arrest brought Mary, Catharine and Anne to the door. It was pitch black, and a thick, damp November fog crawled up from the channel. But the light from within his home illustrated the three faces, like some tragic scene by Caravaggio. He saw, he sensed, their fear and confusion.

"John!" Mary tried to reach him, arm outstretched, but the constables held her back.

"Please," he begged. "Just let me say goodbye to my family. You could keep me under guard here for the night, or at least give me five minutes with them in my own home. Show some mercy, man."

"What, like your rabble showed at the Westgate, you mean?" the clerk sneered. "Shooting at soldiers who were doing nothing but their patriotic duty. Take him away, men!" And he smirked as John looked back over his shoulder for as long as he could before they bundled him into a cart and out of sight.

STAPLETON, BRISTOL
1877

He couldn't continue. The memories were too raw, even after all the years.

"Fifty injured, Anne," he sighed. "And more than twenty dead. Old men, young lads! Dead. And for what?" He shook his head. "Families had to bury them quickly, at night, in unmarked graves. It hurts even now to think of that."

She helped him to his bed and kissed him on his forehead.

"No more for now, Father. It can wait," she said.

"Not for too long," he murmured. "Not for too long. There's so much more to tell."

He kept to his bed the next morning, turning defiantly to face the wall. Anne read again her father's account of his trial, and altered some of the pages she had written the day before. She tried to imagine, to travel back to that world: the torrential Welsh rain on the barren mountaintops, the terror of gunfire from inside the Westgate, bodies bloodied and lying on the wet cobbles. How could her pen ever capture all that? What had she ever done in her narrow life to provide the right words?

Several days passed when John barely spoke but spent hours sitting gazing at the fire, or remained in his bed. Anne, restless and needing to do something useful, cleaned the brass plates and jugs which sat on the Welsh dresser in their parlour. John's mother, Anne's mamgu, had brought them from Newport when she came to live with them four years before, just prior to her death. He had sold The Royal Oak twelve months ago, for £1500, and the brass was what remained of that chapter in his past. Sometimes as Anne worked, a word she had struggled to find earlier would come to her, and she would move across to add it jubilantly to the parchment left waiting on the writing desk. Then she would go back to her brass.

"You should get a woman from the village to do all that for you," John said, surprising her as he came down the stairs.

"Perhaps," she sighed. He had no concept of their finances, or how hard she found it to manage, determined as she was to eke out carefully that money from the sale of the inn. There was little else. Always the cheapest cuts, disguised and seasoned with the herbs she grew herself. The same two dresses she wore, and the interminable mending she did which he could no longer see.

She changed the subject. "Will you sit outside a while, Father? The sunshine is quite warm."

"Not today," he replied. He seemed to have more energy. "We need to carry on. Can you bear to write again?" He avoided her gaze and added, "I do know how painful a time it must have been for you all."

"I remember that night," she said, replacing the gleaming brass on the dresser. She turned to face him. "Mother made sure we were ready when the men came demanding your papers. She hid most of them, telling me to watch the street for the constables. Catharine helped her, and when the men came, they waved their weapons and asked her to hand over all your documents." Anne laughed in spite of herself. "You know what she did? Cool as ever, Catharine smiled at them prettily, as only she can, and gave them what she knew would never cause you harm." She shook her head, remembering what happened next. "And then you were there, suddenly, outside in the dark, held by constables, and we could not speak with you. We could do nothing." Anne paused, lost in the memory. "Mother sat for hours afterwards, and kept saying 'He's a dead man, girls. He's a dead man,' over and over. I don't think I've ever been so frightened."

She sat and steadied herself to write again.

"Fear was in the air men breathed after that night," John added. "It festered in the valleys and towns for weeks. No one knew who to trust. Rumours held court everywhere. In Usk, Abergavenny, Merthyr and Monmouth, all the damn men in power were terrified of further marches and attacks. They set curfews on public houses and shops. Some disappointed men still wanted to march on other towns, even to London, but there were soldiers and constables everywhere, and the bosses were alert to the faintest whiff of rebellion. And where was I? In gaol, with no way of talking to the men who had marched with me. That was left to loudmouths like Price, in Pontypridd, the wild bugger who burnt his dead son. He was quick to point a finger in my direction."

She stopped writing whilst he puffed on his pipe, his cloudy eyes staring out to the garden. It was a long time before he continued. "Later I learned that many of them felt betrayed, disillusioned with the cause, and who could blame them? I had promised no bloodshed. I had told them the soldiers would not fire. I had told them the Charter would be ours. And yet men died... You've read the newspapers from that time, Anne. You've seen how those noble working men are described... as an illiterate, vicious rabble. And they are ridiculed. Savagely. They laughed at me too."

"I remember people cursing us in the street," she said quietly. "And some shopkeepers refusing to serve us. It went on for months. In the end we had to leave." They sat in silence for a while before she said, "When things go wrong, it's easy to blame someone who's not there, no longer able to defend himself. For a while it seemed as if all the leading Chartists were in hiding or behind bars. Only the people in power had something to say, and they did so with such a fanfare, Father! It was unbearable, but one thing's for sure: we truly learned who were our friends."

She was holding a copy of *The Merlin* from that month. "Listen, Father. Just listen to what Prothero wanted everyone to think:

"*I've never read of anything like this in the history of civilised nations... savages all... only Providence saved Newport – through the rain. We should be on our knees in gratitude. If insurrection here had succeeded for a day… nay, even two hours… the signal would have gone forth and we would have heard of similar insurrections."*

John suddenly smiled at another memory. "I would love to have seen Prothero's face when he heard how they rewarded his former protégé Mayor Phillips. Bastard was lauded everywhere as a hero, Anne. Knighted by Victoria, would you believe, and invited to dine with her. Given the Freedom of the City of London. Must have driven Prothero mad with envy!"

He was quiet for some minutes, then sighed. "But he got me in the end. The charge of treason would never have held but for Prothero. James Hodge swore he'd heard me say we were going to blow up Newport Bridge and attack the town. Apparently I'd confided in this man, whom I barely knew, that I was going to stop the mail and start a nationwide rebellion! Turns out Prothero was alone when this 'confession' was extracted from Hodge. Conveniently no other witnesses heard it… oh, and another small matter, Anne. Prothero just happened to have offered Hodge employment the week before! So much for justice, eh?"

They spent the evening poring over newspaper stories of the trial, checking names and details from the published account by Gurney, then re-reading letters John wrote about it years later. Gathering the facts, Anne realised for the first time how important a role Prothero had played in the prosecution and conviction of her father, cleverly inveigling his slithery self into the service of the London prosecutors. The odds were heavily weighted against John from the start, the shadow of his past darkening every day.

MONMOUTH
November 1839

He had been here before, of course. Seventeen years before.

As the prison cart rattled up Monks Way, John could see Monmouth Gaol ahead, a brooding presence just beyond the turnpike cottage on the narrow road to Hereford. Built some fifty years before, its turrets and high stone walls stood impenetrable as a medieval fortress. In its sad environs lived the debtors, the vagrants, the murderers and the scoundrels alike. Grey shapeless uniforms offered no warmth in winter and were flea-infested in summer. Sick inmates were treated perfunctorily in the infirmary and then, more often than not, buried in the cemetery lying in an adjoining field.

The gatehouse was ominous, incongruously grand with its flat roof ideal for hangings. These would be observed, often in an atmosphere of great festivity, by mawkish onlookers cheering the executions from a convenient grassy mound on the opposite side of the Hereford Road. The gatehouse also housed the hangman's drop, and two condemned cells eagerly awaited their next guests from just inside the huge wooden door with its overhanging portcullis. The whole place had delusions of grandeur.

A turnkey with greasy grey locks and a limp pushed John roughly into a cell in the main block, and John recognised the smell of cheap spirits on the man. Stumbling blindly onto a straw mattress, he heard the key turn in the door, and shivered, suddenly afraid for the first time in days. He was completely alone. Cold air filtered through the grill which covered a narrow aperture high in the wall. It was pitch dark, the silence broken only by occasional cries from neighbouring cells, and the ubiquitous rats who came respectfully to inspect their new cellmate. With heavy heart, John pondered the fate of the other leaders.

Later he would learn that Jack the Fifer, reckless as ever, had favoured a second attack and tried unsuccessfully to regroup the retreating men. He'd been heard bragging how he had intended to kill the mayor, and that he had "got a few" soldiers at the Westgate. His card was marked, but with his usual devil's luck he eluded trial and escaped to Virginia. It was fifteen years before John saw him again.

William spent some time in hiding, but was soon captured and taken to Monmouth. He and John were joined by Zephaniah, spotted in Cardiff by one of the many who saved their own skin at that time by reporting erstwhile friends to the authorities. John was not surprised. Not even angry. He knew 'twas ever thus.

The wheel's final turn and the end point of a journey, a cause, a dream that had led the three of them to nothing more than a trial in Monmouth for high treason, the rarest of charges. So rare in fact that Solicitor Maule for the Crown was forced to study old legal cases in search of useful precedent. He also took advice from the local men assisting him with the interrogations, none other than John's longtime adversaries, Prothero and Phillips. The clerk T.J. Phillips busied himself squirrelling evidence from three hundred "witnesses", many of whom were employers, professionals, policemen and residents of Newport. Some, though, were disillusioned Chartists, and tongues were loosened by the threat of the workhouse. Arrests were commonplace, gaols and police stations were full to overflowing, anxiety was everywhere, trust was nowhere, and some informants needed police protection.

Zephaniah brought news to his friends as they met together for the first time in the icy cold of the exercise yard: "There are bounty hunters everywhere," he whispered. "John, you'll remember Thomas Watts? Farmed above Blackwood? He reckons he's helped find over twenty Chartist marchers. Earned a fortune from it, I'll wager."

William was unimpressed. "Won't win him friends up in that valley… He'll be blacklisted, could lose his farm. Folk thereabouts don't forget betrayals. Never."

At the mention of betrayal, John was tempted to say something about William's absence at the Westgate, but remained silent. What was the point, now all was lost?

Zephaniah continued. "Prothero is cutting deals like there's no tomorrow. You both know Tom Saunders, the draper's assistant. He's been grovelling around Prothero too. Claims he followed me on the day of our march, and saw everything. Truth is he was never there!"

"His word will never hold, surely," William replied. "Saunders is a well-known opportunist. He'd swear to anything if the reward suited him. He's not the only one though. I reckon nine tenths of the 'evidence' they're collecting is lies."

"Shall I tell you what I fear most? So few of the poor buggers the Newport magistrates have sent on to trial will have the means to defend themselves." Zephaniah shook his head in despair. "Last I heard before they found me was that even those who did have legal support were denied access; bail was refused and paperwork from the magistrates was held back. They'll make it as hard as they can, won't they? We, none of us, stand a chance."

John tried to lift the moment. "Friends," he pleaded, "we must stay strong. We've come so far and achieved so much, far too much just to lead us to the gallows. What we have done has threatened the men in power, and they're bound to hit back, but believe me, the cause does not end here."

The other two said nothing.

Darkness was falling and a cold drizzle covered the cobbled yard.

"Stop your jabber, you traitorous filth!" the wizened old turnkey snarled. "Back inside now!" And he hustled them grumpily back to their cells.

***

A weak morning light filtered into his cell and John woke with a fever. At some point between dream and waking he saw his grandmother. He could smell lavender, and reached out from his bed, but then suddenly he was with Francis Place in his London library. The turnkey bringing the morning gruel found John pale, weak and rambling, calling for Mary, then cursing others whose names the man did not recognise. He feared that this famous prisoner might die before the trial, and went swiftly to the prison doctor. A dour and indifferent man, the latter claimed John had contracted a "binary derangement" following the exposure to the elements on the night of the march.

"Give him arrowroot with his gruel," he told the turnkey. "That'll see him well enough to meet his fate."

For several days John lay on his straw mattress, barely conscious, just able to lift himself to use the bucket to void his stomach or his bowels. At one point the prison chaplain was called, and readied John to meet his maker.

Then suddenly the fever passed. Hungry, John called through the door for food. The turnkey pushed open the small serving hatch cut into the cell door and John took the opportunity to ask, "I want to see my wife."

The turnkey scoffed, shoved a dirty tin bowl of foul-smelling gruel through and rubbed a skinny arm across his face. "Not a chance," he replied, grinning. "Governor's orders."

"Then I demand to see the governor himself." John summoned all his energy to sound confident, but was still surprised some hours later when the cell door opened and the man in question appeared, silhouetted against a bright lamp light which blinded John temporarily.

"Mr Frost, delighted I'm sure!" This was one to take his pleasure in power. He spoke slowly, relishing the moment. "I regret we are unable to grant your wish to see your wife. However, I too must bow before my Christian duty to show some mercy, and I have granted you a visitor this afternoon. Your stepson, Mr Geach, has asked to visit. As your defence counsel, he has some justification for seeing you. One hour only, mind. "

He turned to go. "Oh, I almost forgot. They tell me you like to read, Mr Frost. You desire some light diversion to while away the time till your trial, perhaps?" A saccharine smile as he threw down onto the filthy mattress a small pamphlet, dated 1832. John recognised the printer's name and, holding the booklet close to the light still outside his cell, read *Rules, orders and regulations for the government of the Gaol in Monmouth.*

Oftentimes the cruelty of men is coated in courtesy.

John had always held his stepson in great affection. A clever lad, handsome and with his mother's eyes, William Geach had his own family now and had made a name for himself as a fine solicitor. Until that is, he was declared bankrupt by some devilish machinations linked to Prothero and Phillips. He had since launched his new practice in Bristol, was again building up a reputation, but here was a chance to defend his stepfather and to face in court the likes of Prothero. It was irresistible.

"Thank you, William." John choked back tears of relief at the sight of a familiar face. "This means so much to me."

William saw how thin and tired John looked, older than his fifty-four years. He needed to offer some good news if he could. "First, let me reassure you that Mother and the children are all well cared for and send their love. You have many supporters still. Some in London and elsewhere, like O'Connell, are collecting to pay for the defence of the others to be tried for treason. But I will do what I can for you, Zephaniah and William."

"How many others are accused?" John asked.

"Of treason, twenty-one, all here in the gaol. There is much interest across the country, and all the newspapers are full of the story. Not surprising really, given this is the first high treason case in twenty years."

"What are they saying? I fear the papers will have found us guilty already."

William tried to sound positive. "O'Connor wrote in his *Northern Star* that 'the cause of Frost is the cause of the whole nation'."

"And the others?" John did not need an answer. William's face said enough.

John sighed. "Iesu Mawr, Prothero must be loving all this."

"I have argued for more time to prepare a proper defence before the trial," William continued, "but all those local men with means and influence are keen to proceed quickly. The special commission is set to open on December tenth."

"Who will preside?

William was hesitant. "Justice John Williams," he said, avoiding John's eyes.

"Christ no! He was the bastard who did for the Tolpuddle men. We might as well walk to the scaffold now!"

"Do not think that way," William replied. "The Lord Chief Justice, Sir Nicholas Tindal, will also sit. He's a fair man, a deep thinker and known for acts of kindness. The third will be Sir James Parker. Justice Williams will not be the only voice."

"And for defence?"

"Pollock and Kelly. Brilliant, both. They'll put the so-called 'witnesses' through their paces. I'm doing all I can digging up dirt to discredit the likes of Hodge and Tovey. What they told the magistrates… sounded as though another French Revolution had been intercepted! By the time they are questioned at the trial, they will be exposed for the liars they are. I'll make sure of that, I promise you. It'll wipe the smug grin off Prothero's face too. Besides, some of his informants have already jumped bail and fled. It all weakens the prosecution case.

"And to find you guilty of treason," William continued, "they will have to prove you intended harm to the Queen. *Intention* is paramount for the charge to hold, not what *actually* happened at the Westgate. For that, I remain optimistic you will be freed."

John remembered the looks of the magistrates when they sent him to Monmouth Gaol, the sneer on Prothero's face, the governor's grin. Local men with axes to grind cared little for the technicalities of London law. They had him. This was their chance. He wished he could share William's certainty.

"Have you some paper and ink?" he asked. "I would like to write to Mary."

He feared it might be his last chance to do so.

STAPLETON, BRISTOL
1877

Her fingers hurt. Anne had given up trying to remove all the ink staining her middle finger, and rubbed now at the callous forming there. She lowered the silver lid on the glass inkwell and was struck by a sudden memory. Catharine had won that inkwell at school for writing the best story. Anne remembered how proud their mother had been when Catharine brought it home, and her own hidden envy.

The night before she left for Australia the second time, Catharine had given it to Anne. "In case you decide to write something," she had said, dismissively. Anne wondered what Catharine would think of the story she was writing now. Then stopped herself. What did it matter? Her sister had made her choice and was no longer part of their life.

She checked the nib of her dip pen. It was wearing thin, and she would need to replace it soon. Her supply of paper was dwindling too, and she sighed at the thought of the expense. Chewing her lip, she considered how she might manage their meagre budget to accommodate such extras.

Anne rose, stretched and placed her hands on her hips. Her back ached from long hours hunched over the manuscript. She had been rereading the sections covering her father's arrest and charge, altering a word here and there, and she rubbed her tired eyes. She wished she was younger to tackle all this. She had in her possession a great deal of material about the trial, some she did not trust, and some of such intricate legal detail its meaning eluded her. Anne knew it would confuse her readers too, who might then abandon the story, so she needed to be selective. She had to ensure a reader continued to care about her father, as if he were a friend.

She refocused. Clearly the Chartists had secured in Sir Frederick Pollock and Fitzroy Kelly the best defence for her father, and she understood the judges' directive that the trial should focus on "object, design and intent". She believed her father when he said he had not wanted violence in Newport, just a peaceful show of strength to demonstrate support for Vincent and the Charter. But there was always a whispering doubt which accompanied her writing, like the bitter, lingering taste of something eaten many hours before. Try as she might, she could not bury the niggling question about weapons. Her father was not naive; he surely knew people like Jack the Fifer would use them if they carried them. And he'd read for himself the men's mood at Blaina.

At breakfast the following day, John asked her, "What do *you* remember of the days around the trial, Anne? You were just a girl, but you must have some recollections."

Anne thought for a moment. "Soldiers," she said. "There were soldiers everywhere, in Newport and Monmouth. And I remember William calling to see us and bring us news. He told us about the jury, selected from influential people who hated and feared the Chartist cause – the iron-masters, or Morgan from Tredegar House. Enemies all.

"Mother refused to go near the courthouse, afraid of what she might hear. But Catharine went, observing everything from high above in the public gallery. She would come home with such anger towards those who gave evidence against you. It was so obvious they were lying for their own gains. But she told us about Pollock and Kelly and how clever they were, and how brother William's help was invaluable.

"Catharine said she heard witnesses testify *for* you too. They reminded the jury of your time as magistrate, of your peaceful nature, and one said you were 'the most unnatural and unprepared revolutionary in history'.

"From articles in these," she said, handing some old newspapers to her father, "I learned the Chartists nationally wanted the trial stopped. The papers tell of angry meetings across the country, and rumours everywhere that the trial would be interrupted by violence – hence all the soldiers, I suppose. The magistrates who had sent you to trial received anonymous letters threatening their lives, and there was a feeling of real danger everywhere. See for yourself."

He read silently, old news now, of violent protests in London, Manchester and Bradford, and of the campaign to save the accused. *"If Frost is unfairly treated,"* he read, *"no crown in Europe will be worth one year's purchase."* He read too that some newspapers, supportive of Chartists, papers such as Vincent's *Western Vindicator* were seized by government agents in the shops. Fear led to the suppression of anything remotely deemed seditious.

"They petitioned the Queen," Anne added. "Thousands signed it. People everywhere saw the injustice of your charges. They wanted you free."

"They did, yes, but *she* certainly did not, nor the men who sat in that courtroom in judgment of me," he said. "Theirs was a mission to prevent any such future rising. No amount of petitioning or clever legal debate would move them. I always knew that, Anne. William Jones didn't often inspire me with his ramblings. Quite the contrary, and I despised his infantile posturing. But on the first morning of the trial, as we were leaving in the prison cart for Monmouth courtroom, manacled together, William remembered some lines he had once delivered as an actor.

"He told us that for the jury we were nothing more than three 'flies to wanton boys'. Zephaniah and I were irritated by his prattling, Anne. It was hardly the moment for his type of nonsense, but he persevered, asking if we remembered the words from *Lear*. When he saw we were still baffled, he scolded us for ignorant illiterates, coughed, adopted his deepest stage voice and declared:

" 'Like flies to wanton boys are we to the Gods.
They kill us for their sport. '."

MONMOUTH
December 1839 – February 1840

The last day of 1839, and the first of the trial. Eight days taking the three men from one year to the next, from one life to another.

The scene is set. A packed court, entrance by ticket only. A wood-panelled room, too small by far for the magnitude of today's business, stuffy with the smell of clothes dampened by heavy December rain, a cloying miasma of stale sweat and fear. On one side, the judge's bench sits magisterially above the proceedings, lit from behind by large, ornate windows, through which a pale winter sun sends accusatory rays like pointed fingers. A central oak table displays leather bound tomes of ancient law, a few unconvincing weapons to be submitted as "evidence" in the trial, and several large, well-travelled leather bags holding the legal arguments of the London lawyers.

Noises from the square outside provide the accompanying soundtrack. Horses. Hawkers. Hangers-on. Men using the occasion as an excuse to find oblivion, noisily, in The King's Arms. Sounds more typical of the annual May fair.

Inside, a court artist sent from London will later sketch the accused with skill, catching their differences: Zephaniah struggling to accept the reality of his surroundings, eyes darting madly around the room; William waving and greeting familiar faces up in the gallery, playing his best role yet; and John – reserved, watchful, resigned. Three men chained together in their fate, but linked with all those present to a shared moment of history.

Before dawn, the three prisoners had stumbled out of the cart from the gaol and been pushed unceremoniously down a narrow, winding, rough stone staircase to the six small holding cells deep beneath the courtroom. Only the flickering of a turnkey's torch showed each man the grim reality of a cell just big enough to stand in, with no possibility of moving more than one pace in either direction.

"How long must I stand here?" John could hear the desperation in Zephaniah's voice. He had noticed his friend shaking as he stumbled down the steps to this hellhole.

"Till it pleases the judge," the turnkey muttered and slammed the cells' shutters.

Left then in the cold darkness, John tried to control the nausea brought on by an overpowering smell of stale urine and damp. There was freezing water beneath his feet, and he heard everywhere the scuttling of the now familiar cellmates. He knew it then, in that blackness, knew with an intense clarity, that they were dead men, that the efficacy of their defence mattered little. He visualised the days ahead, and prepared. He would try to stay calm for Mary's sake, for Catharine in the gallery, for his sanity.

The judges, accompanied by trumpeters, had arrived in the town with wigs dusted, robed in ermine and scarlet, like royalty. Proceedings began with a service, the message borrowed from 2 Peter ii 19 and directed at the accused: *"while they promise them liberty, they themselves are the servants of corruption."*

The prosecution was determined to show the 4th November rising was not a gathering about a private issue such as pay or food, or even to demonstrate about Vincent, but was to attack, gain possession of Newport, spread rebellion, change the law and ultimately the government of the country. Intent therefore was insurrection, plain and simple.

The defence applied the letter of the law with astute intensity, tackling the four "witnesses" for the Crown, tearing at their statements.

Fiercely.

Mercilessly.

Successfully, to such an extent that the Crown was forced to withdraw some of its "evidence". Pollock was a clever orator. He reminded the jury constantly that they should focus on *intention*, not the outcome of the march, then discredited the claim about the apparent plan to stop the mail. That, he said, was simply absurd. Frost would know full well the mail went from Bristol to Birmingham, and nothing he might do in Newport would influence that. At one point, Pollock flicked a dismissive hand in the direction of the few rusting guns sitting on the table, turned to the prosecutor and said, "Is this all my honourable friend can find? It's hardly the weaponry for a revolution, is it?" Responding to the supportive sniggering audible in the gallery, he looked up and added, "I ask you this, gentlemen of the jury. Why would men march to the Westgate Hotel if the intention was to seize the town of Newport? Would they not have blown up Newport Bridge first? All this so-called 'proof' is nonsense. The prosecution is based entirely on hearsay and uncorroborated tittle-tattle. Gentlemen, do you really think Frost would confide his plans in a man like Hodge anyway?"

It was a strong argument.

Kelly then spoke for over five hours, revisiting Pollock's remarks, trying to shake the jury's convictions. The defence was strong, clear, logical, and John knew he could not have asked for better. It demonstrated that there were flaws in the prosecution's case, but yet, but yet… no real alternative was proposed by the defence as to the definitive purpose of the march on Newport. In the cold light of a courtroom day, the rising seemed to be lacking one clear coherent plan. Whereas another jury in a different town may have hesitated, claiming reasonable doubt, nothing would convince this group to budge from conviction.

When the Lord Chief Justice summed up, he caused a sensation, embarrassing the Crown legal team by referring to the weaknesses in the prosecution's case and clearly hinting for an acquittal.

The Attorney General wrote later of his surprise that "Tindal summed up for an acquittal", and he was discussing the potentially disastrous outcome of this with his team when the jury's decision was announced.

John always remembered the wait in that holding cell until they reached the verdict – a thirty-minute visit to purgatory. Thirty to judge a man's deeds; thirty to decide a man's future; thirty to take his life. By 6.20 p.m. on 8th January, his fate was sealed. Within the next few days, the other two leaders were also found guilty, unanimously, with a recommendation for mercy.

***

Nine a.m. on January 16th. Chief Justice Tindal had been shut in his small room at the side of the court for hours with just his thoughts, his Bible and his conscience for company. In the courtroom spectators stood shoulder to shoulder, elbowing for a better view, the whole crowd holding its breath as one when the sentence was declared. A sombre man, his face lined and ashen, Tindal reminded the assembly of the enormity of treason and, as if in slow motion, lowered the black cloth carefully over his wig, cleared his throat and sentenced the three men to death. The worst type of execution would be theirs, he added, a hanging before their heads were hacked off, then their limbs severed and distributed.

"God save us!" Zephaniah was breathless, pale and trembling in the dock. "This cannot be."

William smiled, looked up at the supporters in the gallery, waved again and yelled, "Long live the Charter!"

John felt somehow dissociated from the scene. The gruesome reality had yet to dawn. He read later some journalist present in the court had written of how he had stumbled in the dock, that he had shed tears. He did not recognise that account as true: he had merely tripped on his ankle chains, and cried out in pain.

The three condemned men were moved to a cell in the gaol's gatehouse and made to share the one small space. They smelt death waiting. Completely cut off from everyone, they listened to distant shouts of support from the crowd outside the gaol walls, but after a few days, that slowly diminished as people drifted back to their lives, and another sound replaced the cries. They were building the scaffold on the gatehouse roof.

"How do you wish your limbs to be passed on?" The governor was enjoying this. "The thinking is we should send them around the county, but if you have any preference I'm happy to oblige."

Later the turnkey came calling to cut their food, knives being forbidden.

"Your special visitor's in town," he laughed. "Best hangman in Wales. He'll make a clean show of it." When the men did not rise to his words, he lowered his voice and said, "Now, if you'd prefer to meet your maker *before* the last walk up to the roof, I can *accidentally* leave the knife here, or get something to add to your gruel. Just say the word, gents." Turning to John, he grinned and added, "Your pretty daughter can pay me later."

Anxiety and regret stalked the dark corners of their dingy cell. They were there twelve days while legal technicalities were disputed. Twelve long days till death.

"Why did I not see where this would lead us?" Zephaniah asked himself aloud, fighting tears. "Do you think there will be an appeal?"

"Can't say I'm hopeful," William grunted. "Execution date's set for February 6th so there's no time."

John said little. He was tired, having barely slept during the days of the trial. He wore blame like a cloak. It kept hidden his shame and regret, and silenced his pain. It was his fault men had died. His fault other, decent men were being sent God knows where. He had let events take over after that Blaina meeting, too weak to stand up to Jack and the others. Then came the storm, the poor communication, the men's drinking and the crazy belief that soldiers would not return fire. It had left futile and fatal any march intended to show solidarity. He did not fear death now, but feared more a lifetime remembering the pain he had caused others.

When the prison chaplain came, Zephaniah prayed with him, clutching the man's robe as if he was holding life itself. John worried increasingly about his friend's state of mind. William by contrast examined his nails, indifferent, bored.

"Do you wish to pray too, my son?" the man asked John, who closed his eyes and tried, but saw only Mary with his children. What he wanted was *their* forgiveness, not some futile plea to his maker.

"Can you take a message to my wife?" John asked and, aware of the others in the cell, whispered in the man's ear.

The following day, the chaplain returned. "I have something for you," he said, "but keep it hidden from the governor… and the turnkey." From his sleeve, he pulled out a long, thin piece of old leather, which John recognised at once. It had come from his grandfather's shop. "She said you must wear it to remind you of the love which binds your family to you, always."

John wrapped the leather thread around his wrist and knotted it tightly. It would go with him to the scaffold, he thought. In reality, it was to cross oceans and continents with him, a link to all he loved. Much later, whilst a clerk in Van Diemen's Land, he had touched the worn leather, faded then by the interminably hot sun, and reflected on his part in the rising, writing in his journal:

"I was not the man for such an undertaking. From the moment I saw blood flow I was terrified and fled. But what was I to do? I went up to the mountains and men asked me, 'Mr Frost if you won't lead us, neither you nor your family shall live in Newport. We are beginning to suspect you'."

But through the long, dark January days of 1840, a heavy silence fell on their cell, broken only by John's persistent cough. Their initial postmortem of that fateful November day, and the search for blame, had only led to futile acrimony. Now, each man sank into a private despair. Words had brought them here, trapped them and branded them as traitors. Enough with words, then. Besides, what was there left to say? The three believed they had no future, and any hopes for a reprieve or pardon before February 6th were best left unspoken.

John listened to the carpenters overhead, the wind sometimes carrying their curses down to their waiting customers. Once he heard them call out crudely to the washerwoman who repaired the prison linen. Other sounds: the bells of St Mary's summoning the faithful, children playing far off, horses and cattle in the fields around the gaol.

Sounds of a normal life, one he suddenly craved. He was not yet ready to die.

But he tried not to think about what *might* be.

Anticipation only made any disappointment far worse.

STAPLETON, BRISTOL
1877

Anne watched nervously as her father read what she had written. He had spoken softly to her about his experiences in the condemned cell, and she had tried to capture faithfully that time of bleak anticipation.

"You have been kind to me, lass."

Still that "lass", in spite of her grey hairs.

"But you're wrong about one thing. I didn't collapse and cry out at the sentence, as the court reporter claimed in that paper you showed me. The verdict had come as no surprise to me. It was Zephaniah. He could barely stand when Tindal put on that black cloth. So distressed was he that proceedings were halted for a while. Then, when the worst was uttered, he fell. Chained to him, I stumbled too."

Anne altered what she had written just as he wished, aware that accuracy about his behaviour in that courtroom was important to him even now. A man of pride still.

"It is difficult to imagine those days now," she said. "We were so afraid for you. Mother was inconsolable, and Catharine spent her time rallying your supporters. People across the country were demanding a pardon. Mass meetings in all the big towns. You were not forgotten, Father."

He was turning the scrappy leather thread still tied around his wrist. It had become looser last winter and Anne had tightened it for him. He sighed.

"We did not hold out much hope, you know. They say Melbourne and his ministers were tough, immovable when asked to show mercy, even after thousands petitioned on our behalf. Our executions were seen as necessary, Anne. An example to deter anarchy. But then apparently they suddenly mellowed, and bowed to Tindal's summing up... Or did they? In retrospect, Anne, I'm not sure that was the reason. I think it was something far more mundane. Making martyrs of three ordinary Welshmen, condemning them to a brutal execution, would not look good, would it, reported in gruesome detail on the front pages of the newspapers on the same day as the Queen's wedding?"

"I am certain those in power feared a nationwide revolution," she concurred. "There was such a strong feeling everywhere. Whatever the reason, we were relieved when we heard you were spared death."

They walked outside to sit on the bench in the April sunshine. Life was returning to their garden, and they smiled at each other when the neighbour's lad passed, hand in hand with the fresh-faced daughter of the local landlord.

Anne was worried. She had fewer resources available to inform the next section of her father's tale. One or two letters written to Mary from Tasmania, some references to the journey in John's journal, and a few unsubstantiated comments from visitors to the prison ship before it left British shores. For accuracy, for credibility, she needed her father's memories. Recalling that time was bound to be difficult for him. She saw sometimes how frail he was physically, though his mind was still sharp. This required a careful path, a gentle touch.

That evening, she tried to distract him from his memories for a while, fearful that it might all be too painful for a man of his age. She brought him the daily newspaper.

"Look at this, Father," she laughed, hoping to lift his mood. "Have you ever seen anything like it? This is Zazel, or rather Rossa Richter, shot from a cannon in London. At the age of fourteen! Imagine!"

John glanced briefly at the artist's sketch, but did not register the story before him. All that mattered now was his own, and Anne listened carefully as he revisited another dark memory. She would record it later whilst he slept.

"They came at midnight on February 2nd," he said. "We were shoved out of the cell, barely awake in the darkness, afraid we were going to our deaths there and then. It was raining heavily, I remember, but I could see a large number of armed militia, and realised we were being moved. We were in heavy leg irons and handcuffs, escorted by lancers to we knew not where, Anne, and had no time to write farewell messages."

He was speaking fast now, the memories vivid, his eyes shining as if he was back in that life. He lit his pipe again, and continued.

"The cart took us at great speed to Chepstow, then on the steamer *Usk* to Portsmouth. God, I was weak, could barely sit upright, and I coughed persistently. Weather was foul, I remember, and I suffered mightily on the rough seas for two weeks."

A minute passed. "We had to seek harbour more than once before joining the *York*, the prison hulk where I spent the worst of days. I had smelt mankind at his most bestial before, I thought, in that London gaol in '23, but on the *York* we were packed together, unwashed, covered in vomit and excrement for days. You never forget."

Another pause. "I fell ill again, delirious at times, and could stomach nothing but water and a little bread. Ten days we spent in that hell, Anne. Then we were moved again, to the convict ship The *Mandarin*. No one aboard expected me to survive. They threw a rough tarpaulin over me, and lay me in the ship's sick bay, to die I suppose. Though I am loath to use the word, Anne, The *Mandarin* would serve the two hundred or so of us on board as *home* for five months and fourteen thousand miles."

"I remember William went to meet you in Portsmouth," Anne interrupted. "He told Mother you were in good spirits but later told Catharine the truth, that you were declining in health. He feared you would not see the journey's end."

"Dear William. He wanted to go on appealing for a reprieve, but I told him not to waste his time. Men had been transported for lesser crimes than a riot in Newport. But I had another visitor in Portsmouth, you know," John added. "The town's governor came, and advised me quietly but firmly to stay out of any trouble on board. He sent his companion out of earshot and told me he had it on good authority that the government was waiting for the least excuse to authorise my rapid demise at sea. It was to prove sound advice."

THE *MANDARIN*
February – July 1840

So battered was the ship by the winter storms off the south coast that its topmast was shattered and it docked at Falmouth for a refit. John was being surprisingly well cared for by the ship's surgeon-general, a Dr McKechnie, and slowly he began to gain strength, enough to join Zephaniah and William in a secure cabin set apart from the other convicts, one normally reserved for the most dangerous criminals. Though some of the convicts on board were petty thieves or unfortunate wretches driven to crime through desperation to feed a family, others were brutes, murderers and rapists who would not hesitate to kill a fellow convict if looked at the wrong way. Every day in such company carried an underlying threat, and no one trusted his neighbour in chains.

On the second day in Falmouth, a visitor boarded the vessel. Barclay Fox was desperate to see these three notorious rebels for himself, and so, disguised as a missionary, he came offering religious and moral tracts to the deprived souls on board.

"Have you any preference, Mr Frost?" he asked, commenting later on the Chartist leader's wan and furrowed face, his haggard expression.

John asked the man for a copy of *The Pilgrim's Progress*.

"I expect you are relieved to be spared the hangman's expertise?" Fox probed.

"In truth, I should vastly prefer hanging to this slow, lingering torture to which they have condemned me now," John replied, much to the visitor's surprise.

Fox was about to leave, but turned to add, "I'll bring you the Bunyan, Mr Frost, but take care you are not lured too soon into that slough of despair. Life may surprise you yet."

Before the ship left Falmouth, John persuaded McKechnie to prove materials so he might write a final letter to Mary.

"My love," he wrote. *"I am travelling now to a future I cannot yet imagine. If God wishes, I will see land and serve my sentence far from home. I beg you not to follow. Instead, look after our children. Catharine is strong, and will be of great comfort to you, but the others will need all your love. It is my hope that I will return to be with you once more, and until then, know that I love you, and cherish our years together. If we do not meet again, then you should also know that I am resigned to death. It matters not when it comes. The value of life depends on the use we can be to others: if we cannot use it for the good of family or society then it has hardly worth having.*

"When I hear the gulls' cries, I think of my childhood. When I see the stars from the ship at night, my love, I think of you, the children and home. A home that will be with me always, and I swear that wherever this voyage casts me ashore, each night before I sleep, I will remember your face, and pray for you all. Be strong. Kiss the children for me, John."

They were dressed now in the same coarse uniform as the other convicts, all of them male, whose quarters allowed just eighteen inches for each man to sleep. Conditions on prison ships had improved marginally since the First Fleet, and as the surgeon on board was paid according to the number who survived the journey, McKechnie was dutiful in distributing whatever was necessary to prevent scurvy or the spread of disease.

Nevertheless, the men spent long hours each day under the deck, with what little air there was filtering through the bars of the hatch. In warmer climes it was near unbearable, and they relished their brief exercise period on deck. There were deaths, inevitably, a few older men unable to bear the airless confinement. Others just wanted escape. One young prisoner, a delicate boy of no more than fourteen years, was teased mercilessly by some of the older men who groped him as he passed, blew kisses at him and made lewd remarks. On an insufferably hot day, ship becalmed, deck scorched and the crew dazed by lethargy, the prisoners were allowed to exercise without chains on deck.

John watched as the boy leapt overboard and found release.

In weather which improved as the days passed, the ship sailed across the Bay of Biscay, down the west coast of Africa towards Simon's Bay on the Cape of Good Hope. Long days, with nothing to break the aching monotony of the ship's rhythm, the creaking deck and the cursing of the men in chains. During those precious moments outside, John watched the sea creatures which followed the ship, or listened to the cries of the circling birds which swooped low above his head, then flew off, high into an unbroken sky, mocking the men trapped far below.

Once, he woke having dreamt of his grandmother and thought he could smell lavender. In the following hours of darkness, he lay awake and felt overwhelmingly close to Mary and the children. He could see again the bluebells in Bettws Woods, touch her dark curls and remember her warm body. He closed his eyes and, in bright light, heard voices singing a familiar Welsh air, sad in its lilting soulfulness. He cried himself back to sleep. In the morning he asked William what date it was. His friend had kept a tally scratching on the wooden bedpost with his belt buckle every night.

"We have been at sea over three months," William replied. "It is May 25th."

John smiled. It was his fifty-fourth birthday.

He watched the life of the crew and officers on board with interest, and soon realised the full extent of the surgeon-general's influence. He not only dealt with sickness, but acted as chaplain, as mentor, as magistrate in charge of sanctions, including any floggings. McKechnie wielded great power, and John, who from long experience was suspicious of men with too much power, found himself holding back. He could not trust this man as Zephaniah and William did, even though on the surface, he had shown them kindness.

One night the suffocating heat made him restless, and he heard a woman's cry from the other side of the ship. Only four women were travelling on the *Mandarin*, wives of the soldiers accompanying the convicts. John had noticed in Falmouth that a young, fair woman who had struggled up the gangplank was expecting a child, and he had feared for her on the journey ahead. Now he recognised the cries of labour, cries which turned to screams shrill enough to freeze the southern skies. "God help her!" he whispered, and had a sudden memory of James, lost to him for ever. Locked in their cabin, the three men could hear running on deck, and other cries, shouts of men desperate to do something. Then silence.

"I have not heard a baby cry," Zephaniah said sadly. "That augurs ill."

Later, when Dr McKechnie called to check on them, he confirmed their fears.

He was clearly shaken and exhausted from the night's events. "I couldn't save her," he said, head in hands. "The baby's head was stuck... I have little experience of childbirth, and no instruments on board here to help. I might have otherwise saved the mother..."

At noon they heard the soldiers gather on deck, and the sound of the body as it was jettisoned into the deep. The three men said little for the rest of the day, each man remembering his own wife and children, holding their memories like an aching loss.

STAPLETON, BRISTOL
1877

"What is it, child?" He saw she was troubled. She had stopped writing, was pale, scowling again, her hand trembling. "Have I said something to upset you?"

Anne hesitated before replying, averting her gaze. "Those books you used to read before your eyes weakened, about Spiritualism, and the power of the mind, and that lecture you went to about people sending thoughts to each other… I thought it all nonsense, you know, just the ravings of charlatans. But there is something you do not know, Father, could not have known. It is written nowhere but in my memory."

"Then it is *your* turn to share a recollection this time, child," he said, and sought the comfort of his favourite chair.

"On the first occasion of your birthday after you left us,' Anne said, her voice wavering, "Mother insisted we all gather together. John came with his family. He closed the shop for the day. All of us were there – Elizabeth, Sarah, Ellie and Catharine, all in our finest dresses, and the house was ablaze with candles. Mother got out your grandmother's Bible, the one with the lavender pressed in the covers, and we sat praying for your safe return. Then Catharine, with her sweet voice, and Henry Hunt, just eighteen at the time, sang for us. That sad Welsh song Mother always loved…" She paused, then raising her eyes to his, said, "It is just as you saw it on the ship, Father, exactly like."

They sat in silence until daylight faded. What was there to say?

It was a moment beyond the confines of mere words.

The next morning the rooms were filled with a spring sunlight. Outside, early flowers were pushing through a winter soil. Anne knew she needed to do something about the weeds, but her back ached so, and there had been more headaches in recent days. She felt her age and sighed.

Over breakfast, she said, "Mother kept that letter you wrote from Falmouth in her book of poems. She read it often, always believing you would return."

"Like Ulysses, I suppose!" He smiled as she handed him the flimsy letter he had scribbled on the convict ship over thirty years before. "But I was no brave hero willingly seeking adventure."

She walked to his chair and knelt before him, taking his hands in her own in rare intimacy. "Heroes come in many guises, Father," she said, and he kissed the top of her head, aware that they had become closer in recent months than ever before.

Returning to her desk, Anne reread her recent work and asked, "Was it true, Father, what you told Mr Fox in Falmouth? Did you really wish you had not been saved from the scaffold?"

He was quiet for a time, then said softly, "At the time, I believe I did. You cannot imagine the monotony on board, Anne, it plays with your mind. Hour after empty hour. Cramped conditions, the smell of unwashed, sick men, the tasteless, meagre rations, and above all the fear. Fear of the other convicts, fear of disease, fear of where we were headed. We all knew what was waiting in Van Diemen's Land. We had read the stories and reports. Death had to be better than a life there in misery and pain."

He saw she was shaken by such thoughts. "What strengthened me were the memories of home, and all of you," he added, touching her hand briefly. "There were dark moments, moments when I despaired, but I would hold the leather thread around my wrist and remember your mother telling me 'not to yield'.

"For the others it was different," he continued. "William always disguised his fear by jest. Once, when an albatross visited the ship, he entertained us with a recitation of that Coleridge poem. You know the one – 'water, water everywhere...' Even the worst criminals on board were held spellbound. Whatever else I thought of William, he was clever like that.

"Zephaniah, however, was a worry to me. He had not been himself since the trial, and on board he became more and more reticent, lost in his own world. I would find him rocking back and forth on his bunk sometimes, muttering God knows what, and whimpering about what horrors were waiting for us. What happened next was no real surprise to me. Every man is capable of the worst when self-preservation calls."

"Do you really want to talk about that tonight?" Anne asked. She could see he was tired, but knew his stubborn determination too. She changed tack. "Because *I* am so very tired, Father." She yawned loudly. "I would prefer to write about Zephaniah tomorrow. Shall I get your bedwarmer ready?"

She smiled at her small victory as he followed her without complaint.

THE *MANDARIN*
1840

The soldiers were ever watchful as the prisoners exercised, nervously alert to any sign of dissidence. So John was surprised when a convict with whom he had never previously exchanged a word, an ape of a man with one eye and a scar the length of his face, bent over as if to spit then thrust some paper into his hand. He hid it swiftly under his loose shirt, until he was back in the cabin with his two companions.

"It's a letter asking us to join some of the convicts in a mutiny," he read. "They're planning to seize the ship and sail to South America."

William was immediately interested. "I say we join them. What have we got to lose? You know as well as I what life awaits us in the Colonies."

Zephaniah agreed. "I just want this nightmare to end. We have a good chance of success, I'd say. What can a few soldiers and crew do against the combined anger of two hundred prisoners? I'm for joining them. What about you, John?"

John remembered the warning he had received in Portsmouth.

"I disagree, my friends. This could be nothing but a trap to lure us into another act of rebellion. There are those back home who are waiting for us to err, who want us dead… and we would be quickly disposed of on this ship, no questions asked. It plays perfectly into the hands of our enemies. "

He could sense them hesitating. "Besides," he went on, "if we joined the others, what do you think will happen? I'll wager their first act would be to raid the liquor store, after which we three would be swiftly sent overboard. You've heard the grumblings about us having special treatment and this space to ourselves."

"I still think it's worth the risk," Zephaniah added. "Anything is, to avoid what waits in Hobart."

"Think, I beg you, my friends." John's tone was more aggressive now. "If anyone wants to write a letter like this on board, how does he acquire his writing materials? How would one of the common convicts get to write this?" He waved the letter at his companions. "Why, it's clear as day, isn't it? Only by acting as a stooge for the powers that be… in the guise of McKechnie, I fear, for it is he who authorises all the writing materials."

Zephaniah and William conceded, with some reluctance, and nothing more was said until a day or two later when all the convicts were gathered on deck to witness the brutal flogging of a sailor and a convict who had apparently been found guilty of planning a mutiny. John recognised them both. The sailor was often the worse for wear, lazy and unpopular with his fellow crew, the convict a simple-minded youth prone to singing loudly at odd times, and spinning tales of his adventures as the paramour of a duchess. The two men accused were stripped, and, crying out for mercy, each was whipped repeatedly until the deck was vermillion. John was certain the two had been selected randomly, and he carried the bloody image back to his bed, angry and unable to sleep. He could not know then that he was to witness many such random acts of injustice before he saw home again.

But John always maintained his assertions about what lay behind that clandestine letter. Some months later, leaving behind him the *Mandarin* and McKechnie for ever, the doctor leaned towards John on the Hobart quayside and whispered in his ear, "Welcome to your new life, Mr Frost. I'm glad you survived the journey. It was touch and go for a while back there, but I didn't want the famous Chartist leader dead on my watch."

The surgeon contemplated with an air of disinterest the ship's human cargo as it disembarked, a ragged batch of lost souls.

"Careful how you go here, mind. You did well to ward off that mutiny ruse. Remember you are being watched always, Frost, so don't trust anyone here too easily, will you?" His smile was ice. Before turning to go he added, "Know that you've said nothing and done nothing since you boarded the ship with which I have not been made acquainted."

That was 30th June. Previously, at the start of the month, Zephaniah had continued to decline. He had spent the days lying on his straw bunk, staring at the wooden slats of William's bed above. He rarely ate, and at night would cry out in his sleep or weep inconsolably. John was saddened to see this man so fallen from the articulate, clever friend he had once admired.

After one particularly bad night, when Zephaniah's cries must have woken all on board, McKechnie took him away to the ship's sick bay. Zephaniah did not return for three days, and when he did, he ignored his friends' greetings, lay on his bunk facing the wooden panels which separated them from the main quarters, and said nothing. More than twelve months would pass before John learnt exactly what his friend had been telling the ship's surgeon-general.

But in the days immediately following this incident, there were other problems to face. The weather turned and the ship hit gales of such force no one was safe on deck. The noise was insufferable. Forked lightning immediately overhead, and deafening thunder bringing an apocalyptic deluge such as John had never seen before. Waves peaked and fell, the gales playing with the ship like a toy. Sea water swept over the decks for hours on end, and the ship rolled and cracked as if begging the elements to cease their torment.

All hatches were battened down against the tempest, and through the thin wooden wall which separated them, they heard the other men fighting now to keep their quarters from flooding. There were screams of terror, curses to a vengeful God, and often John could hear the hardest, most brutal men cry out for their mothers. He had long since voided his stomach and given up any semblance of decency, but retched now on bile, the cabin reeking of vomit and humanity at its most exposed. For the first time since the trial, John tried to pray.

When the storm calmed a little the next day, John tried to eat some convict beef, holding a wooden post with one hand to steady himself. He heard chuckling, and looked up to see the boatswain laughing. "Ah, Mr Frost," he said. "This voyage will be worth a thousand a year to you; it will teach you something of life." John remembered the words years later whilst writing to a friend, and added thoughts of his own: *"I have seen life now in almost every form; it is something to see in a convict ship – something to see in a penal colony. However, at last, which is something hard to believe, it may turn out for the best."*

STAPLETON, BRISTOL
April 1877

An unforgiving spring sun exposed the neglected corners of their home where dust had gathered over the last few months, unnoticed in draughty corners. Anne lifted her face to feel the sun's warmth, and donned her apron. Time for some cleaning. When she reached her writing desk, she stopped. The wooden surface was hidden completely by all manner of papers, open journals, pamphlets, and an old map of Hobart. This too needed her attention.

Carefully, she made a pile of all the resources she no longer needed – accounts of the march in Newport, newspaper reports of the trial, early journals and letters, and Francis Place's documents. She was about to add her mother's copy of Tennyson but hesitated, and placed it back on her desk where she could see it. When John found her, she was still in her apron, feather duster on her desk, an errant curl falling around her face. It always annoyed him when she left tasks unfinished, one of those unspoken irritations which accompany life spent in close proximity to another. She had not seen him approach and jumped when he spoke.

"May I help?" He knew he sounded brusque.

She dropped what she was reading, and distractedly pushed the loose hair behind her ear. "Goodness, you startled me... I started to give some order to the papers on my desk, but then began to read one, and forgot myself again... but yes, you can help. These can all go back in your chest now." And she indicated the pile at her feet.

He needed several journeys to complete the task, limping painfully each time he crossed the room.

"I have almost finished with the dusting," she said, "and I am anxious to start telling of your time in the Colonies. But I need your memories of what happened to Zephaniah on the ship. I can find little reference to him in your correspondence from that time."

"You won't," he replied. "Go finish your chores, Anne, and I'll tell you what I learned."

A while later, she poured him some ale, and he sipped slowly as he travelled back, accompanied by the scratching of her pen.

"I'd been in Hobart a year or so," he started. "News from London reached us slowly, and the papers were always four or five months old when they came. I had not seen Zephaniah from the day we arrived, when he was sent to supervise the coal mines, being a geologist and all. I hadn't thought much about him, just hoped he had found some peace in this new life. Then I read the news. On the *Mandarin* that time, in those days with McKechnie, Zephaniah had 'confessed' – at least that was the word the papers used – admitted what we'd all three been charged with, namely high treason, insurrection, an attempt to harm the Crown and cause a nationwide revolution."

"He betrayed you." She was scrutinising his face. "You must have felt much anger."

John shook his head, took another sip of beer. "Not anger, Anne, not even surprise really. Just sadness. The Zephaniah I sailed with on that ship was a broken man. He was terrified of his future. Wanted some easy route by which to lessen the burden. McKechnie's kindness was deceptive, I can vouch for that. But it would have been enough to persuade Zephaniah into admitting whatever was suggested to him. Otherwise, why confess *after* the trial? Makes no sense. No one at the Home Office gave it credibility either... in their view, it was just a rambling statement from a desperate convict on a prison ship."

She remembered the articles in the papers, the verbatim reports of the trial. "Witnesses swore Zephaniah *never* extolled violence. In fact, didn't he warn the men not to damage any property on the march? Doesn't sound much like a revolutionary to me. Tell me, did he ever leave Van Diemen's Land?"

"Never," John replied, "and his years there were eventful, to put it mildly. I'll tell you later, and what happened to William, poor man, but now we must focus on my own story. There is still so much to tell. I am just about to step ashore in Hobart…"

A New World

"Yet all experience is an arch wherethrough
Gleams that untraveled world whose margin fades
Forever and forever when I move."

Tennyson, *Ulysses*

HOBART
1840

He could not stand without falling. So accustomed was he to the months of constant movement that he felt the solid earth move like quicksand and grabbed the nearest post to steady himself. The blinding sunlight on the bustling port, and the sounds of whaling ships unloading and loading, of a myriad shouts and orders. This was Hobart, just three decades old, born unceremoniously to accommodate the lawbreakers from a world away, here on land taken from others. He could see strange trees around Sullivan's Cove, and hear the cawing of exotic birds seeking the cool of the Derwent, which flowed gently into the sea. In the distance, beyond the meadows, rose Mount Wellington, giant of this landscape, capped with snow.

He staggered ashore somehow, and was taken roughly with his two friends to a crude brick building. Shading his eyes from the sun, he looked around at this new world he had joined. He took in the wooden huts for the surgeon and the chaplain, the ensign hanging limp in the square outside Government House, the unwelcoming nature of the place.

Was this where his life had been leading him? Was this where he would die?

They were greeted by a tall, portly man in naval uniform, stern but not hostile. He had the air of one accustomed to giving orders, a man who knew precisely the nature of his role in this new world.

"Sit, gentlemen, you must be weary," he said, John detecting a faint accent, which he could not identify. Sir John Franklin had fought Napoleon, had sailed to the Canadian Arctic. He was not an easy man to impress.

"Welcome to Van Diemen's Land, gentlemen. You have come far, but your reputation reached us before the *Mandarin* docked, and your arrival has already caused a stir in these parts. Here, see for yourselves."

He pushed across his desk a recent copy of the local paper. Their portraits sketched at the trial were on the front page, with an article highly critical of their trial and punishment, supportive of the Chartist aims. They were surprised by this glimmer of hope for what lay ahead.

"I presume we will be treated with respect here," Zephaniah asked, barely concealing the desperation in his voice. He looked shiftily at the other two before adding, "Dr McKechnie has spoken with you, I trust?"

William looked at John and shrugged. What devil's deal had Zephaniah done on the ship during those three days' absence?

"I have not spoken to anyone from the *Mandarin*," the governor continued, barely registering Zephaniah's interruption. "You are all three political prisoners here. As such, you may wear civilian attire, and will not be subjected to hard labour with the others who arrived with you. But" – and he shifted uncomfortably in his seat – "I have my orders. You cannot stay in Hobart. You are here to be punished, after all. Convicts spend their sentence digging, cutting stone, building to improve this place, and so I have considered what each of you can also do to contribute to our community. Now, let me see…"

He consulted some documents on his desk, and without looking up said, "Mr Williams, you are an engineer and geologist I believe, well used to the search for coal. We are in need of a supervisor in our coal mines, and there is a cart waiting outside to transport you there. Goodbye… and good luck."

John had just enough time to shake Zephaniah's hand before his friend was hurried out of the door.

"And you, Mr Jones," the governor continued, moving his finger down the document before him. "Yours has been a colourful life, I see... a travelling actor, no less."

"One of the finest of our time at your service, sir," William joked, with a sweeping bow.

His bravado made little impact: the governor remained inscrutable. "There is nothing obvious here to match your... errr... *skills*, Mr Jones. But your capacity to capture the attention of an audience may be of some use to us, nevertheless. At Puer Point we have a correction facility for boys too young for hard labour. I am assigning you there today."

William was getting up to leave when the governor added, with just a whisper of sarcasm, "You will find your sense of humour of great assistance to you, I feel certain."

William winked across at John and saluted. "Au revoir, my leader!" Then, turning to the portrait of Victoria behind Franklin's desk, added, "Long live the Charter!" His echoing laughter hollow in his wake.

Suddenly there was just John, and he felt a strange sense of loss. The three had endured so much together, a lifetime of disappointment, anguish and fear in just eight months. Who knew if their paths would ever cross again?

"Now, Mr Frost, what have we found for you? We haven't much call for drapers here you know!" John's thoughts were broken by the governor, who was standing now, looking out of his window down to the docks. He was silent for some time, then said, "I admit I was tempted to keep you here. Hobart needs clever men, men who can write, competent at administration. Besides, I have plans for this place and need a secretary. But the decision is not mine, alas, so you are bound for Port Arthur this afternoon. I have arranged for you to act as clerk to the commandant there, a Captain Booth. My advice is to stay out of trouble and, who knows? A recommendation from me might lead to your being free to work where you choose one day, though leaving these shores is an unlikely prospect. Best keep that out of any dreams you may still have."

Franklin held out his hand. "Good luck, Mr Frost. God be with you."

John was strangely touched by the gesture, and was turning to leave when he spotted a portrait of a young woman in a silver frame on the governor's desk. Next to it lay a book John recognised instantly.

"You read Tennyson?" John asked, pointing in disbelief to the familiar green cover.

"Mr Tennyson is married to my niece Emily," the governor explained. "She sent me this. Told me I reminded her of the wandering hero in her husband's account of 'Ulysses'. Do you know the poem, Mr Frost?"

John smiled.

A sign from home.

"I know it," he acknowledged, and left for the newest chapter of his life.

***

No roads linked Hobart to Port Arthur sixty miles away, just water. John's small bark sailed down the Derwent estuary into Storm Bay towards Cape Direction. Seated on coiled rope amongst the packing cases and barrels transporting supplies to this remote outpost, still in handcuffs with a solitary armed guard, John gazed in awe at the exotic foliage along the banks. Insects plagued him, and he wondered at the creatures living in the water and beyond its banks. Man was not the only danger in these parts.

Once he thought he saw a strange naked figure in the bushes, black skin and a flash of a spear. Then the landscape changed dramatically and a wilder sea took him past tall, grey, strangely crenellated cliff faces. He was suddenly reminded of the organ he had once seen in St Paul's, its pipes, like hands in prayer, pointing heavenwards. He had gone into the cathedral to avoid a sudden shower on his way to visit Francis Place, at a time when a haunting evensong was caressing the dome. He wrestled to remove the memory from decades earlier. If he was to survive here, then too many thoughts of home could prove dangerous, and were best avoided.

"Men call this Hell's Gateway." It was the first time his guard had spoken. "From what I've heard, they could be right."

John heard the dogs before he saw the dock. Vicious, snarling, half-fed packs were led by armed soldiers in constant patrols, preventing any chance of escape.

"Most of the men here are real villains," the guard continued. "Guilty of crimes committed in Van Diemen's Land itself. Rumour has it that more than one has made a mutual pact with a fellow guest."

"Pact? What sort of pact?" John asked.

"One'll murder the other in plain sight so as to be hanged himself. That way they're both set free from this place. Watch your step here, won't you?"

He said nothing more till they reached the dockside.

Everywhere there were signs of building in progress, and the area resembled a child's unfinished puzzle. Convicts hurried by carrying planks, or hammered furiously, if not in the shells of new constructions then in the shipyard itself, visible across the natural inlet with its small harbour. There was a strange energy to the place, a sense of purpose which John found encouraging.

Captain Charles O'Hara Booth was waiting for him in an edifice marginally better than others around the bay. A man of some forty years, with almost twenty of those spent in service, he wore his uniform proudly. John noted the long face, receding hairline and bushy eyebrows. Like Franklin, this was someone used to being obeyed.

"Mr Frost," he said, his voice sharper than John expected. "Please sit."

He turned to the guard and said summarily, "You may remove those. Mr Frost will no longer be needing constraints." The guard did as he was told, and John rubbed his wrists, touching briefly that thin leather thread. "You may go now. The boat back to Hobart will take you. It leaves soon."

Alone, they looked at each other in silence for a while, each weighing up the other. "Well, Mr Frost," Booth continued. "You and I are to spend some time together it appears. Sir John suggested you act as my clerk. God knows I could do with some help. You will record convict arrivals, punishments, deaths and… departures, of which I admit there are but few. You will note all expenditure, all materials bought for new constructions and so on. There are many projects underway here, Mr Frost. I am building a tramway, you know, and clearing swamps for farmland. All that needs an administering eye, and you will be busy. Time passes quickly that way, but rest assured: whatever may be thought of you and your Chartist traitors locally, I have no sympathy with your rebellion. Do not expect any preferential treatment from me. You may be a political prisoner, Mr Frost, but the emphasis is on the second of those words. Do you understand me?"

John nodded consent.

"You will not find Port Arthur an easy place to live. It was barbaric when I arrived, uncultivated, hostile," Booth went on. "The men sent here are a special breed of monster: most have committed heinous crimes, but I call them my lions to be tamed. Beatings, though necessary, have little effect. My intention is to change the savage men who arrive here, give them skills, make them useful. The best behaved work in the shipyard. You will have a chance tomorrow to see for yourself how we operate here. Oh, and one more thing. No one ever escapes. The dogs see to that."

"May I make a request?"

The other man raised an eyebrow, clearly surprised. "What?"

"May I have writing materials in my quarters? I should very much like to write to my wife and, with your permission, to keep a journal of my time here."

"A man needs the support of a good wife." Booth grunted. "She may decide to join you here, you know, Frost." Then he added, almost proudly, "I keep a journal myself. Find it useful to sort out my thoughts at the end of a day... so yes, I agree to your request. But don't expect other favours. You're here to work. The sergeant will take you to your quarters now, Mr Frost. I shall see you at eight a.m. tomorrow morning sharp."

John entered the crude wooden construction that was to be his home. Its one room held a wooden bed with coarse mattress, a wooden table and chair and a small stove. There was some bread and cheese on the table, which John devoured greedily. A single window looked down to the harbour and he was suddenly back in his grandparents' house. Again he cursed his memory. He needed now to be disciplined to live only in the present.

Some time later, he was surprised when the sergeant arrived with a large pile of paper, rough but usable, some ink and a pen. For John, it was a priceless treasure. As the sun set on his first day in Port Arthur, he lit the lamp and started to write a letter to Mary. He would reassure her, tell her he was treated well and was engaged in a meaningful activity.

"July 21, 1840. Dearest love," he began. *"I write to tell you I am well..."* He described the strange creatures he had seen on the sea journey, but spared her the rest. He assured her Booth was not as bad as the stories made out, wrote of the work in place at Port Arthur, and begged her again not to join him, reiterating his belief that he would earn a reprieve and come home. Before concluding, he added, half in jest and almost as an afterthought, *"I hope that if the Colonial*

Secretary, my old friend Lord John Russell should break the seal of my letter he will have so much of the gentleman about him as to send it according to the address."

Matters of great moment sometimes originate in the smallest of actions.

He kissed the letter, comforted strangely in the knowledge that Mary would one day touch the paper too. His letter would be on the next barge to Hobart, read first by Booth, and possibly Franklin.

It would travel for at least four months before reaching Mary's hands, perhaps more. A reply might take a year to reach him.

STAPLETON, BRISTOL
1877

Anne woke with a start. Someone was talking across the corridor in her father's room. In the darkness, she fumbled for the lamp and lit it carefully. She wrapped the quilt around her night shift and crept out onto the landing. It was John she could hear, calling out names of long dead people and distant places, then mumbling incoherently. She opened his door a little, and could see his eyes were open, though he slept on. She waited until he turned and fell silent again, and heard his breathing steady itself into the rhythms of a deep sleep. This journey back into a difficult time was testing him, its painful memories troubling such an old man. She could give up, of course. Say she no longer wanted to write. Blame herself. But she saw how desperately he wanted to recall and recount what he had lived. It would break him to stop now.

She was wide awake. The clock in the hallway struck three, and she edged her way down the stairs, careful not to trip over the quilt. Catharine's quilt, this, bought from some settler's wife in America. Anne cajoled a fire into life and boiled some water for tea, pouring it into a china cup. She held it in both her hands to warm them, and sipped, savouring the tang of lemon. Her mother's cup, chipped now, with its faded painted bluebells around the handle. She felt the two women's presence strongly tonight, and realised how very alone she was.

She had a difficult decision to make.

On the desk before her sat her father's letter sent in July 1840 from Port Arthur, the letter they had spoken about when last she wrote. With it was a copy of *The Times* dated January 1841. It told of the insolence of Mr Frost towards Lord Russell and the outrage to think a revolutionary was allowed to live and work relatively comfortably as a punishment for treason. She knew her father believed it was Booth who had sent a copy of that letter to the Colonial Secretary, and always blamed him for what came afterwards, but Anne knew the truth. The dilemma was whether to reveal that truth to her father.

As with many acts of great moment, it had not seemed so at the time. Mary had many visitors after John was sent away, supporters offering material help if they could. Near the anniversary of the Newport march, Henry Vincent called. He was different somehow, had lost the swagger and was teetotal. Prison had altered him, he said, and he no longer approved of violence to achieve their charter.

But he had not come alone. His companion was a younger man, a Londoner, well dressed, clever with words as Vincent had once been. Anne had hated him from the moment they met, loathed his sneer, his grey gaze, his patronising flattery. She despaired to see Catharine fall under the spell of this stranger as she had done with Henry years before. Anne came across her sister huddled in a corner with him on more than one occasion, and asked her mother's opinion.

"Leave Catharine be," Mary had scolded. "She's a grown woman. He'd make her a fine husband, that one. He's not short of a penny, I'd wager. Your father's gone, Anne. We need to be practical."

He was clearly in no hurry to leave Newport, this stranger, even when Vincent moved on. He and Catharine attended meetings and lectures together, discussed political pamphlets late into the evening and walked unchaperoned in the autumn fields. When John's letter had arrived, Mary read it to the family and there was much joy in the news he was well and sounded positive. She laughed as they all did at the reference to Lord Russell, one of John's old critics. They were pleased to see such evidence of his good humour. It was a welcome moment of family unity and hope. So how did the outside world ever get to see a copy of this personal, private letter?

Anne knew. She had been in the hall, cleaning the floor, while Catharine entertained her new beau in their parlour, the door ajar.

"May I see the letter?" he had asked, casually.

"Of course." Catharine had not hesitated, such was her trust.

"Damn!" the man swore. "I have forgotten my spectacles. They are in my room in the inn. Do you think I might borrow the letter tonight and return it tomorrow?"

Again there was no hesitation, and Anne watched from the hallway as her sister removed the letter from their mother's desk and placed it into the hands of the smiling stranger.

The landlord's young son brought it back the next day, and it was in Catharine's hands then Mary's desk before anyone apart from Anne knew it had been moved. And the stranger was gone. No message. No forwarding address. Just a broken Catharine, lying inconsolable in her room for hours. It was some weeks before the truth emerged, before Henry Vincent wrote, telling them how mortified he was to discover that his companion had in fact been sent by the government to infiltrate and spy on the Chartists and check for further insurrections, particularly around the anniversary of the Newport rising.

Anne had never told a soul but saw how such a betrayal affected her sister. Catharine realised how her father would now be punished for his rude remarks, seen by those in power only because of her own vanity and stupidity. She was bereft, moping around the house, refusing to eat, unkempt and sullen, barely speaking. Once or twice, Anne was on the verge of confessing she knew the truth, but everyone, including Mary, believed the letter had been copied by Booth in Port Arthur. No one suspected Catharine in any way, and believed her current gloom was the result of romantic disappointment.

"She'll get over it," Mary had said, "but we must be more careful in whom we trust."

Anne was angry with Catharine for causing their father further misery, very angry, and if she dared to be completely honest with herself, she rather enjoyed seeing her sister suffer for once. The truth was, however, that Catharine could never forgive *herself*. She lost some of her lustre and joy, stopped attending lectures and became something of a recluse. Within a few years, on a spring tide, she had set sail to join her father.

So now Anne had to make a choice: to remain honest to his story as she had tried to do to date, only ever embellishing the basic facts with some occasional embroidery when she believed her readers would benefit, or to keep sacred an old man's love for his favourite?

In the end, she kept her counsel, believing the truth might break his heart.

PORT ARTHUR
1840–1841

John soon became attuned to the rhythms and routines of his new life. A heat by day unbearable in the stuffy little workspace, not much bigger than a cupboard, tucked away from life in the rear of Booth's house, which sat in eminent pomp on the hilltop above the settlement. But it was better than the cell in Monmouth or his bunk on the *Mandarin*, and he tried to think positively. There was indeed much to do, so he worked hard and kept out of Booth's way when he could. His status as a political prisoner allowed him a limited freedom around this remote outpost, where attempts at escape were anyways rare. He could dress as a civilian and his rations were good. He was surprised to find fresh vegetables and fruit readily available from the settlement's burgeoning farms.

He knew being busy would help fill the empty, monotonous days waiting before him and soon learned the finer points of ordering and transporting goods, of shipbuilding and keeping convict records. In the years since Booth had arrived, convict numbers had expanded exponentially and records had been sorely neglected.

"I like things to be well organised," Booth warned. "No sloppiness. See to it that you cross all the Ts, Mr Frost."

Booth was not easy to know. A man of contradictions, sometimes he would bark orders at John, be morose and reticent, shut in his office scribbling in his journal. He would remain like that for days, then emerge a different man. At other times, he would suddenly start to sing raucous, bawdy music hall songs from his desk and engage John in lively discussions on the philosophy of crime and its punishment.

He was an inventive man too, and John transcribed a careful record of the plans Booth made for a crude but effective semaphore telegraph system to be used should any convict attempt escape. Booth had a fondness for puns, which he would repeat endlessly to any passing ear.

"It was the bier that carried him off," he would announce, amused at his own ageing joke. Heaven help some hapless sergeant who failed to respond to his wit.

But to his credit, he had plans to improve the place. John had seen for himself the smallholdings outside the settlement, where well-behaved convicts cleared swamp and dense bushland to cultivate what food was needed in Port Arthur. It was impressive, he had to admit. Drawings in Booth's office depicted plans for a huge flour mill and a hospital, the Commandant studying the sketches for hours. Once, he called John in to see new drawings which had arrived from Hobart with the mail.

"Come see these!' he yelled. "Destined to change punishment in Port Arthur for ever."

John was unsure why he was suddenly entrusted in this way, except that there was no one else around and Booth needed desperately to share this moment with someone.

"Do you know Mr Bentham's work?" he asked, breathlessly. "The panopticon? The all-seeing?"

"I do, sir," John replied, remembering his evenings with Francis Place and their long debates into the night. He had once met Bentham there, but it was not a detail to share with Booth.

"Well, cast your eyes on this." And Booth unrolled a detailed drawing of a strange star-shaped building with a central hub. "This is our future. No more floggings. Prisoners will spend their time in solitary confinement, each cell visible to just one guard in the centre. The inmates will never know if they're being watched, so will be constantly vigilant. They will have numbers, not names, and will eat alone. They will not talk – ever. They will not look at each other, and will be hooded to exercise. Any rule-breaking will receive a swift response: a blackened cell for a period of reflection – up to thirty days." He paused to savour the concept. "We will subdue them through boredom."

John chose his words carefully. "Extraordinary," he said, trying to sound impressed. "Quite extraordinary. But permit me to ask... why would you think silence is the answer?"

"These are evil men," Booth pronounced. "They need to look into their souls and find peace." The Commandant was clearly proud of his plans. "'It will be known as the Separate Prison, because the inmates will be alone, always. This reform will be some years coming, Mr Frost, but it is the future, I'm telling you. And just think – you will be part of it. You will help with the not inconsiderable administration ahead, and then will see the benefits for yourself."

John prayed silently that would not happen, believing that what lay on the table before him was a representation of hell itself.

Occasionally, John would find Booth doubled up over his desk, clearly in pain. He learned from one of the more friendly guards that Booth had been lost in dense bushland three years before and had spent four nights in bitter cold, suffering frostbite. He had never fully recovered. It explained in part his irascible moods, but John felt little sympathy, and wondered sometimes if he too was losing compassion for his fellow man.

What John did recognise in this new master was a man who desperately sought approval and recognition, some way in which to make a name. Once he told John of the time he needed to face down almost four hundred prisoners. "I put on my annihilating countenance," he bragged, "raised my stentorian voice and made them quake." Yet John heard him more than once reprimand a guard for swearing at a convict. A man of contrasts.

Booth relished deference, enjoying his power and position, just like so many others John had known. Nothing pleased him more than to don his bright red captain's uniform – a little frayed now, John had noticed – and entertain the few "elite" members of Port Arthur society, namely the surgeon – his own wife's father – the chaplain and the master shipwright. He would regale them with tales of his hunting, how he had bagged sixteen brace of quail in one day, nine kangaroos on another. He carried always a purse he had made personally from a kangaroo's scrotum.

Though things might change once the Separate Prison was erected, at this point, discipline at Port Arthur was notoriously brutal, Booth himself admitting he "took the vengeance of the law to the utmost limits of endurance". He believed what he had told John, that the answer was to give convicts a trade, some skills. But many of those sent to Port Arthur were already broken men, far past repair in most cases. Offered a chance, therefore, woe betide any who rejected it. The whip, soaked in sea water and dried in the sun to maximise effectiveness, was used as housemaids might use a feather duster, simply a tool to serve a purpose.

Outside of his long working hours, John would wander around the settlement. He had been pleasantly surprised to see so many engaged in making shoes, a lucrative trade in those parts. He would stand to watch the skilled craftsmen mould and cut the leather in a manner he remembered from many years before, and once saw an older man hide several pieces under the floorboards when the overseer was distracted elsewhere. There was a lively black market in operation, he soon learned, with shoes made clandestinely to order and bartered for food or tobacco. Inventiveness thriving where men need their wits to survive.

Evenings he would walk to the quay, watching scenes familiar to him since childhood, but so very different here, with row after row of tall masts and huge vessels silhouetted against the sunset. Later he would lie on the patch of scrubland outside his hut and stare up at the heavens. He had never before seen such stars.

"She's a fine looking lass, is she not?" The man's broad Scottish lilt took John by surprise as he stood by the quay one evening. There were few females here, mostly soldiers' wives, and John looked around to see who might be passing, before realising the stranger was staring at the large new whaling ship nearing completion in the dock.

"A splendid ship indeed, sir," John replied, noting the man's silk waistcoat and fine cloth trousers, training from so long before not yet lost to him.

"I'm David," the man introduced himself, holding out a hand. "David Hoy. Master shipwright here these past five years. And you are the infamous John Frost, I presume?" he asked. John noted the twinkle in the man's eyes. "How're you doing with Blunderbuss Booth?"

Since McKechnie, John was instinctively wary of anyone offering friendship, and he muttered, "Perfectly well, thank you, sir."

They stood in silence for a while watching the convicts scramble over the skeleton of the new ship. "Those men," Hoy said, pointing, "all criminals of the worst type – murderers, rapists, men with violence in their souls – they all now have a trade. Never give me a minute's trouble, you know. And why? Secret is, treat them like humans, not beasts. Most have washed up here from poverty and want, with little chance in life. See that young lad there?" He indicated a skinny youth working at a delicate piece of carving. "Best I've seen at that craft in a long time. I have high hopes for him. If he can earn his ticket-of-leave, even given its limited liberty, he can make a positive contribution around here." He turned to John and added, "You might make that your aim too, Mr Frost. Good day to you." And he left John wondering at the strangeness of this place of punishment where lives might still be changed.

And yet. And yet. He could not ignore the dark side of life in Port Arthur.

A terror, lurking beneath the landscape of paradise, like a dormant beast.

John was walking to his work some days later, listening to the strange morning birdsong, when he saw guards dragging a young man to the place notorious for its public floggings. He recognised the prisoner as the youth Hoy had held in such esteem. Horrified, John watched as a burly guard tied him spreadeagled onto the triangular frame, exposing his back, and, ordering another convict to administer the lashes, he counted out thirty-six. Silence. Just the whistling of a whip and the thud against soft flesh, until the young prisoner fainted and the dry earth beneath him ran red.

"What had he done?" John whispered to another convict.

"Had his hand in his pocket when Booth passed," the convict muttered, careful not to be seen by the guards. "Same every time," he whispered. "The fourth lash will split the back, anything above fifty exposes the backbone." His words were clinical, detached: he had seen all this so often. "Bit of hog's lard on the wounds tonight, then it's back to work tomorrow."

A second prisoner was dragged out to the square, an old man John knew to be blind and almost completely deaf. Why in God's name was he being beaten?

"Didn't acknowledge the bastard," the convict whispered, anticipating John's next query. "Couldn't see him, more like."

Again it was another convict chosen to administer the beating, and it was only his plea to show the old man mercy which broke the silence around the square lined with convicts. Mercy had no home in Port Arthur. An eternity later, his back ripped apart like some animal carcass hanging in the sun to dry, the old man collapsed lifeless in his own blood. John asked himself what sort of tyrant would punish someone *unable* to obey?

He never saw the beaten old convict again.

And these were not isolated events. Days later, John saw a man whipped brutally, another thirty-six lashes. Booth was outside to watch this time, in full uniform despite a midday heat. But this man did not cry. In defiance, in some desperate attempt to retain a scrap of dignity, he kept silent and smiled.

"Insolent dog!" screamed the Commandant. "Give him thirty-six more."

They were impossible sights to forget. Images which ached behind his closed eyes at night, scars themselves which refused to heal. How could he survive in this world of excessive, pointless cruelty? Was this what humanity had become? He feared above all that he would grow accustomed to it, immune to the suffering, accepting of the regime, unquestioning. To him, it made little sense to provide constructive training, but then resort to sheer brutality in order to maintain control. He had learnt long ago about loyalty, and how best to tame wildness. It was not like this. And those new plans for total, silent isolation would surely serve no purpose but to drive men mad.

His whole being began to rail once more against the injustice of things. That passion, dormant now a while, cowed by the demands of his own survival, was stirring again, his convictions as strong as ever. John lay on his bed at night and resolved to somehow record the life of these convicts. Who knew if he would ever see the freedom to share what he would write? Who knew if he would see liberty again in any shape? But at least he would have some purpose, some cause to fight for. Some reason to live.

The wheel was back in motion.

Around Christmas, he accompanied Booth to the settlement at Point Puer to visit those whom the Commandant mockingly called his "poor boys".

"Get it?" he would spit at the sergeant. "Puer/poor?" exasperated by the dull man's vacant expression. There was little of amusement where they were headed.

It was a place for juveniles, originally designed to keep the young boys apart from the hardened men at Port Arthur. But it was no more than another anteroom of hell. John knew that they were there to investigate a serious incident. A group of boys in chains had, in a mutual pact, thrown themselves off a cliff together. He shuddered to think of his own sons ever being so desperate.

"Do the boys ever leave?" he asked Booth as they sailed close to the quay.

"Only when they can prove they are literate," he replied, then turning to John added, "Doesn't happen often. If a boy acquires a skill, though, he might be moved to Hobart… but only if he knows someone there."

John was surprised by the change in William's appearance. It had been less than a year since they last saw each other, but the inveterate entertainer had long since left the stage. His fellow Chartist was now gaunt, his hair thinning and grey, his eyes dull. He barely greeted John.

"Make careful notes, Frost!" ordered Booth. "This is a trying situation indeed. We'll have to send a report of the unfortunate business to London, and I'm damned sure I won't be blamed for it."

Booth was anxious to leave at the earliest opportunity, but walking back to the boat, John took in the hostile, barren place. The boys who shuffled by looked half starved, ragged, eyes kept on the ground. It was a place devoid of hope. John wrote that night, *"If I had twelve sons and it was left to me to decide whether they should be transported or hanged, I should at once say to hang them sooner than allow them to go to Puer Point."*

In March, he had a letter from Mary. She told again of her desire to join him, reported that the family was well but that she had disturbing news of William, John's stepson and legal assistant at the trial. That old nemesis Phillips had tried William for some trumped-up forgery charge. Even the judge had complimented William on his self defence, and the jury had real difficulty reaching a verdict. But Phillips was more powerful than ever, and William had been transported to Van Diemen's Land, soon to be joined by his wife and children. Mary hoped by God's will they might some day be reunited with John. She ended the letter, *"My love, I have decided to move across the water to Stapleton. Anne will be with me and Catharine of course. Henry Hunt has not been well, and I feel it wise to move from the damp vapours of Newport. And from the reach of Phillips too. It is a comfortable cottage, with a small garden, and I pray you will one day join us all there. You are in my heart always, my love. Be strong, my hero, my Ulysses."*

It was depressing news about William, and he turned the leather thread round and round his wrist thinking of them all. His stepson was paying a heavy debt for association with the Chartist leaders, and John felt the old familiar cloak of guilt fold across him.

He was at his desk the following day, deep in thought still, when a voice he recognised said, "Mr Frost, good day!" David Hoy stood before him, some documents in his hand. He looked anxiously at the Commandant's door. It was shut, the man currently in one of his dark moods.

"These need the Commandant's signature," he said, then, lowering his voice, added, "There is something you will find interesting at the bottom. But be careful old Blunderbuss doesn't see it!"

When he had gone, John lifted the documents tentatively and found a copy of *The Times*, months old. He did not dare read it immediately, but hid it in the folds of his jacket. Later, in his room, he lit the small lamp and read of a huge nationwide petition calling for the return of Zephaniah, William and himself. There had been a vote in Parliament, only narrowly defeated. They had not been forgotten. He read the article several times, but it left him strangely numb. It was as if he was reading about a different man, of another time, in an alien land. Looking around his room, and out to the harbour beyond, bathed in the brilliant red which accompanied evenings in these parts, he understood.

This was his world now. He had a different war to wage.

STAPLETON, BRISTOL
1877

"It must have been lonely." Anne had been thinking about her father all afternoon while he dozed, about the life he had led so far away from them. "And you could never be sure who to trust." They were sitting at the table, Anne spreading his favourite homemade blackberry jam on fresh bread she had made while he slept.

"Aye, lass. I missed home, tried hard not to think of it. But then some small object, or a whispered sound, would spark a memory, and such heaviness would creep on me... it could last days. What helped was writing. It was time alone with only the voice inside me for company. God, it was precious, privacy being of a premium for a convict. It was a time when my thoughts were not subject to any master, were free even if I was not."

Anne understood. She too had come to love the solitary world of paper and pen.

"Thank God Booth was a man who liked to scribble too," John continued. "Paper was scarce, mind. I had to limit myself and use tiny print. Probably didn't help the eyes much. Sometimes, I used the back of letters and documents Booth had drafted and then discarded. He didn't seem to mind much... but he might have, had he known I was recording the abominable things he did."

He chewed slowly, savouring the sweetness of the berries. "There was a woman prisoner who worked as domestic help for the Commandant. Welsh, she was, with dark curls. She had a way of saying, 'I'll put this over by here, right?' when she brought Booth his victuals... The music of her voice reminded me sorely of your mother." He sank quietly into his memories for a while, humming softly some old melody.

"Sundays we were all in the church built by convicts. I had never been that much of a churchman; I've seen too many use religion to control and subdue. But I confess I found some comfort singing with my fellow exiles. A few were from home, and one lad, a tenor with a voice to make angels envious, would give us a Welsh hymn. First time I understood the meaning of hiraeth, Anne. It was all I could do not to cry. But the number one rule of convict life was never to cry…"

They cleared the table and settled near the fire. It was still light outside, and a sudden April shower had left the new spring grass glistening. Anne waited. When he was ready he would tell her about this next stage. It would be awkward, heavily dependent on his recollection. She was asking him to relive the pain, to shed any reservations, if she was to complete the next chapter. Anne realised she was frowning, and picked up some darning to distract herself.

"I had no idea why he wanted to see me that day," John said, as if there had been no break in their dialogue. "I thought maybe some wild new idea, or a pun he wanted to share, or even an invoice I needed to file. But I could tell from his face it was serious."

VAN DIEMEN'S LAND
1841

John made to sit down as he usually did before the Commandant.

"I'd prefer you to stand," Booth barked. It was clearly one of his dark days. "It's about the letter."

"Letter? Which letter?" John had recently written one or two on Booth's behalf, to suppliers and the like. "Is there a problem?"

"Most definitely, Mr Frost, for you at least. You have offended gravely the Colonial Secretary with your flippant insults. You have caused uproar in the Commons because you are seen to be living a good life here instead of being punished for treason. You are therefore summoned immediately to Hobart to stand trial before Sir John Franklin."

He felt he'd been struck with a hammer. This he had not anticipated. He'd only ever written of Russell in the letter of... how many months ago now? But that had been a private letter to his wife and children, not meant for other eyes. How could his remarks have been seen in London? Who had betrayed him?

He looked across at Booth, and believed he knew.

"Clear your things, Frost." Booth avoided his gaze. "You leave immediately for Hobart... I doubt you'll be coming back."

He just had time to bundle a few meagre items into rough sacking before the boat left. But he was careful to protect the pages which began the account he was compiling about convict life. He wondered how he would fill the next pages, or if they would ever be written at all.

John's "trial" was a meeting with the governor, recorded by a convict acting as clerk. Franklin was waiting in his office, looking decidedly uncomfortable, and John noticed the book of poetry had been removed from the desk. He indicated for John to sit, avoiding any eye contact, and looked down at an official-looking letter before him.

"You seem to have upset a few people, Mr Frost. Important people." Franklin paused. "Regrettably, you have also cast *us* in an unfavourable light, presenting yourself as someone enjoying a carefree life here, meaningfully employed, relatively free, not engaged in penance and reform."

"The letter was for my wife, sir," John interjected. "I was trying to sound cheerful and not to worry her. And the reference to Russell was a joke, nothing more."

He watched as Franklin kept reading the edict from London.

"No one outside of my family, the Commandant and yourself was meant to read what I wrote," John added pointedly.

"And I can tell you I sealed it without any copy being made," Franklin replied, looking directly at his prisoner for the first time. John believed him.

"Well, the deed's done now, and my strict instructions from England are that you be sentenced to two years' hard labour. It is so ordered in the hope you will contemplate the folly of your arrogance, Mr Frost, and learn humility before your betters."

He stopped reading and in a softer tone added, "My hands are tied, Frost, and in all honesty I regret the necessity. It will be hard where you are going. Especially hard for a man unused to physical labour. You will see much suffering, but mind you hold your tongue. Question nothing. Challenge nothing. Keep out of trouble, keep your wits sharp, and I shall see you when your sentence ends. We may yet have useful employment here in Hobart for a man of your talents."

John knew it was pointless to argue.

"May I at least ask you one favour, sir? Could I speak with my stepson, William Geach, before I leave? I realise it is highly irregular, but I learned he was here in Hobart, and he may have news of my wife. God knows if I shall have another chance, ever." He hesitated briefly before adding, "It is my wife who admires Tennyson so much." It could not harm to try.

Franklin paused, then nodded, and John was sent to wait in a small anteroom whilst a guard went in search of William. Then he was there, and John held the younger man close with an intensity of affection which surprised both of them. William had not been hugged often by his stepfather, but for John this young man meant home, or as near as he could get to it. He fought the tears.

William spoke first. "They are sending you to the gangs?" he asked. "It is an outrage. What crime have you committed to be so punished? Were it not for my own restrictions here, I would challenge this at the highest level."

"Hush, William," John said, amused by his stepson's defiance. "There is little point in being angry. Life's path meanders so, but I accept this as the next step for me to take. Do not worry yourself; I shall stay strong, ever mindful of home and those I love. But what of you?" John was pleased to see William looking well, leaner perhaps, but his face tanned by the sun.

"A clerk here, as you were in Port Arthur. And Agnes has opened a little school calling herself 'Mrs Foster'. Our two girls attend, along with the others in the town, sons and daughters of the trusted convicts, those whose families joined them and who will settle here. It is well received."

"I shall visit when I return, I promise," John said, though he saw in William's gaze a flicker of doubt that the pledge would be kept.

"Time's up, Frost!" Franklin was calling him back, the guard anxious to get going.

"One minute!" John shouted, then, whispering to William, asked, "Will you write to your mother for me? Tell her all is well... and add that I continue 'not to yield'. She'll understand!

And could you keep these till I return?" He brought out of his sack the carefully tied pages written in Port Arthur. The next part would have to wait, its details reliant on memory alone.

As William left, turning away so his stepfather would not see the tears, John wondered if that was to be their last meeting.

Life was slipping out of control again. John watched with heavy heart as Franklin signed the papers for entry to the "gangs", well known for providing the hardest labour in Van Diemen's Land. Alongside the signature, Franklin wrote the date.

It was 25th May.

Another birthday.

"I think it better not to include the next part of my life," John announced when Anne had finished writing about his meeting with the governor and William. "Just mention it vaguely perhaps, in a passage or so. It is not something to be read about by someone of a sensitive disposition. When I lectured about it in later years, I always asked the ladies to leave at this point."

Anne laughed. "I am over fifty, Father, not an innocent child. I grew up with brothers, I read the newspapers, I heard the men's conversations in The Royal Oak. In truth, I may be a spinster but I am not naive, and I know how the world moves, what man can do to man."

"They published my lectures in a—"

"—pamphlet, yes, and I have read it," Anne interjected, producing a copy of *The Horrors of Convict Life* from beneath a pile of other papers. "You cannot exclude this part of your life, Father." She was firm, resolved. "I will not let you. You must be true to your history. It's not a fiction where you are free to pick and choose what helps the story. You are not Mr Dickens. What is written about you in my pages will be uncensored, and I am prepared to tell of the worst, however painful or unpleasant."

John was surprised, but moved too, proud of her. There was a force in her he had not previously noticed, the resilience of her mother, perhaps, but something of him too. A refusal to let the world win.

"It will be more than just unpleasant," he warned. "Much more. But promise me you will stop if you cannot bear it."

"Do not trouble yourself so," she mocked. "I have never been one to be overcome with the vapours."

And so he began. "They took me with two others up a rough cart track to a thick forest high above Impression Bay. Blue gum eucalyptus trees taller than you can imagine, tops far too high to be seen from the ground, acres and acres of them. We reached a rough camp cut into the forest, a dark place, oppressive from the trees around."

He looked down at his hands, embarrassed. "They stripped me, took away my few belongings, left me exposed until a guard threw at me a dirty grey uniform. It was stained with what looked like blood and smelt of urine. I kept my right hand over my left wrist, determined they would not take this." And he indicated the thin leather thread. "It was suddenly the most precious of things: a last vestige of self. Then they put the irons on my ankles… could barely move at first, stumbled, falling over my own feet, bruising my legs against the metal. But when one of the other new arrivals tripped and fell flat, I couldn't get to him. They beat him, Anne. Beat him till his arms bled."

Anne stood to fetch him some cool water from the pitcher. "Our hut was too small by far for thirty men. Hellish place, with no air, smelling always of sweat and effluence. Stained straw mattresses on bare boards, and rats, larger than any I ever saw in London. Crawled over the bunks, they did. That first night I could not sleep, so terrified was I of the men around me. Men whose eyes told a terrible history. Men bereft of any morals. Lost men."

Anne was trying not to picture leg irons on this frail old man sitting before her.

She saw he was trembling, tearful, moaning softly to himself, so she stopped writing. This would have to be done slowly.

"My, my," she said. "Just look at the time. If I do not stop now, Father, we shall have no supper. Why don't you put your overcoat on and sit outside a while? The sunset is beautiful this evening. I shall call when it is ready."

IMPRESSION BAY, TASMAN PENINSULA
1841–1843

They were woken roughly at daybreak and queued silently for a piece of coarse bread and a cup of water. Waiting his turn, hunger clawing at him, John was approached by two men.

"What have we here?" one asked, nudging John till he almost fell.

"Looks a gentle sort, don't he? He ain't seen much labour, this one. Look at these soft hands." And the man laughed, blowing kisses in John's direction. "Got something here for those hands," he leered, grabbing his crotch.

His companion laughed, bent towards John and said, "Best sleep with your back to the wall, eh?"

It was more than jest: there was menace in the threat, a vile promise.

The men did not see the blows coming. Both were sent staggering backwards, and John was faced with a giant, well over six feet, with a bald head, broad shoulders and huge hands. "Fuck off, the pair of you!" he yelled. They did not need a second warning.

John stared at the huge hand that was now held out towards him. "Iolo, Mr Frost, Iolo Edwards. It is an honour to meet you, sir."

John recognised the familiar Welsh lilt. "I was at Blaina, sir. Heard you speak. Walked behind you to Newport."

John took his hand. "Dear God, did they send you here after the Westgate?"

"I would have preferred it if they had," replied John's countryman. "Never got more than half way down Stow Hill. Saw what was happening and went home. But we can't talk now. Overseer's coming. Stay close to me, Mr Frost. I'll see no one gives you trouble. I'm Top Dog here."

John soon realised what Iolo meant. A "gang" Top Dog played a critical role in the business of felling trees around Impression Bay. A "centipede gang" of anything up to fifty convicts carried the felled grey tree trunks on their shoulders down to the settlements. Wood was precious here, in demand for buildings, ships, furniture. The "Top Dog" was the tallest man, out front, bearing the heaviest weight. The "bottom dog" was in the pit at the end of the saw. Iolo made sure John was positioned where the weight was lighter. No one seemed to question this gentle giant. When the overseer yelled at the men "Straighten your backs or you'll feel my whip!" Iolo stood still, turned and glared at the man, who then moved away, allowing the caterpillar to continue as before.

By the end of his first day, John could barely move. Every muscle ached, and he was covered with insect bites. He sought his bunk, but Iolo stopped him.

"Food first, Mr Frost," he said. "You will not last a week here unless you eat."

Reluctantly, John complied and, suddenly overcome by hunger, devoured greedily the grey liquid in which floated some vegetables and fatty lumps of a meat he did not recognise.

"Could be possum," Iolo surmised. "Seen a few hereabouts recently."

In the cramped hut, the men slunk off into their groups, and John sat with his newfound friend.

"It's not right you're here, Mr Frost. You're no criminal. Shame on the bastards who sent you to this place!"

"Call me John, please," he replied, "and remember, I very nearly lost my life after Newport. I should probably count any blessings there might still be in this outpost of hell. But what brings you here?"

Iolo was examining his hands, and held them out towards John. "These caused the problem," he said. "Miner I was, not afraid of hard work for a fair wage. But I was sick of watching the overseer bully the weaker ones down there in the dark. The man was a brute. Swear to God I think he enjoyed causing the pain in others. You know the type… Then one day he starting beating a boy no older than my own lad Evan. He'd died of the typhoid a year before, God rest his soul. I couldn't help it, Mr Frost… broke that stick over the bastard's back, then smashed his head against the mineshaft. I had to be pulled off him else I'd have killed him and been sent sharpish to the rope.

"I have years to serve yet," he continued. "But I will not let them win. I *will* get home again. I have promised Myfanwy. But I will do what I can to keep you safe here, Mr Frost… sorry, *John*. You were our hero back home, acting for the likes of we miners. Always on our side. It is my turn now to do my bit for you." He paused, moved to go, then hesitated, bending to whisper, "You need to be careful, John. The sins of Gomorrah are rife in this place. Some seek solace with each other out of sheer loneliness, but others – many others – have been so scarred by life they now have no sense of what's right and what's wrong. They give in easily to urges of the flesh, take what they want where they find it, and are ruled by lust. Such men have lost their way to God."

"Dear Lord, how does anyone survive here?" John suddenly felt despair sweep over him, cold, dark, heavy.

"When the world of the body is unbearable," his countryman advised, placing his huge paw on John's shoulder, "dig deep inside. It's always where the richest seams are in a mine. Think of those you love, and find a space for your maker. He will send you strength."

Few in the gang could read, and the only book was a worn copy of the Bible. Some nights, when the men had settled in exhaustion in their bunks, Iolo would read aloud his favourite psalm. A vermillion sunset would close yet another miserable day and the silence would creep through the stale air as all the men, even the hardest, would listen to that deep baritone voice promising a better life beyond their earthly hardships. Promising forgiveness.

"I shall lift up mine eyes unto the hills...."

In years to come, whenever John heard the familiar psalm, he would remember Iolo, and how grateful he had been for the warmth of unexpected friendship in such a loveless wasteland.

***

Each day dissolved into the next. Little broke the routine of this hard, hard struggle which challenged all human endurance. John learned quickly who to avoid, which overseers were the cruellest, which men the most depraved. At night, he learned to block out the sounds of their coupling in the darkness. He dreaded the arrival of any new, young, handsome convicts, knowing the certain fate awaiting them in the conspiring dark. He covered his ears so as not to hear their cries, aware that the fragility of his own safety depended solely on the other men's wariness around Iolo. Fights were common, and he learned to look the other way and to have seen nothing if asked. He was shamed by his reticence, but understood. Men do what is necessary to survive.

July, and the weather turned. Days were cold, the temperature at night often below freezing. No sunlight reached the forest floor as they worked, and accidents with the saw were common. The men dreaded a visit to the hut laughingly known as the "hospital". Few left alive. John kept close to Iolo, fighting the cold numbing his fingers, trying to control his trembling body as he shouldered log after log down to the settlement. He would not yield.

One of the gang, a Londoner called Benjamin, had also been a clerk. It transpired he had poisoned his master, a botanist here on the peninsula.

"I reckon he deserved it," Iolo explained when John asked. Clearly selective in his Christian notion of forgiveness, Iolo provided more details. "The bugger raped Benjamin's wife. She killed herself in shame. What man wouldn't have sought revenge?"

In truth, John came to enjoy the company of this poisoner who, each time he spoke, reminded him so much of the apprentices he once worked with in that London draper's. Who could have guessed then, four decades before, that one day he would seek out the company of a convicted murderer?

But it was Benjamin who could tell him which birds provided the strange, exotic backdrop to their daily labour, and Benjamin who knew the names of the plants and creatures living in the woods around them. Besides rabbits and lizards, they shared the forest with beetles the size of small mice, wombats and strange Tasmanian devils.

And, deep inside the dense undergrowth, lived a platypus that would sometimes spy on these unwelcome intruders.

One day, a convict in the "caterpillar" collapsed screaming, causing all the others to stumble and the tree trunk to roll off their shoulders. The overseer was livid, but the man continued to clutch his leg in agony. Benjamin recognised the marks.

"Tiger snake," he said. "Venomous. Fatal. It'll paralyse him. He won't last long."

By the evening the convict was dead.

And so John lived each day aware it might be his last, his fear unrelenting, normal as breath itself. Moments of joy were rare: sunlight filtering down the tall tree trunks onto a hidden pool; a shy koala clutching close its eucalyptus leaf; the iridescent glory of a butterfly; and once, in a shady hollow, the surprise of wild sun orchids, the colour of bluebells. Colours and sounds from paradise, now consigned to hell.

Not long after his arrival, the gang were sent to Slopen Island to gather timber for a new convict settlement there. It already had a tramway, and they carried some additional logs down to the jetty for transport. John gazed spellbound at the white sands, the seals basking on the headland, and the calm, clear water stretching to the far horizon.

"Look!" Benjamin cried, pointing out to sea. "Dolphins!"

They stood with Iolo and smiled at the antics of the creatures until the overseer noticed their tardiness and shouted at them.

It had been a reminder of another type of life, a rare moment of pleasure.

Months passed. The wheel turned slowly. Then one day, John was summoned to see the chief overseer.

"You have a visitor," the man announced.

John had not known this happen before in the settlement. "Who?" he asked.

"Some writer from a magazine." The overseer was clearly annoyed, preferring to keep the outside world away. "Franklin himself approved the visit... but be careful what you say, Mr Frost. Don't go rattling any cages. You are still here for a long time yet."

John found a dapper little man waiting for him in the outer office. His elegant clothes made John suddenly aware of his own rags, and he realised he had long stopped caring about his appearance. "I'm from *Fraser's*," the man said, holding out a hand in greeting. "James Dawson at your service. My editor thought it might be interesting to find out how the famous Chartist leader is doing here in the Colonies."

When John did not reply, Dawson added, "Permit me to say, Mr Frost... you look rather well."

Again, silence. John could not register this strange arrival from another time and place. He might as well have come from the moon.

"Fraser's, eh?" he said finally. He looked enviously at the man's thick notebook, his travelling ink pot, the tortoiseshell pen. He missed writing more than he missed good food. "And what might your Tory editor want to hear? That I am a broken man, cowed into submission, confessing the error of my ways as a Chartist? I ask you, Mr Dawson, do I look a broken man?"

Dawson sat back and examined the convict sitting before him. What he saw, beyond the prison rags, was a man sitting straight-backed with his long hair tied back and greying at the sides, a man of a strong, rather muscular frame. He appeared younger than his years, his face tanned and his grey eyes bright. He spoke clearly, determined, resolute.

"You will wonder whether I harbour regrets, Mr Dawson. I suspect it would be much to your readers' satisfaction to learn that I do. Well, know this. I regret the pain I have brought to my wife and children. I regret men died in Newport and that loyal friends have been sent here because of it. But I do not, cannot, will not regret the cause."

He paused so Dawson could make notes. "I remain convinced society will benefit when the vote is available to all men. And I say when, not if, because it will happen. There has been too much injustice, for too long. I see here only too well what tyranny and oppression do to men, what happens when powerful men exercise brutality to keep order. It turns men into beasts. It rots their souls. No one wins."

Dawson waited for further details, pen hovering expectantly.

"What I could tell you today about life here would never be printed, Mr Dawson. I fear it would not be palatable in the reading rooms of gentlemen's clubs. You may wish to see for yourself, of course. Some of the men here would be glad of a fresh young face like yours. They would find you most entertaining, I'm sure,"

Dawson left before sunset. His report simply described the man he had seen to be in sound health and good spirits. Some details are best left unreported, he concluded.

STAPLETON, BRISTOL
1877

When Anne found her father, he was in the garden. It was the first day of May, and he was sitting in their overgrown wrought-iron arbour, its paint long since rusted, his face towards the sunshine.

"It is good to feel the warmth again," he said as she approached. "Sit with me a while."

She fetched her shawl, and settled next to him, each listening to the birdsong, neither speaking for some time.

"You have written enough about my time at Impression Bay," he said, suddenly breaking the silence. "I would prefer to move on now. It has been difficult for both of us, but" – he turned to face her – "I owe you my thanks. No one could have told of my life there in a better manner, Anne. You had to be honest, but without offending any reader."

"I am sure it was far worse than anything I might write," Anne said. "It is so very difficult to imagine you there. We were all worried you would not return from that, you know, and had so little news for years."

"Were it not for the friendship I found I doubt I would be here now," he added. "They took Iolo away, Anne. A month or so before I left… dragged him out of the hut one morning and I never saw him again. Benjamin heard they had taken the big man to the mines near Hobart. He'd been a collier back home, of course, and his strength would have served them well. But the mines were well known as the worst part of convict hell, worked by the most serious offenders. God knows what befell him there…"

"And Benjamin?"

"He got his ticket-of-leave several years later. Had to stay on the peninsula, though, so started working the land. They needed men to do that, and his know-how with plants must have helped. I met him again, just before Catharine and I left for America. He had remarried, his wife a former convict too, and they had a son. He was a good man, Anne, a good friend..."

"And yet a murderer," Anne interrupted. She was bending to pull some weeds from the borders. Buds were forming in her cracked flowerpots.

John took his time before speaking again, looking at the branches hanging over the arbour, seeing shades of green through his cloudy eyes. A promise of life to come.

"You see, Anne, nothing is ever black or white with people. There has never been a society anywhere as depraved as witnessed by me in Van Diemen's Land, but I learned something else in that godless place. A man can find compassion and kindness even where evil has taken root. If you seek hard enough, you can find beauty in the darkest of places."

"A bit like those orchids," she said, and yanked at another weed.

HOBART
1843

He was back before Sir John Franklin, once more waiting to hear his fate.

"It is good to see you, Mr Frost." It sounded genuine. John thought the man had aged, his face lined and sallow. "You look well. Two years in the forest have suited you."

John made no response. What was there to say?

"Hobart has expanded since you were last here. It is quite the thriving town now, with a growing number of warehouses, all needing good clerks and bookkeepers. You have been assigned to one such, and will lodge there. I have informed the authorities back home, who will be satisfied with that decision, I know."

He handed John a slip of paper bearing the name of his new employer and the address. "My hope is that you can now contribute something to our growing community." He picked up the framed portrait on his desk. "Everyone has a part to play. Even my dear wife Jane here. She has opened a little museum, has overseen new botanical gardens, and has dreams of a university for the town sometime in the future. She believes that education is the way forward. I hear your stepson's wife has a thriving little school too?"

"I believe so, though I have not seen William since I left... for the forest."

The door opened and two young girls entered, one indigenous, but both dressed alike in ribbons and fine taffeta dresses. "Ah girls, Papa cannot talk now. I am occupied."

"Hello sir," the fair girl said. "Welcome to Hobart."

"We hope you enjoy your time here," the other added, and they both bobbed, giggling as they closed the door behind them.

"That, Mr Frost, was Eleanor and her adopted sister Mathinna. My wife and I took in the girl, a daughter of the chief of the local Palawa people. She knows her letters now, can add and subtract, do fine embroidery, and is learning the piano. Proof, is it not, that education can civilise anyone? Have you any daughters, Frost?"

John suddenly had a memory of the family around the table in Newport, of small girls seeking his arms when they fell, of the favourite story at bedtime, of their growing into young women all too soon. Of Catharine arguing with Henry Vincent.

"I do, sir," he replied. " They are a great joy."

"Then you must write to them and your wife to tell them you are back in Hobart. "

John got up to leave, believing the meeting was over.

"Before you go, Mr Frost – a word of advice. See out a year or two at the warehouse, then I believe your future will lie elsewhere, perhaps in Mrs Foster's little school. Teaching would be a rewarding occupation for you, one approved by those who monitor these things from London. Earn your ticket-of-leave, then be relatively free to live out your days in Hobart. But I implore you, avoid saying or committing to paper anything contentious and controversial."

John nodded, though he longed to continue his account of convict life. It would have to be a clandestine undertaking now. There was too much at risk.

"I shall scrutinise your letters home – for your own sake, Mr Frost – at least until my departure."

"You are leaving Hobart?" John was surprised. The Franklins had become local dignitaries, something of an institution.

"My family and I return next year to London. I am planning another long sea expedition. Her Majesty has commanded me to investigate a Northwest Passage."

**

The warehouse was an enormous wooden building near the quay. Floor to ceiling cases filled the cavernous interior, and men, trusted convicts, swarmed around loading and unloading from the busy port. John could see a man dressed differently from the others giving orders from the far side of the building, so made his way across.

"Mr Clayton?" John enquired. "I'm John Frost. I'm sent by Sir John. He said you wanted a clerk, sir."

There was something about Clayton that reminded John of Prothero – the same sneer, same physique, same arrogance. Not the most promising start.

"Ah, you're here," he said, barely looking at John. "Well, you might as well know now that I did indeed want the services of a clerk, but I most definitely did not want *you*, Frost. Your reputation precedes you. The last thing I need is rebellion and truculence. Rest assured: first sign of nonsense and you're sailing right back to Impression Bay. Am I understood?" He moved so close to his face, John could smell the man's breath, see the warts on his unshaven chin, and the copious nasal hair.

"Understood," he muttered.

He was shown to his "quarters", a bed, chair and table in a tiny room behind the one in which he would work, his new home not much bigger than his cell in Monmouth.

"Don't think you can swan around the town, either." Clayton had followed him. "You eat with the workers. Wash at the pump in the back there. Evenings you stay here. Do a good job, and you may be granted some time on Sundays. I'm watching you, Frost. I'll have no Chartist shit here."

The work was tedious, each day long and joyless. The other convicts had been warned not to engage in conversation with him, so mealtimes were lonely affairs. But as a clerk, he had access now to paper again, ink and pens. Carefully, a piece at a time, he took what he could from his desk, anxious not to arouse any suspicion.

Alone at night, he started again to record his thoughts on the injustices of convict life and the cruelty he had seen at Port Arthur, at Puer Point and Impression Bay. He thought of the young lads raped, of the lives ruined, of Iolo, of the men beaten to death. He would be their voice, and somehow, someday, he would tell their story to a world made to listen. As the second Sunday approached, he took a chance. Handing a letter to Clayton for signature, he said, "Mr Clayton, sir. I trust you have found my work to be of a standard acceptable to you? If so, I wonder if I may be so bold as to ask your permission to visit my stepson here in Hobart on Sunday? It is his wife who has the little school."

Clayton's lip curled. "Not this Sunday, Frost. Perhaps the next one."

The conversation was repeated twice more in the weeks which followed, before Clayton finally agreed. But not out of charity: John could see the man needed something in return.

"Your stepson Geach... getting a bit of a reputation hereabouts. Lawyer by trade, they say. I need some free advice... Tell him I expect to see him when you return on the Sunday evening. You may have three hours' leave only."

For John, there could not have been a greater gift, and he counted the days until the visit. William and his family welcomed him with hugs and tears, told him of their lives, of the school, and showed him with pride their little vegetable plot. His grandchildren, Emily and Grace, brought him drawings done specially for his visit, and introduced him to their toys, wooden dolls whittled crudely by Will. "Still learning," he confessed, laughing. Agnes presented as close to a celebratory meal as their circumstances allowed.

Family life, and the happiest John had been in years.

"I could not come sooner," John explained. "Clayton is a cold and demanding man, and he's agreed now only because he needs your help over something, William. Be wary of him, mind."

After they had eaten, William took John into the yard behind the house and sat with him, each smoking a pipe in the sunshine.

"I am truly relieved to see you, Father. We all feared the worst when you were sent to hard labour. I have your papers safe, the writings you did at Port Arthur. Take care to keep them hidden… they will not win you many friends in London."

He paused, puffed on his pipe. John felt there was something left unsaid.

"What is it, son?"

From inside his waistcoat, William brought out a letter, already opened. It was many months old.

"From Mother," he said. "I shall leave you to read it on your own. Come back inside when you are ready."

John's hands shook as he read, his heart pounding to see her handwriting after so long.

"Dearest William,

I write to you knowing your father is beyond the reach of my letters. But God willing, he will return to Hobart, and I ask you give these pages to him then. I trust that you, Agnes and the children are all in good health and making the most of your lot on such distant shores. Anne and Catharine are still with me, and John's mother too, though she is frailer now. We miss you so. But we have settled well in Stapleton and life is better where the shadow of the Westgate does not follow us.

Alas, I must now be the bearer of such sad news, the main reason for my letter. Our beloved Henry Hunt finally gave up his long struggle with illness, and has gone to join his baby brother James. We buried him in the cemetery here, in a patch where the

bluebells grow in spring. One day I shall take you and your father to
see the grave.

Kiss my granddaughters for me, and stay strong.
Your loving mother."

He sat clutching the letter to his chest, grief coming in waves, his chest tight, tears silent. Mary had been alone burying their son on the other side of the world. What sort of husband was he? What sort of father for Henry Hunt, that gentle, laughing boy with a voice of angels? The familiar whisper of guilt in his ear again.

"It is time to go." Agnes came out and put her arms around him.

"Remember," she whispered softly, "however alone you feel, you are in our thoughts and always have been. Remember you are loved." And she kissed him lightly on his rough cheek.

William escorted his father back to his room at the warehouse, where Clayton swiftly drew the young lawyer into a private room to talk.

Anne knew it was coming, and had been dreading it. She would have to write about Catharine, and her father would expect nothing less than a flattering portrait of his favourite.

She would try to please.

"When exactly did you learn about Catharine's arrival?" she asked. "I do not have any details or dates. You will need to tell me what you remember."

"It was some months later. Clayton seemed pleased with whatever William had advised, so permitted my Sunday visits more frequently. One Sunday, the girls appeared particularly excited and Agnes unduly anxious to silence them. William was grinning, barely able to contain his joy as he announced, 'Father, we have a visitor... waiting for you.'

"You cannot imagine my surprise to see your sister, there before me. She had grown into such a fine woman, tall and confident. Neither of us could speak at first, but I held her close and blessed my good fortune to have lived long enough to enjoy that moment. She had voyaged alone, all that way. Brimming with tales of the other passengers, she was, where they were headed, the dreams they held. You know what Catharine's like... passionate as ever, eyes blazing. I realised then how much I had missed her."

He noticed Anne was frowning, chewing her lip again. "As indeed I missed all of you," he added hastily.

"And what did she tell you was her reason for travelling so far to be with you?" Anne was trying to sound professional, to show nothing more than the objective interest of any observer to this tale.

"Well, she was always a free spirit, wasn't she? She told me vaguely of some fellow who had let her down, and her decision afterwards to join me. She said she had worked as a governess in Bristol to save her pennies for the ticket, and planned to help Agnes in her school. I was just so pleased she was there… whatever the reason. It took such courage to come."

"Indeed…" Anne replied, noncommittal. "Life certainly changed after she left. Dearest Henry had died, and Catharine took herself off… then it was just me. Nan was often abed poorly, and Mother grieved so after Henry. She sometimes refused to dress… it was not an easy time."

Anne remembered the drudgery: cajoling the older women to eat; dust in the empty rooms; solitary evenings and silent days. An endless routine of domesticity.

A different type of courage.

"Catharine brought letters from your mother with her," he continued, ignoring Anne's words, "and newspapers with reports of Chartist activity – more petitions, more meetings, more rebuttals. Nothing much had changed. But she brought gifts from home too… Wait here a moment." And he limped off to his room. Anne had noticed recently how slow he had become and how, with increasing frequency, he gripped the arm of his favourite chair when the pain became unbearable. She worried in silence, keeping all thoughts of the inevitable well under control.

When he finally returned, he was carrying a large folded cloth wrapped around something square. He revealed reverently that old copy of Paine's *The Rights of Man*, his grandmother's gift, wrapped within a Chartist flag with its three stripes faded.

John held the flag tenderly to the light to see it as clearly as he could. "Blue for heaven," he said, "green for the common people and white for peace. The English changed the blue to red," he added. He was talking to himself now and Anne struggled to hear. "Never understood that. Probably O'Connor's idea." He turned to where she sat and added, "Catharine told me this one was carried to the Westgate, that Henry Vincent gave it to her on the anniversary of the march."

Anne recognised the flag at once. Vincent had indeed brought it with him, the first night he came with the stranger. The night that sentenced her father to hard labour.

"Such a thoughtful gift." She was trying to sound genuine, trying to sound as if she cared. "So how exactly did my sister occupy herself in her new life? It seems a long way to go to give someone a flag."

"Her arrival in Hobart was a turning point, Anne." Again he had failed to notice that sharpness in her voice. "With Catharine and William close by, life became more bearable. I had been lucky to survive Impression Bay, was more determined than ever to finish writing the truth about what happens there. And however long it took, I would earn my ticket-of-leave. Your sister's arrival gave me energy… a new purpose."

"I'm sure it did, Father… Always inspiring, our Catharine, such clever ways…" She couldn't help herself. It was imperative to find something to do before saying what she would instantly regret. "Now excuse me. There is a good breeze today, and I have your bed linen to launder."

HOBART
1843–1844

Catharine took up lodgings with an elderly widow who lived across the street from William. She kept her rent low by helping with the woman's cleaning and cooking, but spent most of her time in Agnes' school. She had always liked William's wife, a gentle, pretty woman with blonde curls, a not unattractive lisp when she spoke, and above all a big heart. The family lived mainly in the kitchen and two small bedrooms of their timber house, the other room converted to a cramped schoolroom for some thirty small bodies. William promised his wife that as soon as his ticket-of-leave was granted, he would set up a law practice again, and they would perhaps, in time, find a bigger home.

For now they did the best they could, and much to her surprise, Catharine found great joy in her days with the children. She taught them to recognise their letters and numbers. She loved watching their tiny, intent faces as they struggled to copy the alphabet. Little frowns, tongues escaping. The boys she taught to draw, the girls to sew. She loved their questions: "Miss Frost, how old are you?", "Miss Frost, have you ever told a lie?"

Many of the pupils were of convict families, who worked like William, as directed. A few others were offspring of free tradesmen and immigrants whom William had helped with unpaid legal advice, and who had agreed on a meagre amount in fees. But there was growing competition threatening these "private venture" schools. It came from the burgeoning Anglican schools, and the new "public" schools with a larger curriculum, both determined to drive out schools such as Agnes'.

A few weeks after Catharine's arrival, Agnes received a letter from Franklin addressed to all in charge of private venture schools in

Hobart. He warned they were under scrutiny, and to survive, needed to be more focused on moral education, with regular Bible study.

"We need help, William," Agnes said over supper that night. "Someone who might come to give religious instruction to the children, someone who might impress the authorities should they inspect us."

William was thoughtful, then said, "I think I know who. I have this week completed some clerical work for the vicar at St David's. Tasmania's been declared a diocese, and St David's will shortly be a cathedral. But they're building another, smaller church in West Hobart, and its new young pastor has just arrived here. He might be willing to help… at least until his church is completed."

And so it was that the young Reverend Peter Sinclair entered Catharine's life. A Cambridge man, he was tall and gangly with wild hair, and eyeglasses which made him look older than his years. He had not been long on the peninsula, and his pale skin and heavy clerical attire were incongruous in the heat. But he agreed to help William, at least temporarily.

Peter's first encounter with John's outspoken daughter was not entirely amicable. He agreed to observe the two women for a day as they taught, and later announced to Catharine, skipping any pleasantries, "You cannot be heard in the back of the room, Miss Frost, and you are simply too fast when you explain things. Some of the children were not listening at all. When training for my role, I was taught how to project my voice and to direct remarks to those furthest away."

It was unlike her to be lost for words, but this took her by surprise.

"Really, sir? Well, no doubt you will be so kind tomorrow as to show us how it is done?"

Agnes suppressed a smile.

The next day he came clutching his Bible, and Agnes introduced him to her young charges. "Now, children, this is Mr Sinclair. Sit still, and listen to what he has to say."

She and Catharine left him to the children, and he immediately started to read them the story of the loaves and fishes.

"My pa is a fisherman!" The first interruption. "And mine bakes loaves!" The second. That started a lengthy debate on whose father did what and how well. The cacophony increased.

"Quiet, children." He started gently, to no response.

"Quiet, please," a little louder.

"I said QUIET!" His face was red, glasses steamed, hair wilder than ever, Bible closed.

Catharine felt she had to help. She entered, clapping her hands and getting instant silence. "Now, now, children. This will not do. Listen to the story, then afterwards you can tell Mr Sinclair what you know about the fish caught here in Hobart, and how we make our bread. But one at a time, mind, and it's hands up, always."

Before he left, he sought her out. "Miss Frost, I owe you an apology. It appears that keeping the attention of children requires far greater skill than giving a sermon."

"I don't need to tell you, sir, about the value of different talents," she replied, smiling in spite of herself. There was something attractive about this rather gauche young man. "Will you come again tomorrow?"

"Most certainly," he replied, "and I shall be better prepared for my congregation!"

By the time John met him, Peter was already a familiar face in the Geach home. He came one Sunday for lunch after the morning service in St David's, and greeted John warmly.

"Mr Frost, it is both a pleasure and an honour. I have long admired your work, sir, and read many of your pamphlets. Your fight for universal suffrage goes on, you know."

John still found it strange to be known by his past actions. His life had moved inexorably since then, his goals had shifted. "It was a long time ago, all that," he said, and attempted to change the subject. "Catharine tells me you are making quite an impact with the children. Not as easy as it looks, is it?"

"Indeed, sir, though I find there is much to reward my efforts. But tell me, Mr Frost, is there a ticket-of-leave ahead for you? Have you thought what you might do?"

"No ticket for a while, I fear. But as it happens, I have just learnt Clayton is selling the warehouse and leaving Hobart. He has purchased some land and seeks to farm it. William here helped with the transactions I believe. Anyway, Franklin has informed me I am to work next as clerk in a grocer's store, opening in the New Town outside Hobart. Lodgings above the store, so it may mean I can't visit so often."

"Then we shall come to see you!" This was Peter, and John noticed the "we" as the man looked across at Catharine. He saw her blush.

So that was how it was. Well, she deserved happiness.

***

Letters reached him intermittently from Mary, bearing news of the other children, now almost strangers to him, and of grandchildren he had yet to meet. He would read them many times, turning the leather thread at his wrist, remembering her smile, trying to believe they would see each other again, in this life not just the next.

But in truth, daily life had improved. The new store was on a tree-lined street in a suburb of stone-built homes with small gardens, and the grocer was a decent family man called Bill Taylor.

"I'm told you have experience in a shop?" he asked John kindly. "This is a new business, so I welcome all the help and advice you might offer."

"Well, I know about cloth and tailoring," John replied, "but it's my guess that pleasing the customer applies anywhere. I'll do my best."

And he did. It was the most settled and productive time since he'd left the *Mandarin*, each day spent in the little store or bartering over local produce with former convicts now working the nearby farms. He was a diligent bookkeeper, quickly gaining his employer's trust, and each evening, he sat in his room recording his far less happy experiences as a convict, determined never to forget.

Sometimes Catharine came to see him, accompanied inevitably by Peter, who John could see was besotted by his daughter. She, however, seemed much more interested in the goings on in this, her new world.

"I simply must tell you, Father," she announced breathlessly at the start of one such visit, even before removing her bonnet. "Peter had to visit the convicts at the female factory yesterday, to arrange a burial for one of the poor souls there, and I decided to accompany him. It is the saddest of places, dark, dirty and noisy. I hated it… but we had apparently just missed a regular event, something known as 'the ritual of the handkerchief'."

She was holding the stage now, as she had once done before his Chartist friends in their parlour, years before. John was intrigued, urged her to sit, and gave her some tea. Peter sat listening, eyes fixed on Catharine.

"Men come to that factory from time to time and place a handkerchief in front of any one of the women lined up before them. It signifies they wish to marry the one standing by their kerchief, and the marriage is immediate. Can you believe it? It is nothing more than the acquisition of a breeding mare at market such as I saw once in Abergavenny, and it sickens me, Father!"

This was Catharine as he used to know her, magnetic, inspiring, passionate. She ignored the tea and carried on. "These women have no option. No voice, no choice and no chance. How can we justify *this* as penal reform?"

Peter tried to interrupt but she held up a hand to stop him.

"Then we followed the old woman's corpse," she continued. "Cast in a cart, wrapped in a dirty shroud, carried to a foul place called 'The Isle of the Dead'. Do you know it, Father?"

"Know *of* it," John replied, marvelling again at this woman before him.

"Peter and I were the only mourners. He said a prayer, then the poor soul was thrown into a pit in the lower area of that place, where the convicts, lunatics and invalids all lie, their graves unmarked. Further up lie the other citizens of Hobart, tradesmen and professionals and their families, all with headstones carved by convict stonemasons."

She was out of breath, eyes blazing. "You know what that means, Father?"

He could feel her anger, recognised in his daughter that sense of injustice he too had long carried.

"There's a hierarchy even in death," she spat.

Once, some months after changing employer, John was sent by Taylor with a grocery order for The Queen's Orphan School in a new suburb. It was a large stone building, forbidding, hostile. He left the groceries in the kitchen then asked to see the superintendent to collect payment as arranged. He knocked on the oak door and waited.

"Enter!"

Behind the desk was a familiar figure. Booth.

"Well, if it isn't Mr Frost," he exclaimed. "From Chartist leader to grocer's clerk... Quite the trajectory, eh?" The man, dressed in a shabby, poorly fitting coat, looked ill, his skin oily and eyes yellowing. Gone was the champion of music hall and puns. Gone the military pomp. This was someone who had been transferred unceremoniously from controlling the large Port Arthur settlement to running a children's home... but John held his tongue.

"Pass me the bill, man. I'll get what you need. Wait here."

John looked around him and was surveying the books gathering dust on Booth's shelves when the door opened again. This time it was a maid bringing in Booth's tea on a tray. An Aboriginal girl, in a long black dress with a crisp white cap and apron. She kept her eyes to the ground, unaware of his convict status, and at first John did not recognise her, then, as she bobbed to leave, he remembered.

"Mathinna?" She smiled to be recognised. "What are you doing here?"

"She works for me." John had not seen Booth return. "Off you go, girl."

John was stunned. "But she was adopted by Sir John… educated with his own daughter… She can read and write. Play the piano…"

"Yes, and very entertaining all that is sometimes," Booth continued. "Franklin's gone. Left last week for home. Couldn't take his 'little experiment' with him, could he? Can you honestly see the girl joining Her Ladyship in their 'at homes', man, being presented at court or dancing at a ball with her 'sister'? Not a chance. Ever."

"But she has family here. She's no orphan." John was indignant.

"*They* didn't want her either. She's lost to them for ever… so Franklin suggested I took her in to work and live here. There are worse places she might be, Frost, as well you know."

Frost made his way back to the room above the grocer's shop with a heavy heart. Cruelty wore many guises, something life had long taught him, and stories like Mathinna's were destined to remain untold. He picked up his pen to continue his account of convict life, but realised that there were others suffering too, in the margins of his writing. The country's true residents were mourning their lost lives, unheard and undocumented, for ever condemned to the appendix of transportation's dark history.

STAPLETON, BRISTOL
1877

"Have I been fair about Catharine?"

John was reading carefully what she had just written.

"Yes, very." He laughed. "Agnes told me about the first time Peter faced the children and how prickly Catharine was with him. You've captured that well, Anne."

"It seems my sister settled splendidly to her new life." Anne tried to keep the envy out of her words.

"Hobart suited her. She had her work in the school with Agnes, and often accompanied Peter on visits to the poor and sick around the parish. She was popular... she seemed happy. And I liked Peter. Solid, a good man."

Anne remembered another of Catharine's suitors, less solid.

"Women trusted Catharine. She started to teach one or two who couldn't read and write, in the schoolroom after the children had left. Before long she had quite a gathering. Those lessons often became a place of safety for them, somewhere to share their woes – and their dreams."

When her father was asleep that night, Anne finished the sampler she had been making. She had been careful to keep it a secret, finding an excuse weeks before to visit the town to buy the frame and silks, getting just the right shade of blue. She had never been clever at needlework, and this had been a challenge for her. Anne stretched it carefully to fit its wooden frame, and sat looking at the finished product. She hoped he would like it.

She rose early, put a vase of May flowers on the breakfast table and said, "Happy birthday, Father," as he arrived, hugging him briefly and awkwardly. "Ninety-three years today! My goodness... and I have a small gift for you. Something to hang in your room perhaps. I hope it pleases you." She was chewing her lip, brows furrowed. "My stitches are not even, I know, and I had to sew at night when the light was poor. Besides, my fingers are too large for delicate petals…"

She was rambling, nervous of his reaction.

He took the gift and read the words embroidered on it so painstakingly:

"To strive, to seek, to find and not to yield."

She had embroidered bluebells in each corner.

He sat looking at the delicate handiwork for a long time. When he finally raised his eyes, she could see the tears.

"It is perfect," he said.

HOBART
1844

His sixtieth birthday was a memorable one. The bishop was consecrating Peter's new church on that very day, and the whole family attended. Taylor was a churchgoer himself, allowing John considerably more freedom than Clayton had ever done, encouraging his visits to church and family each Sabbath, and the two men grew in a mutual regard.

"They've even named the place after you!" he teased his employee. "Quite a responsibility, that!"

Perhaps it was the grey hair now covering his head, perhaps it was being part of a family again, perhaps it was witnessing the selfless care shown by Catharine and Peter for the desperate souls around Hobart – John could never say exactly why, but something was drawing him to the Bible again. Tentatively at first, he began to seek, and then find, solace in the familiar words, strength from a force beyond his lost self, something outside the limitations of being human. Its pages held hope.

He began to look forward to Sundays, and in particular to services at the new church in Goulburn Street, West Hobart. It was a pretty little stone building, rustic, simple, and reminded John of a Welsh valley chapel. Bishop Nixon, a man almost suffocating from his own self-importance, had opened it officially. He welcomed a full congregation to what he called a "poor man's chapel" now ready for their use. He chose as his sermon Matthew xi, verse 5: *"the lepers are cleansed, and the deaf hear, the dead are raised up, and the poor have the gospel preached to them."* John was unimpressed. Peter would do much better: people liked his zeal, his amiable character, his empathy and compassion.

But that day was one fit to celebrate life, his own included, with Agnes preparing a special meal for them all. There was cawl using her own mother's recipe, and Welsh cakes baked on the griddle she had brought from Wales. The girls sang a version of "Sospan Fach", proud of what little Welsh they had been taught. Surrounded by laughter and the people he loved, John realised what he was feeling was, if not complete happiness, then a level of contentment. He was not a free man yet – he might possibly die before that happened – but there, in that moment in William's humble home, he felt a kind of peace. There was still much about which he should be thankful.

Somewhere in the shadows, however, a familiar guilt waited, stirred by indelible images of his wife and home. As if to remind him, there was a letter which Mary had written months before, wishing him well on his birthday, but also with news of Zephaniah, passed to her by his friend's wife, Joan.

"He has been denied a ticket-of-leave by Gladstone himself," Mary told her husband. *"But he's been recommended for his services to the police. Did you know he had become a constable? Seems he had quite a time of it before that. The story is he was forced to attempt an escape with four men he was supervising at the mines, and they spent days in the bush on the run, till Zephaniah got away from the others and gave himself up.*

"Joan writes me that he was sentenced to two years' hard labour for that, chained between two murderers, can you imagine?"

John could indeed imagine, only too well, and he wondered how his friend would have survived, in mind and body. Wondered also whether the story of the escape not being his idea was actually the truth. Zephaniah had a history with stories shaped to suit his ends.

Mary continued: *"Sixteen weeks of his punishment he spent in a dark cell, in silence. Rats everywhere... and lice. The Zephaniah we knew would have struggled with all that, John. But he found a strength somewhere, as you must have done, my love. I can hardly credit it, but he stayed to help the overseers at that convict settlement find water – and this you will believe – he gave them advice on engineering matters."*

John had a sudden desire to see his friend again. He bore no grudges, and time had long blurred the sharp edges of any wrongdoing around forced confessions. Years were passing like fast-moving clouds – he would ask Peter and William to make some enquiries.

It was William who found him, through a lawyer friend, a former convict who had been granted ticket-of-leave, and who now travelled regularly across the peninsula, often meeting with policemen.

"He's in New Norfolk," William reported, "twenty miles northwest of here. Lot of folk from the First Fleet settled up there, farmers mostly. If you ask Taylor, he may allow Zephaniah to visit you." Taylor had no objection to a constable calling, so John wrote and received a prompt acceptance to his invitation.

The two stood looking at each other for some minutes, each assessing how the passing years had dealt the cards.

"You look well, John." Zephaniah broke the silence. "Greyer, perhaps, but at least you still have your hair, whereas I …" He indicated his bald crown surrounded by thinning wisps.

"But we have survived, my friend." John replied, taking Zephaniah's outstretched hand in both his own. "We are still here. We have faced the worst and come through. There is much to be thankful for."

"Perhaps." His friend was thoughtful. "But I carry so much regret, John. I miss home, Joan, the children. Don't you ever wonder what might have ensued if we had said no to the rabble, that time in Blaina?"

"Life is too short for 'what if', man. I've learnt that here. You live and breathe still, in a place where so many die, my friend. Every day is for some purpose. Use what is left of life as best you can."

Zephaniah shook his head. "Whatever I have here cannot fill the emptiness, John, the ache for home, and I regret risking all I cherished for such a mad enterprise. We were fools, all of us. What in God's name were we doing?"

"We were doing what was, and still is, right," John answered, dropping Zephaniah's hand and stepping back. He was irritated by his old friend's comments. "And it is a fundamental right of each man to play a part in how he is governed. It will come, Zephaniah, even if we will not be the ones to make it happen. And it will reach Van Diemen's Land too. There is injustice found all across this place, men in power exercising cruel brutality and wallowing in oppression. You must see that, man, wearing a constable's uniform as you do."

No response. The man in front of him had become a stranger.

"We may be exiled from our homes," John continued, "we may not be able to publish pamphlets or hold rallies, we may be temporarily silenced, but we cannot – must not – stop caring about our fellow man."

"I just do as I'm told," his visitor responded, eyes downcast. "Arrest drunks, chase escaping convicts, warn women loitering near the public houses. It is hardly the action of a revolutionary... and I won't court trouble now. I've served my time. I stopped a robbery in a store once, more by luck really, but at least that earned me my ticket-of-leave." He was turning his hat nervously in his hands, and John sensed an awkwardness between them. Each man lit a pipe, to fill the void.

"Gladstone may have denied me a full pardon for now, and I can't go home yet, but I'll keep asking Joan to join me. We have to start afresh, John. It's possible to be happy here, comfortable even, if you're willing to work. But first we have to put all that Chartist rubbish behind us."

"And what of our friend William?" John interrupted. "Any news of William? I saw him once at Puer Point, but heard he'd left."

"He's moved around a bit," Zephaniah replied. "Last I heard he was making watches again, but where, well, God only knows.

That writer from *Fraser's Magazine* found his way to me after he'd spoken with you… turns out he'd seen William too. Came across him working in a shabby hotel somewhere, about to move on again – already had a ticket-of-leave. Can you believe it? Seems he earned it as an informant when he was at Puer Point. Told the authorities about someone who was fiddling the books. Nothing he did would surprise me, John… and I still wonder why he never reached us in Newport that night, don't you? Never felt I could trust him."

John was quiet, reflecting on the news about William, but also retrieving a memory of those lost days Zephaniah spent alone with McKechnie on the *Mandarin*.

"It's difficult to know who you *can* trust sometimes," he said, pointedly.

They continued to talk awhile until the conversation dwindled, the silences grew longer, and evening shadows filled the room.

"Well, I must go." Zephaniah rose, replacing his hat. "It was good to see you again, my friend. Stay well, and give my regards to Catharine, and to Mary when you write next. We must meet up again soon. It cannot be too long before your ticket is granted."

"It was good to see you again too," John replied, shaking his friend's hand. "Be sure to stay safe."

As he watched Zephaniah walk down the street and into a darkening distance, John knew there would be no further meeting.

STAPLETON, BRISTOL
1877

They spent most of their time in the kitchen at the back of the house. It was warm there in winter, with the open fire in the large green range where she cooked. John's favourite chair was there, next to the dresser with the familiar brass. The room had a little window which looked out upon the garden, and each summer, the kitchen door would stay open, allowing the sunshine to join them.

But there was another room, at the front overlooking the street. Darker, this "parlour" smelt permanently of damp and had rarely been occupied, even before Mary died. Against the far wall stood an old upright piano, covered in dust. It had spent its life in the taproom at The Royal Oak, and bore the imprints of many unfinished drinks standing to rest on its lid, memories impossible to polish away. The stool in which ancient sheet music was still stored had a fading tapestry seat cover, stitched as a gift for their grandmother years before by one of the girls, Anne forgot which. It would not have been her.

When John woke the day after his birthday, he thought briefly that he was back in Newport. He could hear a familiar sound... a piano? He rose and went downstairs to where something resembling "Für Elise" was being attempted. He smiled.

"I'd forgotten you could play," he said, placing a hand on Anne's shoulder.

He sat in the only armchair which could fit in the small room, leant his head back on the embroidered antimacassar, and closed his eyes until she had finished. The piano was in dire need of tuning, and some of the keys stuck together, but she persevered.

"I have such big fingers," Anne complained. "And I have not played for many years. Mother sold our piano before we moved, but Nan refused to leave this one in The Oak. She was adamant: 'Take me – you take the piano!'"

"Play something else," he urged.

Shuffling through the yellowing, musty music, she found the piece she was looking for, and haltingly played a version of the "Moonlight Sonata", fingers stumbling, notes not entirely accurate, but good enough to be recognisable.

"Mother taught us all to play," Anne said when she had finished. "Usually when you were away. But I was never gifted in the way Catharine was. She used to play this piece *so* well, her fingers light as butterflies on the keys…"

John sat up, could see she was frowning again.

"Catharine is not here, Anne. *You* are, and it is a great blessing for me that it is so. Now play one more piece for me, then let us move to the kitchen. It is too dark here, smells of damp, and you are squinting at the music, even in the May sunshine."

Later, he found her huddled over her desk, papers everywhere. Some had slipped onto her lap and from there to the floor. She jumped when he spoke.

"What is it you are seeking? Tell me, lass."

"Well, when you spoke of Zephaniah and William Jones again, I realised I did not know whether they ever came back to live here. I have no idea what happened to them. There is no mention of them anywhere in all your papers, father."

"Probably because I found out the truth in snippets, here and there over the years. I never met either man again, not that I sought to. We had different paths to tread is all. But I have some details… if you think any reader would be interested."

"Anyone still reading at this point, still interested enough, would want to know," she replied. "It would be odd to make no further reference, don't you think? You were all three charged and sentenced together after all. And it's better to conclude their stories whilst we're still in Tasmania, and before you sail off for California!"

John lit his pipe while she cleared some space on her desk to write.

"Your mother received news about Zephaniah for some years, from Joan... she never did join him, you know. It appears he and William met and fell out, over money I believe. William didn't have a penny to his name, was back performing around the peninsula as a strolling player, and Zephaniah lent him money, which of course was never repaid.

"The next part is a bit vague, but Zephaniah planned an escape to New Zealand. Those helping him in his mad plan shared the details with William, and what did that miserable wretch do? Only went and reported Zephaniah to the police! No doubt money changed hands... So much for old friendships, eh?"

John shook his head. "Again, Zephaniah faced hard labour, but again he survived. According to Joan, he was released around '48. But his story did not end there."

He paused to allow her time to catch up. "I heard from a freed convict who'd been working as a miner that Zephaniah had found coal outside Hobart, but that business venture did not work out too well either. Too many labourers were leaving for the Gold Rush in California at that time. But he went on to discover something he called Tasmanite – you can use it to make paraffin. I spotted his name when I read about it in the Hobart paper... It was quite a find. Made headlines. I believe he did well, sending it to Melbourne. That really was all I knew, until this..."

He rummaged through a pile of old newspapers and found what he sought. It was in the obituary column of a paper just three years old. Zephaniah had died, never having returned from Tasmania even though long pardoned.

"And what of our strolling player?"

"I heard nothing of William for many years," John said. "But when Zephaniah's death was announced three years ago, a journalist, keen to write about we 'Newport traitors', tried to find out whether William and I still lived. I was happy to reassure him for my own part, and the man later wrote to say he'd unearthed news of William. He'd died in '73 in Hobart. Poor sod was given a pauper's funeral."

Anne was pensive. "Strange that you were so close, Father, sharing so much, leading all those men, then suffering together in gaol, at the trial, on the ship... yet such distant strangers at the end."

"The older I get, the less I trust others, Anne. There's no disappointment that way. No betrayals. People let you down always, even those you call friends, and I've discovered that few in this world serve the interests of anyone other than themselves, whatever they claim. I place my trust in God now... and you, of course. Better that way."

HOBART
1845–1846

John's stepson received the news four months after it was sent. An official pardon. He was free once more to lead a life his own way.

They were sitting outdoors the following Sunday, after a family celebration.

"Will you go home now?"

John dreaded the answer.

They continued watching the two girls playing in the sunlight, while Agnes tended the vegetable plot.

"What is this if not home?" William said suddenly. "We have made a life here. Hobart has new suburbs, new constructions, new commerce, all needing legal advice. It is a good time to start my practice here. Besides…" And he turned to face his stepfather. "Catharine may yet decide to leave, and has talked about returning to Bristol. In all honesty, Mother is unlikely to make the sea journey now, and I do not want to leave you here alone."

John put an arm around William, and nodded. "Thank you, son. You cannot know how happy that makes me." But it was a happiness tainted by an unspoken fact hanging in the air between them: Mary might never again see her son, nor watch these grandchildren grow.

One Friday, John was serving in the grocery store when Peter arrived, alone. Taylor greeted the clergyman and told John, "Take the reverend into the back for some tea, John. He looks exhausted, and has probably been visiting folk all morning."

Peter sat in silence while John busied himself with cups, milk, sugar. His back was still turned when the young man suddenly blurted out, "It's about Catharine. May I ask for her hand, sir? I will care of her always, you have my solemn promise. I love her – with heart and soul."

John spun around, amused at the young man's earnest romanticism, but not surprised.

"Whatever took you so long?" he joked. "Of course you have my blessing, Peter, but my daughter is her own person. She will decide for herself, and nothing I do will persuade her either way, I can tell you that now."

The following evening, she called as he was finishing his supper.

"It's about Peter." No preamble. "I know he came to see you."

"Do I congratulate you?" John was scanning her face for clues.

She sat at his table, hesitating, her hands turning and turning the pen with which he had been writing.

"Well?" he asked. "What's it to be? Did you give the poor man an answer at least?"

"I said no," she whispered, almost unable to bring herself to say the words aloud. "I said no."

John has not expected this. "May I ask why? You always struck me as happy together. Compatible, comfortable."

She could not look at him, not yet. "I like Peter. He is a good man, and I respect him... but I do not, cannot love him. Marriage should be about more than being *comfortable* with someone, Father... and Peter is no more than a brother to me."

John sighed. "Love has many faces, Catharine. If you like and respect this man, then perhaps in time—"

"No," she interrupted. "I did love a man once... I know how the very sight of someone can take your breath away, how every waking moment is consumed aching for that person... Peter deserves such a love from someone, but it cannot be me. I have told him so, and I will not change my mind."

After she had left, John sat fingering the leather thread around his wrist. He wished Mary was there to reason with Catharine; he was sure his daughter was making a big mistake, but knew her far too well to argue.

Two weeks later, John heard the news.

"The strangest thing...." It was Taylor, returning from collecting some vegetables. "Went to the reverend's place with some groceries. The woman who cleans for him said he'd gone, upped sticks and left on a ship yesterday."

"Gone where?"

"He told her he had volunteered for a mission to Africa somewhere. Odd, don't you think," Taylor asked, clearly upset by the news, "given how hard he worked to get this new church up and running? Never a word about it to his congregation... Everyone liked him. This is truly a sad day for all in the parish."

"A sad day indeed," John concurred, and wondered about Catharine's future.

William had been right about Hobart's expansion. Whaling and shipbuilding brought new jobs, wealth and a constant influx of free settlers, who soon outnumbered the convicts. But with every ship came disease. Typhoid was already rife in a place where there was inadequate water, no sewage system and poor standards of hygiene. Streets were covered in foul-smelling grime which trailed into the homes on skirt hems and muddy boots.

Into the town came wave after wave of scarlet fever and influenza, spreading rapidly amongst a growing population, taking so many children first. John had seen it all before, in the filth and poverty of London streets, and recognised the familiar stench of death. There was talk from the new lieutenant governor of investment in hygienic systems in the town, but talk alone never saved a child's life. Agnes' little school was sorely affected, and closed more than once.

Then the worst happened.

Catharine came running with the news that Grace was ill. A fever, shivering, sickness and a rash, all the usual symptoms. Agnes and Catharine shared the nursing, night and day, almost losing their charge more than once. As his granddaughter held life by a tenuous thread, John asked William to pray with him, and the two sat in silent communion with their maker, willing some miracle to happen.

When the fever eased and Grace opened her eyes, John went alone to his namesake's little church and wept. He begged forgiveness for the pride which had brought him, and by association, William and his family, to Van Diemen's Land, and promised his God to do some good yet before he died.

But the real tragedy was still to come. On the tail of the outbreak of scarlet fever rode an influenza epidemic. Infection spread across Hobart, the dead left rotting for days before burial, with even the town's doctors too ill to leave their beds. *"The passing knell of St David's,"* wrote the editor of Hobart's newspaper, *"has continually been tolling."*

And it took Agnes.

Kind, sweet Agnes.

John had not wanted to believe his stepson, standing weeping before him. It had all happened so quickly. A headache, a painful throat, then a few days' later, she was gone.

"Why?" William kept wailing. "Why her?"

And so began a dark time of deep sorrow, one that convinced Catharine to stay. She would run the school, she promised, and would provide help for William with the girls. "I think Agnes would have wanted that," she told her father.

They buried Agnes on the hilltop which looked out towards the sea. The sky was the cruellest blue that day, and on the horizon, tall masts and fair winds were taking some exiles back home, penance done. The little church was full as children from her school sang a Welsh hymn she had taught them: lives she had touched in her quiet, unassuming way. Agnes had made a difference, was loved. It was all one might ask of life.

Consumed by grief and sadness, riven by guilt, John arrived at his lodgings to find a summons to see the lieutenant governor. A ticket-of-leave was finally his. It should have brought him happiness.

He just sat and wept.

"We were all so sad when your letter came," Anne recalled. "Mother loved Agnes, as did I. And we were so far away, desperate, unable to help… though you had Catharine, of course." She remembered the black drapes again, dust motes in dark rooms, her mother inconsolable, unlit fires and lonely meals.

"It was a time of great sadness for us," John recalled. "… Trying to explain to two young girls where their mother had gone. Catharine was quite wonderful with them, of course."

Anne bit back her words: "Of course she was," under her breath.

"When William was close to breaking, she would squirrel them away on some pretext or other," John continued. "And there was kindness from those who knew Agnes in Hobart too. People like Taylor who sent groceries and would not accept payment, or the widow who came silently to collect the children's washing and returned it without fuss."

He was back there again, remembering the dark veil which had enveloped them at that time, and the extraordinary kindness of others. "But," he said, "I finally had that ticket-of-leave, Anne, was a step closer to freedom. Provided I stayed in Van Diemen's Land, I was free to choose employment for myself. Taylor offered me a permanent position and a decent wage, and I was tempted. He had been good to me, but with Agnes gone, Catharine was barely coping in the school, and I saw where I was needed."

There was a heaviness in the air between them, and John tried to lighten the mood. "Let's have some tea, and I will tell you about my final years in Van Diemen's Land."

HOBART
1847–1854

John was not the natural teacher Catharine was. It surprised him to find that he was still not fully at ease speaking publicly, and his early attempts left the children fidgeting and giggling.

"Try smiling a bit more," Catharine teased, "and stop looking so terrified."

So he persevered, slowly finding a way to connect with his young pupils, who in turn came to respect this avuncular figure in their midst. He told them about creatures of the deep sea, told them old folk tales of giants, warrior kings and evil queens from his homeland, and read to them his favourite Bible stories. Seeing their upturned faces lost in the power of words gave him a sense of purpose.

He moved to live with Catharine opposite the school, caring for his granddaughters when he could. He went once to the orphanage, hoping to persuade Booth to release Mathinna to help at the school. But Booth had died, of heart failure, and of Mathinna there was no sign. No one knew where she had gone, so for a day or two, John searched the houses and inns of ill repute near the quay, where desperate women waited for lonely sailors. He was simultaneously relieved and saddened not to find her there.

Life adjusted to a new, slow rhythm. Wheels turned again. He carried his ticket-of-leave papers with him everywhere, as required, like some badge of dishonour, and attended the obligatory Sunday services. He began to feel his age; his back and shoulders ached when he tended to Agnes' garden, a legacy from his years in the "caterpillar". Men and women he had known since arrival in Hobart, often younger than he, were dying. He was tired of funerals.

Near their home was a small public house where, occasionally, John would spend a quiet hour at the end of the day. On one particular evening, he spotted a group of familiar local faces at a table in the far corner, huddled conspiratorially over their beer.

"They can't keep coming here," the loudest voice was complaining. "Bloody convicts! We are losing our jobs and wages to rogues and rapists. We have got to stop this, my friends!"

John recognised the passions of local politics, of men on a mission.

"What can we do? We need our own council to have a say in how things are shaped here. This is our land now, ploughed with our blood. It shouldn't be run by strangers from miles away, and we shouldn't suffer so that outsiders thrive."

Familiar themes. Different worlds.

He was listening quietly, head bowed, sipping his ale, when one of the group pointed in his direction.

"Well, look who we have here, my friends. None other than Mr John Frost, Chartist leader. Come join us, friend. You have become a legend in the homeland, sir, the rebel's rebel... none better than you can help we free men of Van Diemen's Land. Tell us how we should proceed. All we ask is a say in managing our own future. How should we best act, sir?"

John was taken off guard. "I can be of no help with all that now," he said hastily. "Politics and I parted company years ago... Besides, I have only recently been granted a ticket-of-leave. I am an old man and have no desire to visit Impression Bay again. But I wish you well in your desire for a council."

"Have you no advice at all?" The man looked disappointed.

"Bide your time just a little longer... It is hard to be patient when you seek change so desperately, but if I learned anything in '39 it was that too hasty a move can lead to disaster. Don't give in to the loudest voices. Take time and get it right."

He had their attention. This old man bore battle scars and deserved respect. He supped his ale and added, "From what I read in the papers, there is talk in London of ending transportation soon anyway. Your jobs will then be safe, but a forum of elected representatives where you might work together to mould the future of this island is worthy of your greatest efforts. Hold firm that ideal. Persevere. Good luck, sirs, and I bid you a good night." He drained his jar and rose to leave before he could be drawn further.

A year passed. Two. William's practice was thriving, and he moved the girls out to a bigger home in a new suburb. He was courting a widow he had met, and they saw him less often. John understood. Life in Van Diemen's Land did not lend itself to lengthy periods of mourning.

A vastly improved education system led inexorably to the closure of their little school, so John found employment with a printer in the town, and Catharine as a clerk at the new hotel. Their financial stability was better than it had been for a long time, and Catharine insisted on putting money aside "for when we sail home".

But a synchronicity of events and people will sometimes influence life's compass.

It started when he received a letter from Mary.

"My dearest love,

"I hope this finds you, Catharine, William and the girls all well. Life must be a little easier with your ticket, though there is still no pardon for you, my love, nor chance of your coming home, I pray for that every day still, pray that we will lie together and I shall see your dear face again.

"With heavy heart, I must convey to you the sad news that your mother has passed. Be assured she did not suffer at the end. She spoke of you often, John, and how she regretted the years you lived away from her as a child. I found her a great comfort when times were dark here. She is buried in the little cemetery, near Henry Hunt. He did so love her stories of the 'old days' in The Royal Oak."

He thought about his mother, but the news of her death moved him no more than would the demise of a stranger. He had tried over the years to understand. Tried to be charitable: perhaps she had simply decided it was better for him to grow up away from the coarseness and squalor of that shabby public house… but then he would remember her flirting with customers – and with "Uncle" William.

Admittedly, she had been kind when James died, and seemed to enjoy her grandchildren in recent years, but it was impossible for John to feel real grief now for someone he had never loved. He turned back to Mary's letter:

"Anne is well, and cares for me now that I am less agile than I was. I have an irritating cough which has lingered since winter, and increasingly I have cause to seek my bed to rest of an afternoon. I fear you would find me very old now, John. Whatever happened to the young woman who walked for miles with you in Bettws Woods to see the bluebells? I have, however, enclosed something I have copied out for you, a poem by dear Mr Tennyson, one to remind us both that old age does not necessarily extinguish hope nor passion. Stay strong, my love, my hero. Always yours, Mary."

Only then did John notice the flimsy paper which had fallen out of the envelope onto the floor. He opened it and found she had copied out her favourite poem about the ageing Greek hero. *"I cannot rest from travel,"* he read. *"I will drink life to the lees."*

He kissed the paper where she had written her name, and read on.

"How dull it is to pause, to make an end
To rust unburnished, not to shine in use."

His hands were shaking. It had happened often in recent months. He saw how they were speckled now with the brown spots which, as a boy, he had tried to count on his grandmother's hands. Blue veins mapped skin cracked by the sun, and his leather thread hung loose now on a thinning wrist. He was old. Mary's "hero" was just an old man waiting for his end. Once, lying in those bluebells, they had dreamed of spending these last years together, surrounded by grandchildren. His stubborn pride had destroyed all that.

Guilt whispered.

He pinned the poem above his bed, and said aloud,

"*'Tis not too late to seek a newer world...*' Ah Mary, Mary, what if it *is* too late…"

He lay on his bed until it got dark, staring at the ceiling. *Was* there something he might still do? Hardly. What future could there be for an old man, an ex-convict, in a foreign land? And how in hell could *he* ever seek a newer world? If so, where was it?

The answer came a short while later. Catharine saw the official stamp on the envelope, ran to him and watched his face anxiously as he opened it.

"Your pardon?" she asked, barely able to breathe. "Is it your pardon, Father? Have they said you may go home?"

An eternity in a minute's wait.

"It is a conditional pardon, lass," he replied, passing her the letter. "I am free to live anywhere except Britain."

A synchronicity of events.

His daughter knew this was a significant moment for them. "So what happens now? Have you thought about what you'll do?" She was suddenly frightened by the idea that he may no longer want her with him.

"I have no clear plan yet, lass, but I know one thing. I am not going to stay here to die. They will not bury me in Van Diemen's Land, Catharine. That I can promise you."

STAPLETON, BRISTOL
1877

"We never understood – Mother and I – why you chose San Francisco, and yet another long sea voyage." Anne was finishing the account of his conditional pardon. "I think she believed you and Catharine might travel as far as the mainland – Victoria perhaps, and start a draper's store, or a printer's, until a full pardon arrived. She was always convinced that would happen, that you would return, you know."

"America was your sister's idea," he said.

Of course it was.

Anne tensed, chewed her lip, and a large blot fell from her pen. "Well, truth be told, I have not yet read your journals from 1854 and 1855, nor do I know anything about the sea journey necessary to get from Hobart to California. If I am to write with any jot of accuracy I shall need to study first."

She was annoyed, but wasn't sure about what. Probably her sister's mad idea to take an old man on such a journey. She bundled together the notes and papers which she had used to write the last section, and handed them to John. "You can put these away for now, and try to find what I need to read before we sail off to America! What on earth made Catharine suggest such a move?"

"Victoria was not an option for us," John clarified. "The Convicts' Prevention Act had just been made law there, and only those with *unconditional* pardons were accepted. But Catharine was working in one of the small hotels which had opened near Hobart dock," he began, settling into his chair. It was early June, a glorious day and Anne had opened the windows so that they might hear the birdsong. "It was a busy place, respectable and clean, used by folk waiting for ships home or for transport to new lives beyond Van Diemen's Land."

"Catharine had noticed the woman staying there alone, still wearing black, and recognised her accent as soon as she spoke. From Merthyr, she was. Had married a miner who was transported for stealing coal. Member of a Chartist lodge. Recently widowed, she was waiting for a ship destined for California. She had a brother there, apparently. He'd gone to find gold, failed like so many before him, but was now working in the docks."

Anne listened, imagining her sister conveying all the details, persuasive as ever.

"The woman's brother said there were many of our countrymen all across America, seeking new lives. There were opportunities for people like us – drapers, printers, teachers. Your sister was convinced we should go, and we talked about it long into the night. There was nothing to keep us in Hobart, though we would sorely miss William and his family."

John winced as he moved in his seat. That hip was painful again, and he often woke now so stiff it was difficult to get out of bed. But he considered the pain as the natural companion of his old age, his body's lingering memory of Impression Bay, a keepsake to remind him to count his blessings.

"And I admit America had an appeal," he continued. "I knew I would find greater freedom in a place which had risen against oppressive tyranny and won. How could I ever feel free if I stayed in a country whose queen still considered me a traitor?"

Anne interrupted then. "And America gave you the freedom to publish your account of convict life."

"That it did. Each year's passing left me more uncertain of how long I had left before I would meet my end, and I was anxious the world should know what I had seen. The government may have stopped transporting convicts around that time, but it was still important to remind people of the corruption and injustice at work.

Above all, I wanted to show how powerful leaders who have no accountability will quickly turn tyrannical."

"But as I recall… and I really do need to check all this, Father… you didn't leave Hobart until December '54, many months after that pardon reached you."

"The hesitation was mine, not Catharine's," he admitted. "At seventy, I had no desire to start a business again and worried about how she might survive alone, should I fail to see the journey to its end. So we hesitated, or rather I did, stalling your sister's enthusiasm a while. But let me find something for you…" John went to his trunk and rifled through yet another bundle of papers. What he brought her was a letter, with a familiar signature. Henry Vincent's.

"I told you about the synchronicity around that time, a jigsaw of events, each piece gradually shaping the picture of my future. Well, this was another. Read it… you'll understand what I mean."

Anne sat closer to the light and put on the eyeglasses she had recently started wearing. Vincent told how he had learnt of John's conditional pardon, granted by the Prime Minister Lord Aberdeen following a series of appeals by Thomas Duncombe in the House of Commons. He hoped John was well, then outlined his proposal:

"Fifteen long years have passed since we last met, my friend, and I know from correspondence with Mary that you have endured much. From the English newspapers which reach you, you will know something of the continuing struggle here for universal suffrage. Good men are making a difference up and down the land, and sometimes paying a heavy price for their endeavours. One such is the lawyer, William Prowting Roberts. Do you remember him? You and I spoke at a meeting with him in Bath in '37 or '38. He has been a true friend to Chartism, John, offering legal advice to trade unions, and defending miners in Durham. They call him 'the miners' Attorney-General'. I asked him once why he

was so dogged in his efforts. Know what he said? 'We resist every individual act of oppression, even in cases we were sure of losing.' Reminded me of you in the years before Newport...

"*He met with me this week with a proposal for you, John. You may not be able to return to our shores yet awhile, but Roberts knows Chartists all across America, many of whom he defended at some point. They would gladly host you and arrange for you to give talks and lectures along the route. You need not fear for your safety, or that of Catharine: you would be with friends everywhere. He mentioned contacts in San Francisco, Kansas City, Chicago and Pittsburgh. This latter has a thriving Welsh community around the new ironworks. You could then proceed to New York where he knows of a boarding house run by a Chartist.*

"*He will write with further details, but I offered to 'plant the seed'. It is my sincere hope you will find the idea agreeable. America will welcome you as a hero, John. Of this I am sure, and you can publish your latest writings without fear of reprisals.*

"*I hope we shall meet again someday. Stay strong.*

"*Meanwhile, may fair winds speed your journey to happier shores,*

"*Your friend, Henry.*"

"Catharine was surprisingly hesitant, I remember, seemed suspicious of the motives of Henry's friend Prowting Roberts, a man she had never met. But for me it was the final piece of the puzzle, Anne. I knew where I wanted to be next, had the answer I was seeking, and to think it came from Henry, eh? He always had interesting contacts, that man."

Anne remembered another of Henry's "interesting contacts" and understood what had made her sister so hesitant, but she kept her eyes focused on the letter.

"When William Roberts' letter eventually arrived," John told her, "Catharine was reassured. It was full of suggested places to visit, complete with names of people who would welcome us, and their addresses, so the matter was decided. In December, whilst the weather was generally clement, we set sail, purchasing our tickets with the money Catharine had saved for a voyage home. We had no idea what was waiting for us, just another distant horizon, but it was new, and exciting, and we were ready. One thing was certain: there was no turning back."

Later, Anne moved the lamp closer to her bed, wrapped her shawl around her shoulders, propped herself up with her pillows and began reading her father's journal entries for the next turn of the wheel.

New Horizons

"Old age hath yet his honour and his toil
Some work of noble note may yet be done."

Tennyson, *Ulysses*

HOBART – SAN FRANCISCO
1854–1855

They took few possessions. One trunk sufficed. Some clothes, his letters, that copy of *The Rights of Man*, the manuscript he hoped to publish before too long, his Bible, and the Chartist flag she had brought to Van Diemen's Land. Before departure, they paid a final visit to Agnes' grave, joined by William, who told them he was planning to marry again. The woman had prepared a special farewell meal for them, and John could see his stepson was at peace and that the girls clearly liked her. It was all he could ask.

William took his stepfather outside as the women cleared the table, guiding him out of their earshot. "When you dock in San Francisco take great care," he whispered. "Last I heard, vigilante groups were boarding every ship to check arrivals. They claim it's illegal for ex-convicts to enter the city. If they ask you, tell them you and Catharine are teachers… it's not exactly a lie."

He moved John further away from the house and lowered his voice again. "You know how gold lured thousands from these shores for San Francisco in '49. Well, I've met a few, back here now, broke and disappointed. They tell of a lawless, uncivilised city living in fear of the 'Sydney Ducks'."

"I've read about them," John said. "They're just gangs of ex-convicts with duck cloth trousers." William was shaking his head. "Look," John continued, trying to reassure his stepson. "I don't doubt the place has some rough edges… but we're used to that, aren't we? Port Arthur wasn't exactly Cheltenham! Besides, I've lived with convicts before. I'm not afraid."

"But you won't be alone this time, Father, nor as young. Some would see an old man and his daughter as easy pickings… so I want you to take this." And he produced from his pocket a small handgun. It was a Colt pepperbox pistol, hand-tooled, expensive, the barrel engraved. "I shall sleep a little easier if I know you have some protection. Please, no arguments."

John had never seen such a weapon. "Where did you get this?" he asked. "It must have cost a small fortune."

"Let's just say it was payment for a favour. It's American. The owner needed legal advice to secure some land for prospecting, out past Sydney, but had no way of paying for my services. He gave me this."

"I'm not a man for weapons, William. You know that, but I've no wish to argue with you tonight. It is a kind thought, and I thank you." John hid the weapon from sight, telling himself it would never be used.

It had been a happy family supper. A memory to pack away and keep: Emily playing the new piano William had installed in his home; Grace giving Welsh cakes she had made on her mother's griddle, "to eat on your journey, tadcu".

But all evening, as the hands moved on the grandmother clock, their conversation danced around the knowledge that these were their last hours together in this life. Parting was intensely sorrowful, beyond any need for words.

The cart came the day before departure, collecting their trunk for the hold. All they had for their months at sea was what Gladstone bags and canvas holdalls could carry. The day had been unbearably hot with not a whisper of air across the bay. As darkness fell, they heard it, an approaching thunder in the distance above Mount Wellington. It brought the lightning zigzagging over the forest of masts down in the harbour, then rain that fell drumming on rooftops and carts, turning streets to sludge.

"Just listen to that thunder!" Catharine said. "I can't remember when I last saw a storm like this."

"I can," John replied. He remembered a mountaintop, and a young boy borrowing his greatcoat. "We'll get a few more out at sea, I suspect. It'll clear the air though." They watched in silence as bright flashes illuminated skeletal ships waiting for the morning tide, until the storm moved out to sea and darkness sent them to their beds.

Tomorrow would be an end and a beginning. An untravelled world, terrifying in its possibilities.

**

The air was cooler the next morning, small clouds scudding across blue sky. As they made their way to their ship, John felt an almost childish excitement, and heard it too in Catharine's voice as she exclaimed, "Just look at all these people!" Everywhere, sailors busied themselves in preparation. Spider-like young boys climbed the masts and shouted to the seamen below. Sails were checked and rechecked. Merchants carried their wares up the gangplank, dozens of heavy crates and barrels, some containing provisions for the voyage. Passengers lingered to say last farewells to loved ones on the quayside, chiding the restless children anxious to get on board. Gulls screamed overhead and somewhere, someone was singing a hymn.

Finances had not permitted a cabin, so father and daughter made their way to the area they would share with others, between the deck and the hold, windowless and rather stuffy. It was not the worst option on board, but was far from ideal. They would be supplied with basic ingredients: oatmeal, flour, rice, tea. Any cooking would be done communally, and there would be little privacy.

"This will be cramped for you, Catharine," John said.

"It is no worse than my last sea journey," she replied, "and we had some jolly times then. It'll be as good or bad as we choose to make it, Father."

John smiled at her resilience. She busied herself securing two bunks in as quiet a corner as was possible, and covered the mattresses with their own bedding as required.

"Can I help?" he asked, but she shooed him away to get some air before they sailed.

He stood on deck watching the final passengers board: a few wealthy families headed for the cabins, the women overdressed for the journey, parasols shading them from the December heat. Others were lone travellers, young men seeking a fortune somewhere else, or couples hoping to grow old together in a new world.

Then John spotted a group of scruffy middle-aged men, their weather-beaten faces downcast and avoiding the gaze of other travellers. He knew instantly what they had been: he recognised the gait and shuffle of men who had spent years in irons. They had the look of spent souls, exhausted, dejected, cowed. One or two had difficulty walking up the gangplank as they headed for the steerage quarters, dark and dismal, alongside the cargo. If these were typical of the "Sydney ducks" in William's warning, John was not afraid. In his experience, the people to fear in this life were more likely to be in the fancy cabins.

Then it was time. Gangplank raised, sails ready, captain at the wheel. A good breeze took them out beyond the harbour, and Catharine joined him to watch Hobart shrink to a dot on the horizon. She squeezed his arm. "This was the right thing to do," she said, as if guessing his concern for her. "California, here we come!"

"Whatever did you do all day?" Anne had just realised how long it had taken her sister and father to reach San Francisco. "Five months is an endless time with the same people, and in cramped conditions. I've read your journal entries for that sea voyage, Father, but it is devilishly thin on detail."

"It had to be," John explained. "I needed to be careful using any ink I had with me. We were not sure when we would dock again – or where. Such journeys often required stops en route for repairs or supplies, but no one knew for sure."

"I'm finding it difficult to imagine, but I don't want to get things wrong either. A reader deserves my best efforts at the truth, so I must ask – was it very uncomfortable for you both?" She was making detailed notes, and he smiled as she chewed her lip again. He was touched by her attention to the detail of his life.

"For me it was luxury compared with my first voyage," he laughed, "but you are right. The hours could drag and, if I'm honest, tedium was the biggest foe. Days started early. Everyone up by seven, and a communal meal of oatmeal porridge. The children on board were schooled from eight, whilst their parents cleaned. Dinner was at one, tea at six and lights out by nine... the same routine every day."

Anne winced. It sounded punitive.

"Keeping clean was impossible. I had long been familiar with the stench of humanity unwashed, but those of a more delicate disposition found it hard. In the bowsprit was a latrine for our use, sea water washing it clean. But in rough seas we could not get there."

She winced again. Tried to imagine how Catharine dealt with it.

"At those moments," he continued, "we had a communal bucket which often spilled onto the floor of our mess area, and many – very many – suffered seasickness. People lay all day on their bunks, moaning, and the children cried constantly. Captain never let us cook then either." John smiled at a memory. "We knew why. Quite early in the journey, when a strong swell tilted the ship suddenly, our dinner, which Catharine had prepared so carefully, slid right off the table."

"I wanted to ask you about food and what you ate," Anne asked, her pen poised over the page. "You have said nothing of victuals in your account."

"Salt beef, occasional ale, nothing fresh after a week or two. The stuff went rancid, or the rats got at it. But I do remember a foul pea soup a fellow passenger used to make for everyone, and endless rice puddings. We used a little of our savings sometimes to purchase an egg or two, a piece of cheese, some biscuits. What I *do* recall, though, is the change in some passengers' taste as we sailed. There were a few in our mess who considered themselves too refined to stomach the greasy lumps of meat we were occasionally given, but before we reached California they were devouring such rarities with gusto!" He smiled. "Funny how circumstances can change you."

He waited until Anne changed the nib on her pen, watched as she tried in vain to wipe away some of the ink stains on her finger. She brought him his pipe, and he carried on.

"The long afternoons were the most likely times to be bored. Catharine had books with her, of course. The latest by Miss Bronte, I think, and I remember her reading to me from Mrs Gaskell. It wasn't light enough for long down where we were, difficult to read on deck with the ship's rocking, and lamps were out by nine, so even time to read was limited. But your sister was very active on board," John recalled, "and very popular."

Of course she was.

"She arranged to teach the children in the mornings, and joined a small committee some other passengers had established to organise our entertainment. There were games on deck, even an occasional boxing match, we played cards, there was some dancing for the younger passengers, and musical evenings. All surprisingly jolly, really. An American gentleman on his way home had a violin, another had a mouth organ, and Catharine would sing, sometimes in Welsh. You could hear a pin drop at those moments."

Anne saw how the memory of his favourite still made her father happy, and she got up to make a camomile tea. She found it helped her headaches of late. When she returned, he continued, "I had *The Pilgrim's Progress* on board with me, a gift from William. I had my Bible, of course, and my journal. Then, two or three weeks into our journey, the committee asked if I would set up a ship's paper for passengers, after your sister had told them I'd been a printer. Seems the captain had experience from a previous voyage of this initiative and had the necessary equipment on board."

Anne remembered seeing in her father's archives a crude broadsheet with details of the weather forecast for 15th January 1855, nautical bearings and deck activities for the following day. She found it and presented it to John, whose face lit up.

"Yes!" he cried. "I'd forgotten I kept this. Each day I needed to consult the sailing master, the navigator if you like, who would show me the maps and instruments he used to steer us. Nice man, from Bristol… We shared memories of the docks there. He was terrified of pirates – they were desperate for men with his skills and knowhow.

"The surgeon on board was an enthusiast for the little paper, and was quite the talented writer. He submitted one or two pieces about places he had visited – China and India, as I recall." He read the broadsheet again, and added, "This paper became far more for me than just a way of passing the time."

"And the others?" she asked. "You had to live for so long side by side with complete strangers. Wasn't it difficult? I would have hated it."

"People are the same everywhere," he said. "There are givers and takers, selfish and selfless."

John was thoughtful for a while. He lit his pipe and watched the thin grey cloud circle upwards to the ceiling long stained by woodsmoke.

"You know, Anne. Life on a ship is a mirror of life anywhere. The captain rules without opposition. Some are better than others at that job: ours was a reasonable fellow, but the surgeon had tales of some real tyrants. Then there was a top tier of 'citizens' on board, hidden away in the cabins with their own private poop deck. They were waited on at meal times, and given the best provisions. A middle group, where we were, struggled but managed to get by. Then there were the poor souls in steerage. In high seas, they were kept shut in the dark as the water washed into their quarters. Their mattresses never really dried."

He stood slowly and painfully. "Catharine once railed against a hierarchy in that Hobart cemetery," he added. "Well, it was there on board ship too. I am for my bed now, lass. Tomorrow, I'll take you to Callao."

CALLAO, PERU
FEBRUARY 1855

It is impossible for anyone who has no experience of a lengthy sea voyage to properly comprehend the vastness of the ocean, to visualise the endless horizons, to feel the sense of powerlessness it creates as those trapped in a flimsy wooden vessel submit to the mercy of winds and weather. Sometimes, becalmed for days, a silence would crawl through the decks and cabins, broken only by the occasional chatter of loose rigging or a baby's cry. Even the seabirds were mute. Crew and passengers alike bowed to the stupor, waiting, waiting. Too much sun on deck: no air in their quarters.

Heat stifling. Light blinding. Blue in every eye line.

Then the storm would come and, like those Greek mariners roused from their lotus eating, the crew would leap around again, remembering their tasks. Such it was off the coast of Peru some two months after John and Catharine set sail.

"It'll be all stations go tomorrow, Mr Frost," the sailing master told him. "There's a storm coming our way. A big one I reckon. Bigger than any you'll have seen on the Bristol Channel, you mark my words. Best stay in your bunk."

Only on one or two occasions in his seventy-one years had John feared for his life: in Monmouth Gaol, in Port Arthur… and here, on this ship. Rain battered and bruised for hours, the strong winds sending mountainous waves over and over the decks. A cacophonous thunder and lightning directly overhead for what seemed an eternity, the noise of parts splitting and breaking above them, and the ship's constant rolling, this way and that, so that possessions were sent hurtling from side to side, and no one could stand upright. The smell of fear in the bunks around him, an awareness of mortality.

For his own safety he was no longer concerned; he had a long life behind him. But he was fearful for Catharine, and opened his Bible for solace. He read aloud from the psalms so that she might hear in the bunk above him:

"He commandeth and raiseth the stormy wind, which lifteth up the waves thereof... they mounteth up to the heaven, they go down again to the depths: their soul is melted because of trouble. They reel to and fro and stagger like a drunken man... then they cry to the Lord in their trouble and He bringeth them out of their distresses. He maketh the storm a calm so that the waves thereof are still..."

When he had finished, he realised his daughter was crying, not something she did often. He prayed that night and begged his maker to spare her, then he held close the leather thread and spoke silently to Mary, hoping she might somehow know he was thinking of her.

But it was not his time.

A bright dawn broke over a calm sea, and he ventured on deck, where the boatswain was inspecting the torn sails. "We lost a lad last night," he said. "Went overboard. Tried to save the mast there." John could see the damage. "Silly bugger. We told him not to play the hero."

The deck was strewn with debris and still awash, strange dead fish knocking against the sides, algae clinging to John's shoes. The ship's carpenter and crew were trying desperately to repair what they could, but a while later the captain let it be known that the ship would limp into land, the nearest port being Callao.

Nothing prepares a traveller on such a journey for the joy of seeing land again. At sea, there is always a feeling of being cast off from humanity, of abandonment. John's mood lifted at the sight of the peninsula and the natural harbour. Beyond would be other ships, warehouses, homes, people. As the ship sailed nearer, Catharine joined him, and they could see an ancient fortress guarding the promontory on which sea lions basked indifferently.

"Surgeon's been here before," he told her. "Tells me it was founded by the Spaniard... what's his name? Pizarro? The one who took all the gold from the Incas. Bolivar landed here too, some thirty years ago now... interesting place."

The bay was impressive in size and beauty. Palm trees lined the water's edge, alongside colourful ramshackle houses and boats of all types.

"Look down, Mr Frost. Look down there!"

The surgeon had joined them, and was pointing into the water.

"This bay was formed after an earthquake," the man continued. "Can you see them?"

Then they could make them out: far beneath the surface of the clear water, preserved like fossils in formaldehyde, the rooftops and walls of homes once part of the city.

They had been told to expect a week's delay at least. Some stayed on board, but Catharine urged they spend time on shore. "It will make the remainder of our sea voyage more bearable," she argued. "Besides, I need a bath and some clean clothes. We can seek the cheapest lodgings." He could not deny her.

Once again he experienced the strangeness of solid ground under sea legs. Like someone the worse for his ale, he staggered, holding Catharine's arm, as their feet touched Peruvian soil. For a while, it was difficult to know where to focus. Just standing on the quay was overpowering: the smells of spices and fruits, the loud cries in a foreign tongue, the exotic dress of locals wrapped in brilliantly coloured blankets. And the music. Everywhere there was music of a rhythm new to their ears. High-pitched pipes with haunting melodies. The place was intoxicating.

They found a modest lodging house near the dock where the landlord spoke pidgin English, enough to provide them with bookings for the bathhouse next door and some warm water to wash a few items of clothing.

"Real luxury!" Catharine laughed, lying on the simple bed, preferring not to notice the suspicious stains.

While she took her bath, John checked that his gift from William was near at hand, and loaded. He had seen some less salubrious types on their way here.

"Your turn now!" His daughter ushered him out of the door. "I'm going to write to William. A woman in the bathhouse said there's a mail boat bound for Hobart leaving tomorrow. I shall tell him about our adventures so far. Now off you go…"

John lowered his aching limbs slowly into the warm, slightly scummy water. "Thank you," he said to the old woman tasked with pouring in the water.

She grinned, her teeth brown from the tobacco she chewed continuously. She nodded, "Yes, mister, yes, yes," clearly not understanding a word of English.

As he felt the liquid caress his sagging skin and ease his old bones, John allowed himself to relax a little, and sighed.

"Feels good always, don't it?" He hadn't really noticed the stranger submerged in the room's other bath. "First time in Callao?"

Why did strangers always insist on starting up a conversation?

"Yes," he replied, wary as ever. "You?" John had recognised an Irish accent.

"Not the first, no. Wife's from Lima," the stranger explained. "Met her in San Francisco. You been there?"

"On our way actually," said John. "Storm damage brought our ship here for a week."

The stranger clearly wanted to talk. "Been in California since '51. Thought I'd find my fortune where they told me the streets were paved with gold! Well, all I saw on the streets was horseshit. Only good thing I found was the laundry run by the angel who's now my missus. On my way back to her now. Just been doing a bit of business here…"

John felt his eyes closing in the warmth of the room, but his companion carried on. "Wife's brother lives in Lima. Got back to Callao this morning on the new railroad from there. He and I have a little trade going in guano. Lots doing it here now."

"Guano?" John had a vague idea he was referring to seabird droppings. "It's used in fertilising plants, isn't it?"

"Not just that," smiled his companion. "Governments need it for gunpowder too… and so you could say those rocks covered with guano really *are* paved with gold!" He laughed at his own joke. "But let me introduce myself. Name's Patrick, Patrick Heaney. Everyone calls me Paddy." He reached a dripping hand across to where John was bathing.

"I'm John," he said, not yet prepared to give his surname, then added, "I'm heading to California and across to New York. I have some people I wish to meet again on the route. I've been – away – for some years." He was being cautious.

"Holiday in Van Diemen's Land, I suspect." Paddy smiled. " I spotted the telltale scars on your ankles when you got in the bath. Snap!" He raised a leg from the water and John could see deep scars above the foot. "Got my pardon in '51 and left for California straight after. Nothing to go home for anyway. Family all dead, and I'd suffered there enough."

John understood. The Irishman was alluding to the famine which killed so many of his countrymen in the late '40s.

"Joined the Irish Confederation in '48, wanted rid of the English bastards controlling us – but that just got me a ticket to hell. I'm wiser, though… looking after my own interests from now on."

John rose slowly and grabbed the rough, thin cloth which served as a towel.

"Where are you planning to eat tonight, my friend?" Paddy asked.

Before John could answer, the Irishman continued, "Only I happen to know the best places hereabouts… clean, with fresh food – and no fights. At least not often. You can try the local Oca wine, and meet some *chalacos*." He smiled at John's puzzled face. "It's the name they give the residents of Callao. Come on, say yes. I promise you'll not regret it. And I'm paying."

"I couldn't possibly accept such generosity, but I'll accept your invitation," John replied. "Just so long as it's a reputable place. I shall have my daughter with me."

STAPLETON, BRISTOL
1877

"I remember that meal."

They were sitting at tea, the door to the garden wide open to let in the summer warmth. Anne had made a sponge, which was not very good. Too dry as usual. She never was much of a cook, however dutifully she studied Mrs Beaton, and besides, she needed to be frugal with the butter.

"You might want to spread more jam on it," she suggested. "Can't see the Queen wanting her name associated with *that* offering." And she passed him the pot.

He ignored her suggestion, his mind back in Callao. "And I remember Paddy speaking Spanish with the locals in the place where we were eating. Handsome people, dark eyes, always smiling.

"I saw from the cut of the coat and his silk tie that this guano was clearly a lucrative affair, so I let Paddy pay as he insisted. There was a fish dish the likes of which I have not tasted since… and red potatoes, as I recall. Yes, red, and shaped oddly. Paddy said the Incas believed potatoes linked we mortals to the gods. Must have heard it from his wife, I suppose."

"Did he know who you were?" She licked jam off her fingers and went to get her pen, ink and paper. She needed to note these details.

"Catharine told him a bit more about my history, but I don't think he recognised the name. He had heard of the Newport rising though, and the aims of the Charter. We had much in common."

He chewed on her cake pensively, not really tasting it. Just as well, she thought.

"But I remember something else about that night… There were other men there, waving their arms, drinking too much, talking loudly with great passion. You didn't need to understand the words. I'd seen such intensity many times… I guessed it was politics."

"Don't tell me they were planning an uprising there too!" Anne laughed.

"On the contrary. Seems they'd just had one. They'd reinstated a liberal president… can't remember the name now… after years of state corruption and reckless spending. Representatives were about to be elected to a National Convention. Sound familiar? They were aiming for universal suffrage within the year." John smiled at the memory. "Within the year! When Paddy translated that for me, Anne, I was truly humbled. I was in Callao like a piece of driftwood cast ashore randomly, stuck in some remote port I'd never heard of before that storm, and what had I found? Nothing less than democracy at its finest.

"Paddy sailed back to San Francisco on our ship, but in a private cabin, courtesy of the guano I assume. We met often. He'd invite me onto the poop deck and we'd put the world to rights, as men do when they have felt the irons around their ankles."

Anne moved the plates aside to start a new sheet, and swore under her breath when she noticed jam on the clean page. It would have to do. She could not afford waste.

"Something else you learn when travelling, lass: how diverse people are, and how they can surprise you. I remember the two of us staring out to sea one day when Paddy asked me if I read poetry. I would never have guessed this Irish ex-convict was a poetry lover, but it turns out he was quite the connoisseur… suddenly started reciting some lines he liked, about the sea. Now, can I remember how they went? Something about 'eternal whisperings' and 'desolate shores'. I remember that much, probably because I'd seen my share of the latter, eh?"

"I know it!" Anne cried, and went to her bookshelf. "I thought so. It's Mr Keats," she announced. "When William wrote to say you had set sail he warned us how long it would be before we had a letter. Mother said something about Penelope having to wait a bit longer for her hero's return, and I asked who she meant. She laughed then, and explained the reference, but also told me it was Mr Keats not Mr Tennyson who had written the best lines about the sea."

John waited while Anne read the sonnet through, and she added, "I remember... Mother particularly liked the lines:

'O ye who have your eyeballs vexed and tired
Feast them upon the wideness of the sea. '"

"I'd much rather feast mine on dry land any day, Anne. But we had a fair wind behind us after Callao and were in sight of San Francisco within two months. Paddy was a good sort, you know. He asked that I stay in touch once we reached the port, but we both knew it would not happen. Friendships made on such journeys are butterflies."

She tilted her head, curious.

"They burn with an intense life for a short while, then die."

SAN FRANCISCO
May 1855

The wheel was turning again.

"You know, Catharine. It sometimes feels as though my seventy years have been mapped by ports." They were standing watching San Francisco approach, each aware of the significance of this new chapter. A sweeping bay stretched around as far as they could see, hosting innumerable vessels, large and small.

He explained further. "Newport... Bristol... Cardiff... London... Hobart... even Callao... and now here. Like signposts. Always the tall masts and the tides. Always the gulls and the salt air. The background to a life, eh?"

"If we stick to the proposals from Mr Roberts, we won't see another port for a long time," she said. "How many months do you think it will take us to travel as he suggests before reaching New York?"

"Difficult to say. So much depends on the reception we get, the route we take, our income... and our good health. A year, perhaps?"

"Do you think you might make this country your home? Perhaps ask Mother to join us?"

"We shall see, lass. We shall see. At the moment, all I want is for someone to be waiting for us when we dock. Our delay in Callao may have scuppered the plans."

But there was someone.

They knew what to expect now when the ship docked, and steadied each other, stepping carefully towards the main terminal. A tall, well-dressed man in a frock coat, silk waistcoat and top hat approached, hand outstretched.

"Mr Frost, Miss Frost, it is a pleasure to welcome you to the state of California. Permit me to introduce myself. I am Joshua Melville, editor of the Alta California newspaper. My dear friend William Prowting Roberts wrote and asked that I meet you and arrange somewhere for you to stay. You must be exhausted – the shipping company alerted the harbour master here of the delay in Callao…"

He hardly took a breath, but his smile was kind and his handshake warm. John was reassured.

"We must retrieve our trunk," Catharine said.

"Already arranged, Miss Frost. May I call you Catharine? We are not so formal here as you British folks."

She opened her mouth to reply, but he continued, "Now you'll stay with my wife and I – she won't take no for an answer. We have a large house, and you'll be comfortable. Tomorrow we'll host a dinner. We've invited some people keen to meet you, and I think you'll find them interesting company, Mr Frost – John." He slapped John heartily on the shoulder, as if he had known him for a lifetime, and continued without a breath. "Then we'll organise that lecture you're keen to give. There'll be no shortage of listeners. All the rage now right across America, these public lectures. Folk seem desperate to know things."

Before John could even thank him, their host was ushering them towards a horse and carriage waiting nearby. "You'll be able to see a little of this city as we ride," Joshua continued. "It's quite the place to be at the moment… gold fever has subsided, of course, but there are still fortunes to be made."

The ride was deliberately slow to enable Joshua's running commentary on the city. He pointed out the upturned ship's hulls around the quay, still used for homes or public bars. "Around '49, '50," he explained, "ships would arrive with their passengers seeking gold, and the whole crew would disappear, off to find a fortune. What you're seeing there is an inventive use of junk… Ah yes, look back now!" They were at the top of Clay Street, which rose swiftly up behind the bay, and Joshua was pointing at two islands visible on the horizon. "Last natives held out there quite a while," he said. "Some of the poor souls starved to death. You won't see many now, but we have folks from just about everywhere else in the darned world."

They passed shops where the signage was in Chinese, the stagecoach office on Kearny Street, St Mary's Church, the new mint turning bullion into coins.

"That there is The Old Ship Ale House," their guide continued, indicating an upturned hull with roughly hewn windows. "Opened by a former convict named Joshua Antony."

John read the sign swaying in the sea breeze: 'Gud, bad and indifferent spirits sold here, 25 cents.' Catharine, who had been sitting silently until now, commented on the contrast between the large, rather grand stone buildings on Montgomery Street and the tents and shacks visible everywhere.

"We've needed to rebuild the place a few times... six fires in as many years... but this is a city of contrasts, John." Joshua continued. "Full of haves and have-nots, a place of aspiration. I've seen the poorest arrive without a cent, speaking no English, nothing to call theirs except grit, determination and stamina. Hard work – relentless hard work, and a good helping of luck – made some very rich. But not all, as you can see...

"Now *that's* someone who *is* going places." Their guide was pointing at a smart shop front. Above the window was a large sign advertising 'George Robinson Fardon – photographer'. "I've used some of his pictures of this city myself. But getting a family portrait taken is very much the fashionable thing to do here, John. You and Catharine should arrange a sitting before you leave. Ah, here we are."

Before them stood a large, elegant stone house with wrought-iron balconies on the two floors. Manicured gardens separated the house from the street, and there were trees of several varieties providing shelter and privacy.

"I can guess what you're thinking, John," Joshua speculated. "You're wondering how an editor of a town paper can afford this? Well, truth is, he can't. It's my wife's money. Now, don't you start thinking the worst of me: I married her for love, plain and simple, but her daddy was an engineer. Made it rich with the railroad out east. Had great plans to bring it here, but he passed last fall. This here was his wedding present for his only child."

They had been accustomed to basic furniture and crude dwellings in Hobart, where even William's impressive new house was insignificant compared with this. Everywhere here was opulence. The fabrics for drapes, the lace, the ornate tables in strange wood from the Orient, the lamps and glassware, the vases and artwork. One large canvas caught Catharine's eye.

"If it weren't for the bison and the native Indians, it might be the English countryside," she said, not entirely sure she liked the incongruity.

"That one was a favourite of my papa's." The voice belonged to a short, pale woman, small-boned with mousy hair pulled back unflatteringly from her face, accentuating her large nose. She held out a tiny hand to introduce herself, and Catharine caught the faint smell of mothballs. "I'm Martha, Joshua's wife. Papa was from England, Warwickshire somewhere. He missed the countryside so." The smallest of voices, to match the physique. John found it hard to imagine the two as a couple.

But they proved to be gracious hosts, providing their grateful guests with the warm water, large beds and soft chairs they so relished after a long sea journey. Martha considered it her duty to commandeer Catharine, and so the following morning, after introducing her guests to sourdough, she whisked Catharine away to a seamstress she knew.

"You must have a new gown for dinner," Martha fussed. "You can't possibly have anything in that small trunk that will do. A lady must always look her best at dinner, don't you agree, my dear?"

Catharine smiled. She had never really given it much thought, but she was secretly pleased with the green satin dress Martha selected.

"Put it on my account," Martha snapped at the seamstress. "And the alterations *will* be finished ready for tonight, I assume?"

The woman nodded. Martha was clearly not a customer to offend.

"Now, let's do something about your hair."

Meanwhile, John had a question for his host. It had troubled him to see a large black woman serving them at breakfast. He had to ask, but dreaded the reply.

"You have slaves?"

"Lord, no!" Joshua replied. "That's Charity, our housekeeper. We couldn't manage without her. She's a freed slave. Came to this city to find a husband... found us instead. She's paid more than she'd get anywhere else, and has her own quarters upstairs. When her duties are done, she's free to do as she likes. She's happy here – you can ask her yourself. She runs this house like a machine, has high standards, and has quite a temper if we disappoint her!" Joshua leant towards John and whispered, "In all honesty, she terrifies me far more than Martha ever could!"

John remained unconvinced. He carried too many painful memories of masters and those who answered to them. This was not how he had expected to feel in the land of the free.

It was a memorable dinner. An oak-panelled room lit by bright chandeliers. A long table with floral centrepieces and candles in elaborate silver holders. So many plates, knives, forks, glasses. Offspring of affluence, their function to impress.

"Why, you have prepared a banquet!" John exclaimed as they glanced in through the open door. He started to feel out of place again: it had been a very long time since he had eaten anywhere near as formally as this, and years since he had experienced such a dissonance with his surroundings. Catharine too was looking a little awkward, alienated even, dress or no dress. They had not anticipated all this; after Van Diemen's Land, it did not seem right.

"Our other guests are so looking forward to meeting you, John. Come through to the drawing room and I'll introduce you. You too, Catharine. May I say you look simply ravishing this evening? That colour is so becoming." He nodded towards his wife. "Good choice, my dear." And she giggled in response.

Six courses. Five too many, in John's view. Every one an opportunity for Martha or her husband to comment on the difficulty they had sourcing the ingredients. But the evening's real interest arrived with the other guests.

"Permit me to introduce the formidable Miss Clappe," Joshua said. It somehow failed to sound like a compliment.

Louise Clappe was around Catharine's age, tall, intelligent, confident, with large expressive eyes. A no-nonsense, independent woman Catharine instantly liked.

"Miss Clappe is a writer, quite well known locally as Dame Shirley," he continued. "Her 'Shirley letters' tell all about life in gold-rush California. Quite witty, I'm told."

"She has written articles for *The Pioneer* too." Martha seemed proud to be hosting such guests. "The latest has caused quite a stir, they say. My dear husband has advised against my reading it."

"It's called 'Equality of the sexes'," Louise explained, a whiff of irritation in her voice, "and you *should* read it, Martha. You really should."

Joshua sidestepped the remark and moved to the man standing sipping a whisky. "This, John, is Mr James W. Towne, best printer and publisher in the city. He's responsible for Miss Clappe being so widely read. Now, let's to table, shall we?"

Catharine had not been introduced, even with her new dress.

"This is truly an honour," James said, over the oysters. "We followed your trial from here, you know. Nothing short of a Salem witch-hunt as far as I could see. And we dismayed of your sentence. Barbaric. You have suffered much in the quest for equality."

John had no wish to share the last years with these strangers. He was not ready yet. "I've not suffered as much as some," he replied.

"We read in *The Times* when it reached us that they added two years' hard labour, and for what? A passing remark about some pompous lord!"

Catharine remembered a handsome man, a borrowed letter, and kept her gaze on her plate.

"Yes, well, as I said, there were those who suffered far worse than I." John did not want his life reduced to dinner-table chatter. "How prisoners are treated is the subject of my lecture tomorrow. Will you be there?"

"Most definitely. Louise has offered to report on the event and Joshua's paper will cover it. I know many other admirers who will attend, Mr Frost. You are quite the hero. Like me, people see much in the Chartist aims which resonate with our own new country here. The right to vote, a belief in democracy... it offers opportunities for everyone."

"Not *everyone*," Louise interrupted. "Just half the population."

Catharine smiled across the table at her father, each remembering conversations from years before.

Louise went on: "Mr Paine wrote that women should be treated equally, remember."

"Here she goes again." Joshua rolled his eyes and tried to steer the conversation away from tricky topics. "Remember what Mr Jefferson advised? Women should not wrinkle their foreheads with politics. Are we ready for the next course?"

"Yes dear," said Martha, raising her hand to summon Charity from the shadows. "And that nice Mr Jefferson was quite right. Whenever would women find the time? Looking after the house takes up enough of mine as it is."

John noticed Charity smile as she collected their plates.

"I have no wish to offend you, Miss Clappe, and thank you for your interest, but I believe my subject matter to be unsuitable for women," John added. "Perhaps you have another, male colleague who might help?"

"That's outrageous!" Catharine was furious. She slammed down her glass, her face red, eyes blazing. "If you believe in equality as you claim, Father, then you cannot banish us from your lecture… or from anywhere else come to that. Such hypocrisy is intolerable."

The table fell silent. Awkwardness hovered over the vegetables.

"This is excellent beef." Joshua again. "You must compliment our supplier, dear."

"I shall be there tomorrow," Louise responded, her voice clear, eyes of steel.

"As will I." Catharine stared at her father defiantly.

"You know, Mr Frost," Louise continued, "women are no longer prepared to be Mr Patmore's famous 'Angel in the House'. We are the most active abolitionists in this country. We may not have the vote – yet – nor be entitled to what is ours after we marry, but change is coming and women are making that change happen. Women like Miss Blackwell, this country's first female doctor, or Miss Stone lecturing everywhere for the antislavery movement. She refuses to take her husband's name."

Martha laughed aloud. "Such stuff and nonsense! More potatoes, anyone?"

Louise was undeterred. "If you open your eyes, gentlemen, you will find us as brewers, woodworkers, innkeepers, tanners… and journalists. We are shaping this new country, whether you men like it or not."

"I'm not sure women are that interested." The printer ventured a tentative contribution.

Catharine could not resist. "That's just not true! For every ten thousand names on the Chartist petition to the British Parliament seven years ago, eight thousand were those of women. We *are* interested."

Louise continued the thread. "Oberlin College has been accepting women for some years now, and women are graduating with honours. For real equality it is only a matter of time, that and a few liberal male minds."

The men sipped their wine in silence, studiously averting their eyes from the women. "And Martha, you might recall Miss Wollstonecraft's advice," she snapped. "'Beings who are only objects of pity... will soon become objects of contempt.'"

Martha had no idea who that was, nor what her outspoken guest meant. She tried to lift the mood around the table. "Goodness, Louise. You'll be telling me to wear Miss Bloomer's creation next!"

"I have met Amelia," Louise replied crossly. "Her suggestion for sensible, serviceable garments was merely a means to an end, to free us as a sex from the restrictions imposed on our bodies by fashion, often to please men. Amelia spoke at Seneca Falls at the launch of the Convention of Women."

Another awkward silence.

"Time for ice cream, I think," Joshua cajoled. "We have the very latest device to keep it frozen. It's real smart, and bound to take off, you mark my words... John, please, tell us about your sea journey..."

And so the conversation shifted to safer territory. But Catharine was transfixed by this free-spirited writer, inspired by her courage and determined to speak with her further.

STAPLETON, BRISTOL
1877

"I'd never seen Catharine that angry before," John mused.

Anne had finished writing for the day, and was ironing his shirts. One flat iron stood facing the fire whilst she used the other. She was uncomfortable in the summer heat and even with her sleeves rolled and the kitchen door and windows open, perspiration trickled down her back, her hair sticking to her forehead. Loose locks fell over her eyes and she blew them away. She remembered old sketches of Miss Bloomer's loose Turkish trousers and short skirts. At this moment, they sounded appealing.

God in heaven, she hated this chore. She had long since stopped ironing her own bits and pieces. Who was going to see her petticoats, anyway? But it mattered to her that her father's shirts still looked as pristine as their age and state of disrepair allowed. She persevered.

"Did Catharine attend your lecture?"

"She most certainly did," he replied with a smile. "I could not have stopped her, nor her new friend… but I was relieved that most of those present were men. You know how unsavoury some of the truths were that I needed to tell."

"Mr Towne offered to print my lecture, to publish *The Horrors of Convict Life*. We could take copies with us across the country, at least enough until we reached New York." John rose slowly, bending to retrieve a shirt from the floor. He winced as he stood upright again. "I am so stiff these days, Anne."

Anne jumped as she burnt the corner of her arm. "How did the Americans respond to your convict tales?"

"I was surprised, Anne… And Joshua was right – these public lectures were really popular. People queued for tickets wherever we went… But you know what I remember most, Anne?" John became thoughtful, a little sad. "Standing there before those well-dressed gentlemen, telling them about what I'd seen in Port Arthur, about the boys in Point Puer, about the prison ships… I might as well have been talking about life on Mars. It all felt dreamlike, as if it had never happened…" He shook his head, then added, "But some came to talk privately afterwards. They had worked for oppressive masters, one or two were freed slaves. They understood how cruelty can thrive anywhere when unbridled power goes unchallenged. They told me of unions formed locally based on Chartist principles, of better conditions fought for by brave workers. It encouraged me."

He paused to help her move his shirts into the garden to air.

"But there was a surprise that evening," he said. "You might want to write about it. I'll fetch your paper and ink."

"I was just leaving. I picked up my papers from the lectern and turned to find someone behind me. It was getting dark, and it took a while before recognition dawned. Sixteen years, Anne. Sixteen. We had both changed, but John Rees still had that unmistakable swagger.

"'Great speech, my old friend.' I remember those were his first words, and we embraced like brothers. Jack the Fifer, there in California."

"And just how did he find himself there? No one in Wales had heard from him in years as I recall. Not since Newport." Anne dipped her pen in the ink in readiness.

"He'd fought in the Mexican War of '35 and still had land entitlements, it appears. He'd been living in Newfoundland, in Virginia and then Texas, and was characteristically vague on what he had been doing there. Best not to ask with Jack! But he'd finally moved to Hornbook in California, drawn by the gold like so many others. He'd taken American citizenship, and seemed to me like a man who had a few dollars put by."

"He took me to a public house and asked for news of William Jones and Zephaniah. He seemed particularly sad to hear that William was not doing too well. They had been friends once. Then, several jugs of ale later, when we were reliving that November night in '39, he let slip a detail I had always suspected. I just never expected to learn the truth in a bar in San Francisco."

John stood to stare out of the window towards the garden. Dusk was falling, and the redness on the horizon promised fine weather ahead. She waited.

"He admitted it was he who fired the first shot that night." John's voice was quiet, his face pensive. "He was the first to race into the Westgate, the first to demand freedom for the Chartists being held there, and the first to fire. He says he *thought* he heard Phillips command the soldiers to fire first, but I don't believe that. It's just an excuse, one he has convinced himself is true as the years have passed. He has blood on his hands, and his confession that night in his cups suggested to me a man with a guilty conscience."

"We parted amicably enough, but watching him walk away down that street in San Francisco, I wondered if he too had regrets and longed for home."

Anne was checking her notes again. "How long did you stay with the Melvilles?"

"We had planned to stay another week," he replied, "but there was an outbreak of cholera in the Bay Area, and besides, I felt I was suffocating in that house, with those people. It was time to move on."

"And Catharine?"

"I think she was sorry to leave her new friend, but..." He paused. " Just a moment. I have remembered something..."

John limped to his room, and returned with a box. "She left this with me," he said, his hand stroking the lid, hesitant to visit the memories. "Yes, they're here." He handed one daughter the souvenirs of another – childish drawings by Emily and Grace, some tickets and postcards, a programme for a concert on-board ship, and underneath, a flimsy copy of *The Pioneer*, dated 1855. In it, Louise Clappe's article on equality of the sexes. There was a newspaper too, with the report of John's lecture, its editorial urging the British government to issue a full pardon. And a sepia photograph taken by one Mr G.R. Fardon, entitled, "The California stagecoach".

Anne realised she had never asked how her father and sister had travelled across America all those years before; she had assumed by railroad. When she asked, John shook his head.

"Hadn't reached the West Coast at that time," he explained. "Hadn't got far at all by '55. All that is much more recent. Catharine and I needed a stagecoach to get anywhere. Now that…" And he pointed at the photograph. "That was a *real* adventure!"

SAN FRANCISCO – CARSON CITY
1855

They were generous to the end.

"You will need this," Martha said, handing Catharine a parcel. It was an embroidered cushion of finest velvet. "Stagecoaches were not designed for comfort, my dear."

"But you've both been so kind to us. I am already indebted to you for all this." Catharine indicated her smart new travelling clothes, which Martha's seamstress had been busy preparing – looser skirts, a sturdy bonnet, fine leather boots and a warm jacket, "because nights in Nevada are cold," her hostess had said, "or so I hear."

Joshua had a gift too, for John.

"And this is for you, my friend… for the road ahead." It was a leather-bound travel journal, with John's initials embossed on its cover. "I hope its pages will record many excellent memories, John, and that you'll begin by writing favourably about your time here with us." He was smiling, but John sensed his host was being serious, and felt ashamed.

They were standing at the stagecoach terminal, just after dawn. In the morning air, an awkwardness, the familiar harbinger of final farewells.

"I will make certain that the letters you have written are sent… and I hope your queen will see sense and give you that full pardon soon," Martha said filling the silence. She took John's hand in both her own. Tiny fingers, protected from the street by her silk gloves. "A man needs his wife," she said firmly, and she looked at Catharine, "no matter what these modern women say!"

Over the days, John had modified his view of Martha. He had a suspicion she was a lot more clever than she seemed.

***

The bustle and noise of departure. Travelling trunks, baskets, even a carpet thrown on the roof. Six black horses groomed and restless to go, steam from their nostrils visible in the dawn light, the stench of fresh dung. A carriage without glass in the windows, with room for four, and two more seats next to the driver. Hard benches with the thinnest of fabric… and many days of travel waiting ahead.

The wheel was turning again.

Two men joined them inside: one, a well-dressed man of middle age, headed for Placerville; another who muttered something neither of them understood. Seeing their puzzled faces, he added "No English," pointing to himself. "Sleep now." And he did precisely that as far as their next stop. Then they were off and out of the city, the driver urging on his team, keen to make good time.

They passed San Andreas and Jackson, sampling the food Charity had prepared for them, glad of the breeze through the windows against the day's heat, but plagued equally by the dust. The countryside became less interesting, its wide open areas holding little foliage. As the sun rose higher, and the road surface turned rougher, their coach became insufferable. Catharine could see how her father was struggling, his body knocked against the side of the carriage. She stuffed the cushion between him and the window.

"Don't fuss, girl!" he pleaded, but she ignored him.

"You are British?" the stranger asked. "Guessed from the accent. Grandfather was British, came on the wagon trains. Where you headed?"

"Eventually, New York," Catharine replied. "But we stop several times on the way. And you, sir?"

"How rude of me," he said. "Johnson, Peter Johnson, tailor and draper of Placerville." And he offered a hand.

"My own trade... many years ago," John said, introducing himself, returning the handshake. "What brought you to San Francisco?"

"You heard of the Sydney ducks?" It took John by surprise.

"I believe I have. Convicts, weren't they?" John caught Catharine's wary look.

"Well you'll know they wear garments in rough duck cloth... ugly, but by God, it's hard-wearing stuff – ideal for any labouring man. I have a friend in 'Frisco, name of Strauss, who's started something I think'll take off mighty fine."

"The draper in me is intrigued," John said.

"Well, Levi and another, name of Jacob David, have been adding copper rivets to the material for some time now, making strong trousers and dungarees. Word's spreading, and they're selling faster than old Ma Lawson's apple pie from that there Golden Gate bakery. There's a call for these garments beyond 'Frisco too. I've placed my order, and I wager I'll sell them all."

"I'm sure the ducks are delighted to be of use," John replied, but the irony was lost.

The road started to climb as they approached the mountains of the Sierra Nevada. Catharine chose to ignore the magnificent panorama, keeping her eyes fixed on the carriage wall opposite her. Fingernails cut into the palms of her hands as the roads narrowed and the earth sometimes crumbled from the edge to a sheer drop below.

Occasionally they would see a wagon train heading west, six to ten wagons with canvas covers, pulled by mules, negotiating the tracks. John would record in his journal the skill they showed to avoid collisions and accidents, these hard-faced men and dishevelled women clutching their babies. Motivated by a dream.

"We stop here for the night," the driver announced. "Be ready at four thirty tomorrow morning. If you're not ready, I leave anyway."

The draper wished them a safe onward journey. "Look out for Mr Strauss's newfangled trousers in New York some day soon." He laughed. "Fashion is a capricious siren, as you know, sir!"

Catharine rather liked the man's idea, but remained silent.

Placerville was a reasonable place, with tree-lined streets of stone houses – and a decent hotel.

"They have ice for cool drinks!" Catharine announced. But she noticed her father's grey hair was covered in a red dust, as was her skirt and shoes.

"We can bathe here," she said, "and order some dinner. Travelling gives me an appetite." They devoured with relish the meat, cheese and bread provided, and the beds were comfortable.

But Catharine found it difficult to sleep for fear of missing the early departure. As dawn broke, she rose and opened her father's Gladstone bag to find him a clean shirt. Her hand rummaged in the half-light then found something cold, metallic... an engraved barrel, an ornate handle. She held the gun in her palm and stared. Across the room in his bed her father snored gently, his wrist hanging outside the bedclothes, the leather thread still in place. The man who once spoke out against weapons was carrying a gun. And he had chosen not to tell her... but why, she wondered?

Catharine considered this revelation for some time, then returned the gun to its hiding place. She trusted her father. She would say nothing, at least for now.

But it shook her, like those tremors deep beneath the California soil: a reminder that the surface does not always tell the full story.

***

John had been talking to the landlord as they waited to board the coach.

"Nice place you have here. Busy too, I should think, with the stagecoach route through."

The man shook his head. "I reckon you're wrong there, sir. As I see it, that there mighty railroad will roll up here pretty soon and turn these old stagecoaches into firewood. Most folks see it as a done deal... just politics, that's all. Final link between states in the west and the east."

"Progress always means change," John mused.

"Who says progress is always what's best for folk?" And the man shuffled off to argue with the driver.

They had the carriage to themselves for the next stage of the journey, so Catharine stretched out her legs on the seat opposite, leaning her back against the carriage wall. She sighed at the filth already casing the edge of her new skirt, at the expensive boots already scuffed and dirty.

Hours passed, dull and monotonous in a punishing heat. John dozed and flies buzzed. Wide empty plains in every direction. Eventually, they stopped to change horses at a wayside house in the incongruously named Strawberry Valley. A simple stone edifice, in absolute isolation, with a rocking chair on the porch. Outside the carriage they stretched and listened to a silence broken only by occasional creaking from the windmill which operated the well, or the scrawny chickens pecking optimistically at the arid soil. The driver took the horses to a barn at the back and attached a new team. A solitary cow looked at them suspiciously.

Inside they sat on hard wooden chairs and supped something resembling beer. It was a welcome surprise to be offered a dish of delicious fresh quail from the mountains, offered by a taciturn woman in a dress that had not seen water in many months. John noted in his journal that the only book he saw in the place was a well-thumbed Bible.

But such stops provided the briefest of respites in what was a perpetually uncomfortable ride. The road led along the shores of Lake Tahoe for some twenty miles, the cool air from the water countered by the midges. They were obliged to lower the leather curtains, creating a suffocating heat in the carriage, and both felt a relief when their driver shouted, "Carson City ahead!"

It was the venue for John's next lecture.

STAPLETON, BRISTOL
1877

John was seated in the garden watching Anne prune the roses.

"I'm surprised Catharine said nothing about that gun. Not like her to keep quiet."

"Story's not over yet, lass," John replied enigmatically, smiling to himself.

"Well, I've looked, and there's nothing in that fancy leather journal about a gun." She sounded annoyed, excluded somehow.

"All will be revealed in due course," he teased, but Anne cried out as a hidden thorn pierced her thumb.

"There were families in Carson City from Cornwall and Ireland," John explained. "Miners by trade. Roberts knew some of them to be Chartist sympathisers so the plan was that I lecture in one of the churches there." He ignored her scowling. She was clearly annoyed about something. "The folk I met had travelled west on wagon trains and were panning the rivers for silver as prospectors had done there for years, but there was talk even then of a likely strike any day."

"And did it happen?"

"A few years later… a big rush for silver, and the lucky winners built a new Virginia City nearby with fine buildings and theatres, an inland San Francisco if you like, but that whole area was nothing more than desert when we were there."

"And was there a hotel?" She was sucking her thumb to stop the bleeding.

"Wasn't that sort of place really. A Welshman called Dai Pugh offered us shelter for a night or two. He spoke to me in the language of our homeland, Anne. It was difficult to respond at first: the years and the distance had intervened. But when Dai lit the oil lamp in the evening and brought me some ale, when the shadows cast shapes across the wooden walls, when his wife started humming a Welsh folk tune as she cleared away our simple supper, I was more at ease than I had ever been with the Melvilles, for all their luxury.

"The lecture was well received," he continued, "and many hung back to ask questions. They were a ragged group of dreamers, really, but hope is a strong motivator wherever life takes you. I left some of the pamphlets, but as only a few of the miners could read, Dai offered to do that for them."

John paused as he remembered yet another example of the kindness of strangers, the generosity of those with little themselves. "The morning we left, Dai's wife insisted on serving us eggs and coffee, and there was bread and cheese for the journey. I offered payment but Dai was adamant. He told me I would always be welcome, that what I had tried to do – and was still trying to do – would not be forgotten. Then he took me away from the women and warned me… told me that just a week before I had used it myself, the stagecoach from San Francisco to Carson had not arrived, held up by armed men, with all passengers and the driver… dead."

Anne had never really thought about the dangers of her father's journey. She was beginning to understand now why William had suggested that gun. She was desperate to hear the rest of its story.

CARSON CITY – KANSAS CITY
1855

The Concord coach was a smart affair, with six glossy horses and red painted wheels. Two additional passengers joined them: one a woman who introduced herself as Miss Fletcher, schoolmistress. She had been visiting an aunt, and as they rode, she tried – unsuccessfully – to eat cake from her pannier without being seen. The second was a man with a wide-brimmed, dirty hat and Indian beads around his neck. He muttered a greeting then proceeded to chew tobacco incessantly, spitting the residue intermittently onto the carriage floor despite, or perhaps because of, Catharine's icy glare. The smell was noxious. They were relieved when he disembarked at what must have been the start of a dirt track to a farm, though there was nothing to indicate mankind had yet reached the place.

At regular intervals the horses needed to be changed, so progress was painfully slow. Passengers could step down from the coach at those places – but for ten minutes only, so any food available was devoured at a pace. A passenger not back in his seat when the driver cracked his whip was simply left behind.

By nightfall of the first day they reached Cottonwood, around forty miles from Carson. Miss Fletcher said her fluttery farewells, cake crumbs still visible around her mouth, and they were alone again. They spent another fitful night dreading the 3 a.m. start.

"I have bad news." It was Aaron, their young driver, appearing in the doorway, framed by an orange daybreak. "We cannot use the coach from here to the next stop… undercarriage is bust, and I can't fix it. We'll use the mud wagon instead. It'll get us there, if a little later than scheduled."

Outside stood their new transportation – a canvas curved over a crude frame protecting a red wooden "mud cart" with hard benches for seats. Their trunk had already been transferred. This cart had been hooked to a team of mules – muddy, bony beasts that looked decidedly unimpressed.

"This is not what I expected... not what we paid for," John complained. "Is this all there is, man?"

"Unless you want to wait here for the next stagecoach, a week from now – which *might* have spare seats... or you could hire a couple of horses and ride to Kansas. You should be there in a few weeks, a month at the most... unless you are attacked by Indians... or coyotes at night... or you could get lost."

"It's fine, Father." Catharine intervened. "We'll be perfectly fine. Thank you, Aaron... We'll just get our bags."

It was a taste of what Dai and the others had spoken of, the old California trail in a covered wagon, except they were heading east. The wagon rolled and rumbled as they felt every bump and rock in the road. Aaron kept a loaded rifle ready for unexpected company, and conversation became impossible. Dust got in their mouth and eyes, requiring them to cover their lower faces with handkerchieves, and the mules stank. The heat was oppressive, and sweat began to turn the dust on their faces to clay.

Mid-afternoon, without warning, the sky darkened. An ominous stillness stretched as far as the black horizon.

"Storm coming," Aaron announced, his face stern.

And it rained, so hard the road ahead became a trench of mud in minutes. They could not see for rain. Could not be heard above its clamour. Without warning, a thunderclap. The mules reacted, terrified, their young driver fighting to keep control. The wagon steered wildly off course, hit something hard – a boulder perhaps – and the wheel was gone. John grabbed Catharine, both now soaked to the skin, each keeping the other from falling out onto the muddy road. Aaron steadied the mules, and the wagon glided to an undignified halt. Catharine watched as her velvet cushion slid off the bench into the mire below.

And still it rained, lightning reflected in the pools of water swirling together under the wagon which was now resting awkwardly on one side like some sleeping drunkard. John and Catharine clung together under the canvas, praying for the storm to end.

Then it did, as suddenly as it started. The sky brightened, revealing the extent of their dilemma.

"How far to the next coaching station?" John was almost afraid to ask.

"Around twenty-five miles, give or take, but roads'll all be bad, like this." Aaron thought for a minute then added, "There's a homestead not far from here. I say we take the mules and head there. Owner'll have tools to repair my wheel… Shouldn't be too difficult to fix. We've been lucky."

Catharine looked down at her ruined skirt, her sodden boots, her cushion. "Yes… very lucky," she replied.

They had ridden before, of course, up steep Welsh hills and through deep valleys, or in Van Diemen's Land where Catharine had taught her nieces to ride on a scruffy donkey, but this was different. John's old bones were already aching from days on the stagecoach, and now he was expected to ride a stubborn, filthy beast who had no desire to go where John directed. Catharine had somehow converted her skirt into trousers, looping the back through her legs, so, dishevelled and muddy, drenched through, and not quite believing what had just happened, they set off for the promise of shelter and help.

***

It was nowhere near Catharine's definition of "homestead". Little more than a wooden shack, with a small lean-to barn and a windmill serving the well. A solitary, unwelcoming dwelling in a dip, shielded by a few skeletal trees. An old horse was tied outside the front porch, and smoke rose from a chimney in the neglected roof. Outside the front door, the carcass of an unidentifiable animal was swaying this way and that, disturbing the hungry flies. John shivered; he had a bad feeling about the place.

"Are you cold, Father?" They were both still in damp clothes, and Catharine feared he may have caught a chill.

"At least there's a fire here," he replied. "Let's hope we can dry our clothes and get what's needed for the wheel."

Aaron had gone ahead to talk with the owner. "He'll give us a night's shelter," he said after riding back to them. "For a small payment, he'll fix the wheel and share supper with us. We're lucky again!"

"You keep saying that," Catharine muttered to herself. Her skirt hem was caked with mud, and her hair stuck to her head.

Fire was the only welcoming feature in the place. The main room was dark, dirty and smelt of tobacco and rotting meat.

"Welcome, strangers. Name's Red. Sit yourselves down and make yourselves at home."

He had not washed in many months, his long, lank red hair hanging over bloodshot eyes. A beard the colour of damp hay carried the remnants of yesterday's supper. Of large build and an age anywhere beyond forty, he used the back of a hand to wipe his nose before drying it on his filthy trousers. He had no front teeth.

Catharine and John sat on a wooden settle next to the fire, ate some grey, tough rabbit and sipped from tin mugs a thick black liquid Red assured them was coffee. A rifle sat suspended over a broken dresser, and John noticed the knife in his host's belt. He had met men like this before, in a London gaol, on the *Mandarin* and in Van Diemen's Land, danger like a vapour emanating from their skin. He used a foot to nudge the Gladstone bag a little closer.

"Can I offer you folks some?" Red was holding out a bottle of whisky.

"Thank you, no," John replied. "But I would be glad of some sleep now. It has been a long day."

Aaron went to feed the mules. He would sleep in the barn with them, he said, and repair the wheel in the morning.

The only other room in the place contained a crude bed, covered in stained rags. Red leered at Catharine and whispered, "For you, miss... Sweet dreams." She was too tired to fuss, but removed her outer clothing, placed the muddy, still-damp cushion between her head and the bed, and fell asleep instantly. Seated in a chair opposite John, Red continued drinking.

John battled to keep his eyes open, desperate to say alert until Red was asleep, but his fight was lost to the warmth of the fire and the exhaustion of the day, and he was in a deep sleep when Catharine's cries woke him.

"Get off me! Stop... GET OFF ME! Leave me ALONE!"

John dived out of his seat and ran. He found Red on top of his struggling daughter, her arms pinned above her head.

"Come now, darling. Stop those fancy English antics." His vile breath in her face, his spittle in her eyes. "Only fair a man should be rewarded some for his hospitality." And he pressed his body over hers.

"Get off her, you bastard!" John cried, pulling at Red's shoulders.

Whenever he tried to recall what happened next, John always saw things in some sort of macabre slow motion. Red's arm lunging back to throw John off balance. John stumbling and grabbing an object – Catharine's boot – to strike Red on the side of his face. The man turning again, fury in his eyes, blood above his eye, to punch

John across his face, hard, several times. Dizziness for a minute or two, then a knife flashing in the man's hand, before the image of Catharine, standing by now, pronouncing with the calmest of voices: "Leave… him… alone, or I fire."

She was holding the gun in both hands, aiming at their drunken host.

The knife was raised to deliver its blow, Red's arm suspended mid-air.

"Why, you ornery bitch!" And Red lunged towards her.

The tableau froze.

"Catharine!" John heard his own voice cry out. "No!"

Several futures suspended in a split second.

Then she fired.

"Was he…? Had she…?"

Anne had never heard this story before. Catharine had said nothing, and there was no mention of Red in her father's American journal. She held her breath.

"No, lass." John was chuckling. "Catharine could never aim straight, not even with a ball as a child… and mighty thankful I am for it. But she grazed the bugger's elbow badly enough for him to cry out. He stumbled, fell forward over the boot – and gave me the chance to sit on him! We were using her stockings to tie his hands behind him when Aaron came running from the barn. He'd heard the shot."

"And then?" This had all the elements of a penny dreadful… Who of her story's readers would believe this? she wondered. "Did you report the assault?"

John chuckled again. "Report to whom?" he asked. "Lord knew where we'd have found the nearest sheriff, lass. Days away probably. The West was a lawless world twenty years ago, remember… and besides, no real harm had been done."

"So what did you do?" She found all this so difficult to imagine.

"Catharine was more charitable than I. My first thought was to let the drunken bastard rot, but not her. She washed and bandaged the wound while Aaron sought something stronger to secure Red, who by then was beginning to sober up.

"At dawn, Aaron repaired the wheel and went to collect our damaged wagon. We told Red we were 'borrowing' his rifle, and Aaron covered me whilst I untied our captive. We made a swift departure, I can tell you. Seems that at some point in our travels, your sister had spotted William's gun in my bag, and I can't say I'm sorry she did. Proved William right too, I suppose. Anyways,

I thought it best not to argue when Catharine decided the thing was *her* responsibility for the rest of our journey. Now, it's bed for me... too much excitement for one day!"

***

Anne sat staring ahead of her for some time, watching the sun set over their garden bursting with June flowers. Catharine had been close to killing a man. Was prepared to do that to protect their father.

Would she, could she, have done the same? she wondered.

Probably not.

She lit the lamp and opened her father's American journal again. The entries for the spring and summer of 1855 were irritatingly vague. After Carson City and until Kansas there was mention of a few towns, some names, dates, but in no order. Just scribbles, really, incomprehensible notes. Anne had sought clarification, but John could not recall the exact itinerary, and she had no knowledge of the geography of America. Yet authenticity mattered to her; she had promised to be faithful to the truth wherever she could in her father's tale. There was only one thing to do, and it meant a visit into the city, which she loathed, but it might be worth the effort.

After arranging with Joe to call, ostensibly with her father's dinner but in reality just to check on him, Anne took the better of her two dresses out of the wardrobe, found some coins for the journey and brushed her bonnet. She chose not to brave the newfangled railway: would not know what to do about tickets, nor how to travel on from Temple Meads. She opted for the more familiar tram, boarding outside Holy Trinity Church and travelling to the city centre , close to King Street and the library.

It was a grand edifice with Palladian columns and sweeping stone steps so that it sat in judgment on the less appealing buildings below it. She had been once or twice before, prior to her mother's death, and liked the wood-panelled silence broken only by the clocks. It was almost empty and she found a helpful librarian who took her to a dusty corner of the main room.

"You're in luck," he said, peering over his half-glasses. "A local landowner left these for the library in his will. He'd travelled west for the gold, I think. They were drafted late '40s, early '50s." From a high shelf the librarian retrieved several large leather-bound tomes containing hand-painted maps of the "American new world".

"Best wear these," the man said, and handed her some fine white gloves. "The paper's fragile – easily damaged."

She sat making notes all afternoon, enough to create a feasible route her father and sister might have taken through '55. She was amazed at the sheer distance and vast emptiness of the land at that time, surprised to discover some places – well-known cities now – not yet included on a map, or if they were, then no more than a name in tiny print, barely visible. One thing was obvious: the route between Carson and Kansas in 1855 would have been wild, sparsely populated and dangerous. As perilous as anything he had faced in Van Diemen's Land. She began to see this part of her father's story in a very different light.

THE ROUTE TO KANSAS CITY
1855

They were avoiding the midday sun in the shelter of some boulders, the mules chewing on some scrawny grey bushes, tails warning the flies to steer clear.

"Best drink some," Aaron said, offering John water from his pouch. "This heat can kill."

John was grateful for the kindness. "My next official stop is Kansas City," he said. "People are expecting us there. But God knows how long that's likely to take. Is there no chance of another stagecoach? Horses would give us more speed than these mules allow."

Aaron considered the options. "We could head north of here, to Salt Lake City," he said. "You might get a stagecoach there, headed east. But it means going right out of our way… and I'm not sure about that place."

"I know of it," John responded. "In Liverpool in the '30s, hundreds of men with no work converted to the Mormon faith and went there, some pushing hand carts all the way. Chartist papers in the north carried their stories."

Catharine had been listening and couldn't resist a comment. "You cannot take us there, Father, please. The Mormons treat women like trophies to be collected, as vassals to serve the menfolk. I couldn't bear to see that."

"You are too quick to judge sometimes, lass. They are a devout people who live peaceably enough," John replied.

"Can't say I agree with you," Aaron interrupted. It was rare for him to voice an opinion. "For folk who supposedly live by the Lord's Word, there's a goodly number who support slavery in their midst. Are you sure that's a proper place for your talks about equality, Mr Frost?"

John thought for a while, then asked, "What's the alternative?"

"We stay on this route," Aaron explained. "No troubles reported with the local tribes hereabouts for a while now, and I know of some places to rest up and replenish our supplies… not big cities, there are none, but we could do it. It'll be slow, but less risky."

"Then it's decided," John concluded.

Catharine remembered Red; risk came in many shapes.

***

Each sun-baked day melted into the next. Each stop resembled the others. One-street towns of wooden shacks, dirt roads and taciturn, suspicious locals. Once on the outskirts of such a town they disturbed the crows around a makeshift gallows from which dangled a rotting corpse. Once, they just missed a gunfight outside a saloon and waited until two scantily clothed women came out to drag the bodies away. Several times they stopped to read the headstones of small family cemeteries near wayside farms. At all times around them, as far as the eye could see, stretched the evidence of hard lives and empty hopes.

It was a journey punctuated by dust, perfumed by horse dung and wrapped in a nagging fear of the unexpected. Aaron kept his rifle close, and Catharine never let the Gladstone bag out of her sight. At the first general store they found, Catharine disappeared and emerged dressed in a leather jerkin, breeches and lace-up boots. To complete her metamorphosis she sported a large-brimmed hat, secured under her chin.

"Why, you look just like the rustlers we passed yesterday!" John laughed. They found a blacksmith to shoe one of the mules, and sat listening to the mournful dirge of an old blind man with a banjo.

"*I know dark clouds will gather round m*e," he sang. "*I know my way is hard and steep…*"

"That there tune's the 'Wayfaring Stranger'," said Aaron. "Guess you could say it's 'propriate right now?"

They laughed, but John suddenly pictured his home, so far away, so long ago. He rubbed the leather thread on his wrist, and as if she could read his thoughts, Catharine took his hand.

Sometimes there were beds, rarely clean, in a run-down "hotel"; sometimes they slept under the stars by a fire and ate rabbit thanks to Aaron's rifle. They answered his youthful questions about their English queen, sea travel and convict life. Reluctantly at first, he unfolded his own tale... a small boy on a wagon train surrounded by a hunting party of young braves, a father shot, a mother's screams... two days spent hiding under a canvas sheet alone... the preacher who found him and brought him up as his own. All he wanted now from life was a few acres to farm.

Slowly, with each passing sunset, bones ceased to ache, muscles grew accustomed to the demands of the ride, faces bronzed. At times it was almost enjoyable.

Almost.

***

At Colorado Springs, another thunderstorm hindered their progress, but a red sun silhouetted behind them an extraordinary rock formation.

"That's Pike's peak," Aaron whispered. "Cheyenne have another name, of course. Folk say this place was sacred to them." The travellers watched a new day open in reverent silence. At Topeka, they met three sisters who operated a ferry service to pull their cart and mules across the Kansas River, their fortune guaranteed by the constant flow of wagons on the Oregon Trail.

John had not written in his journal for days, and realised he had no idea of the date or of how long they had been travelling, but he felt nothing but immense relief when, at the top of a steep incline, Aaron pointed down to a large group of buildings in the valley and announced, "That's Kansas City."

STAPLETON, BRISTOL
1877

"All that's written here under 'Kansas City' are the names Keen, White and Van Horn." Anne was studying a page from the journal. "Presumably they were friends of Mr Prowting Roberts? You'll have to help me with a few more details, Father," she pleaded.

"The joy of taking a proper bath again. That's what I remember most, lass. But it was difficult to adjust... The city was just so noisy after the time we had spent crossing Utah and Colorado. We'd spent hours in silence, not a sound beyond the mules and the cart. But oh, the delight in seeing green pasture again – with wild flowers, Anne! I picked a few to send in a letter to your mother. You and she had not heard from us in so many months."

Anne remembered his letter bringing news that they were both alive, that they still had many months of travel ahead, and recalled the sad, dead flowers which had made her mother cry.

John was thoughtful for a while, then continued, "As for those names... Let me think... Charles Keen was a Londoner, an exiled Chartist. We lodged with him... rather dour man, a bachelor. His friend Van Horn... Robert, I think... had just arrived. I remember him pontificating at length over a dinner about the future of America being in the railroad."

"And White?" Anne's pen scratched the paper as she made some notes.

"Now George I already knew, from London meetings years before... he'd written articles for the *Northern Star*. Giant of a man, he'd been one of O'Connor's henchmen before seeking exile. You wouldn't want to cross that one! He arranged the lectures in the city, and I left some of the pamphlets with him."

"From there you must have travelled to St Louis," she said, consulting her notes from the library.

"If you say so," John replied. "What does my journal record?"

"Just the name John Hinchcliffe. Do you remember him?"

"Vaguely, alas. He was a lawyer, I think. I remember the fancy buildings in the city, and the steamboats on the river. Lots of Irishmen working around the docks, most of them sympathetic to the Chartist cause. My talks there had quite an audience – men angry about the slavery still operating around them… a lecture about the evils of tyranny and oppression touched a nerve."

"The next names you scribbled down were Weaver and Lloyd, and the town 'Belville'."

"Oh yes!" he exclaimed, a distant memory returning. "The German town, not far from St Louis. Extraordinary place… miners mostly, but German spoken everywhere. Many had fled when their revolution failed in '48. Can't recall the actual names of those two you mentioned, but they were very active politically in the area. Lord, this is bringing back some memories, Anne!"

"Then it was on to Chicago. Catharine wrote a long letter from there, which I've got."

She stopped suddenly, a blinding pain behind her eyes. She removed her spectacles and rubbed the lids. Her vision was blurred, not for the first time in recent weeks. Too much time reading and writing in poor light, she thought. She needed to stop.

"Shall I make us some tea now, Father? You could probably benefit from a rest."

But he was not listening, lost in his memories.

CHICAGO – DETROIT
1855

They said their farewells to Aaron on the quayside in Belville, just before boarding the steamship. They had grown fond of the young man who had guided them so well, and they promised to write from New York.

They were having to exercise caution now with expenses, even though supporters had been generous in their donations at John's lectures and the Melvilles had paid for their journey as far as Aaron could take them.

"I'm afraid we can't afford the private cabins on the upper deck," John said, "but it's not that far to Chicago, and there will be no rough seas this time!"

The steamship was much dirtier than Catharine had imagined. She and John would share space with pigs and cattle, general cargo and dozens of other passengers on an exposed deck with few seats. The stench from unwashed bodies, the chimneys and the cattle was overpowering, at least until they set off and a cooling breeze made their journey more bearable.

They were prevented from accessing the upper deck where there were fine dining rooms and gambling tables. "Mind your bags on there," Aaron had warned them. "Floating honeypots for thieves, these boats." And he tapped his hat brim, turned and was gone.

"It seems the good people of this land of the free are also fond of their hierarchies," Catharine mused, examining the "No Entry" sign to the upper deck. She was chewing on some bread and ham they had purchased on the dockside. "Every man in his place and all that…"

But Chicago was waiting – a vibrant metropolis with a huge population, a busy transport hub on the shores of an oceanic lake.

John had the address of the man with whom they would stay, a lawyer called Matthew Trumbull, a Chartist sympathiser and very well-connected, according to Prowting Roberts. They retrieved their trunk, which still smelt of the filthy hold, and hired a cart and driver. The lawyer was an affable, well-spoken man in his fifties with a warm handshake.

"Welcome, both," he said. "We have waited so long for this, and I am deeply honoured to meet you, sir. We began to wonder if you had met some awful fate on the journey."

"We had our moments," John replied, and smiled at Catharine. She had been staring at the longest beard she had ever seen, a soft white down which bobbed around as he spoke. But the smile above it was kind, and the eyes twinkled.

"I will show you Chicago tomorrow, and we'll arrange some lecture dates for you," he added, "but for now, rest and a good meal, I think."

Again they were in the care of an excellent host, and the following day, he took them to see a truly extraordinary sight: hundreds of men turning dozens of jacks in unison to replace the foundations of existing buildings.

"I doubt you'll see this anywhere else on your travels," Matthew explained. "Rain makes our streets impassable, so my wise friends in the city council are raising the buildings by adding earth underneath. It'll take us twenty years, they reckon. See that building there?" He pointed at a large edifice already towering over its neighbours. "That was raised hydraulically by an engineer friend of mine, John Lane. Impressive, isn't it?"

John suddenly recalled the shabby, half-built "towns" he had passed through over the last few months, all the abject poverty and despair he had seen, the illiterate panhandlers, the ill-fed, barefoot children. Such contrasts everywhere made this enigmatic country an unfathomable, albeit indestructible hydra.

The venue for his lectures, a grand stone building, was full each night. Lots of those attending were German immigrants or Irish Catholics, some encouraged to be there by the families he had met in Belville, many sympathetic to the Chartist cause. They gave John a rapturous welcome, clamouring afterwards for copies of his pamphlet, but Matthew was not at all surprised.

"They know about Newport and what you tried to do with the Charter, John," he explained. "Just a few months ago, these men also had a march and riot. It was the stupid mayor's fault. The fool closed the taverns on Sundays and raised the liquor licence. Sunday's the only day working men around here can rest and enjoy a stein or two, so the taverns ignored the edict, police got involved and there were arrests. All that led to a march and riot… and some deaths. I'll wager that has a familiar ring for you, John?"

"Sounds to me like another attempt to control the working man," he reflected. "Doesn't matter if it's weavers, dock workers or miners, doesn't matter if the men come from Blaina, Galway, Hamburg or Chicago, they will only take so much before they turn if they feel emasculated and powerless. But I admit I am saddened to see it on these shores after the struggle for independence. America embodies the Chartist aims, after all – manhood suffrage, no property qualification for voting, payment for members of Congress, equal constituencies, and yet…"

"And yet," concluded Matthew, "we are in many respects less free. We are actively discouraged from challenging anything. The recent business here left a bitter taste, even though the idiot mayor backed down. I defended one or two of the rioters, released without charge. But the working folk don't trust anyone in authority now, especially police. There is a strong sense of injustice hereabouts."

"I am of the opinion that a good many arriving on these shores, brimful of hope, have not found the paradise they anticipated," John mused. "I have myself been saddened by the tales of lynchings, shootings, stabbings… by tales of cruelty in the prisons, similar to my own experiences… by the duplicity of politicians here too."

His host became thoughtful. "Politics in a democracy like this one," he said, "is a tale of sound and fury signifying nothing of importance to the labouring poor, alas. But every day those working men are learning new things. In time they will organise their power – and I remain an optimist in this – because real progress takes time… that and the efforts of men of courage. Men like you, John."

After John's final lecture in the city, Matthew hosted a dinner and invited another former Chartist in exile, Allan Pinkerton, a young Scot whose attempt to flirt with Catharine earned him short shrift. John listened with amusement to the man's futile attempts to impress his daughter.

"I'm just about to launch my own detective agency, the first in Chicago," preened the Scotsman. "It'll make the streets safer, putting villains where they belong… and keeping our ladies safe, of course."

"I'm sure your 'ladies' will be eternally grateful." Catharine could not have sounded less interested. "Might I trouble you to pass the salt?"

***

"Whatever is that fan-shaped contraption, Father?" Catharine was standing at Chicago railway station, examining the front of the enormous engine which would take their train to Detroit. The front wheels towered above her.

"No idea." John coughed as a foul smoke billowed in their direction. "To clear dead cattle off the line? Who knows. Let's find our seats, shall we?"

Their carriage was midpoint in the train, its shabby interior housing seats in pairs for forty or so passengers, with a narrow aisle and a stove for charcoal which was already making the carriage stuffy.

"The windows are so small!" she said. "We'll hardly see a thing."

"I suspect it's more luxurious in the back in first class," John admitted, "but we'll be in Detroit in no time, you'll see."

Catharine wriggled on the hard wooden bench, and sighed. She knew it would take them many hours. He saw the discomfort on her face, and noticed the stray grey hairs from under her bonnet. She looked well from her weeks in the open air, but she was no longer young, and he worried about her future, wherever it might be.

"I wonder sometimes," he said softly, "if you regret joining me on this adventure?"

She turned her face away from the window and said, "Nothing would have stopped me. I have never felt more alive than I have since we boarded that ship in Hobart. It has been a privilege to hear you speak again, Father, and I have learnt so much this last year… not least about myself." She leant her head on his shoulder and they travelled on in silence.

***

They were both relieved to reach Detroit, stiff from the cramped, crowded carriage, their clothes smelling of smoke from the stove. Waiting on the platform was their next host, John Bray. A tall, thin man, he always gave the impression of being about to split in two. Sunken eyes peered out of a long face below his bald pate, and above his full beard. The two men met as old friends.

"I had the pleasure of hearing your father speak years ago," their host explained to Catharine. She detected the faintest trace of a Yorkshire accent. "A Chartist meeting in the north somewhere. A lifetime ago, eh John?"

"And I read your *Labours Wrongs* when I got back to Newport," John said. "Are you still in the printing business?"

"Sure am. Best in the city, wouldn't you know?" He smiled. "I've printed another set of your pamphlets ready for your lecture here. I know Matthew well, and he sent one ahead so they'd be ready."

John was again struck by the kindness of strangers – Matthew had said nothing to him about this.

The printer's carriage took them up Jefferson Avenue and down wide, tree-lined roads fanning out from the central park area.

"It's beautiful here." Catharine could not hide her surprise. She knew of it only as a mining town.

"There's a plan to build some pretty impressive dwellings soon. Iron ore's brought real wealth to Detroit. Everywhere there are new factories making stoves, railroad cars, ship parts. There's work for everyone."

"As I recall you were a union man in the north?" John asked.

"Still am. We typographers in the city have a union, as do the cordwainers, but there aren't any others yet... it'll come though. Makes sense. Gives a voice to the working man, which is something *you* always advocated, John. A clever boss knows that the *perception* of consultation taking place helps keep things peaceful. Whether it makes a real difference to men's life... Well, let's just say the jury's out."

They pulled up outside a modest house and were greeted by a small child who flung his arms around the printer.

"My grandson, Sam. He and his mother have lived with us since my son's death last year."

A comfortable sitting room, all Morris wallpaper, large pot plants and antimacassars. Sitting stiffly on either side of the huge black fireplace were the women of the house, John's wife Eliza and his daughter-in-law Phoebe. Straight-backed poses, as if about to have one of those newfangled daguerreotype portraits taken, Catharine thought. She noticed the women's uncanny resemblance to the two Staffordshire dogs sitting either end of the mantelpiece behind them, china eyes staring out at her. Except the two women's eyes were fixed on the stains of Catharine's skirt with its residue of meals eaten messily in a railway carriage.

The women uttered barely a word through dinner, where talk centred inevitably on politics.

"I have been surprised to see so much poverty and hardship in this country," John told his host. "For us, back in the years when the Charter was written, we saw America as a fair, prosperous land of opportunity and freedom. I remember the London Working Men's Association called this country 'a beacon of freedom for all mankind'."

"I know, my friend." Bray replied. "And do you remember the front page of *The Charter* in '39? Claimed these Unites States were governed on Chartist principles, that nothing here could stand in the way of the advancement of ordinary people. But it's not as simple as that."

He poured John more wine. The women cleared the table in silence.

"I've always said," he continued, "that universal suffrage is not an end in itself but rather the means towards change… a much greater social change, where the producer of wealth will receive and retain the full reward for his exertions. We're a long way from that here, my friend, for all our so-called democracy, which on its own does not guarantee happiness. Best not get sick here. Best not get old. There is no welfare state to care for you when it's needed. It's no surprise for me when I read of many returning to British shores, disillusioned and bitter."

The mood was sombre as the two men retired to smoke in the small library.

Catharine avoided the women, and instead found Sam in his room. She took great delight in playing with his tin soldiers and reading him to sleep. That night, she dreamt of Emily and Grace, far away in another life. She had not realised how much she missed them.

STAPLETON, BRISTOL
1877

"Do you think any readers will want to know about those visits to Belville, Chicago and the like?" John had read again her latest passages, and had doubts. "I'm not sure that what is little more than an itinerary makes for very interesting reading, Anne."

"But it's all so fascinating!" Anne exclaimed. "You seem to forget that few of us have travelled as you have. Most never venture further than the nearest town. I didn't even know where these places were until I studied the library maps. Besides, it is interesting to read about your impressions of America... some things disappointed, it seems."

He was not convinced people would care that much about his American travels, but had no wish to dampen her enthusiasm.

"Now, let's see. It must have taken you a whole day on the train to New York," Anne said. "Your journal says it was late November. Is that right?"

"Probably," he said. "I remember it was very cold when we arrived. I hadn't felt cold since the nights in Impression Bay, but this New York cold was something else. Catharine hardly left our lodging house fire for the first few days, and we needed coats, of course."

Further memories of New York were interrupted by a knock on the door. Visitors were rare at their home, and Anne did not recognise the man before her. Tall, well-dressed, in his late fifties.

"Your father asked me to come," he explained.

She led him into the kitchen, but John insisted on taking the stranger into the musty parlour. "We'll have some tea, Anne, if you would be so kind." And he closed the door.

Now she was intrigued... and annoyed. Why this sudden desire for secrets? She was recording his life, after all. She banged the kettle onto the hearth and found their second-best cups. All conversation halted when she presented the tea, but when her father reminded her to close the door on her way out, she noticed how the man kept his gaze down towards his hat, which he was turning in his hands. She had a sudden terror that her father was matchmaking. Dear God, no.

He stayed for an hour or so, Anne straining to listen at the door. Nothing.

"Who was that, Father?" Sharpness like a pin in her voice. "When did you invite him?"

"I sent Joe with a letter, that day you were at the library," he replied, giving nothing further.

"Why so secretive? What could you possible want to hide?"

He tapped the side of his nose and grinned. "Time will tell, lass, time will tell. Now let's get back to New York, shall we?"

NEW YORK
November 1855 – May 1856

A November fog coughed up by the Hudson had infected the city. Its smells and sounds took John back to his youthful self in London, before he met Francis Place. Before real life started. Before.

He summoned the first available carriage, paying the driver to lift on their luggage and handing him a scrap of paper on which he had written the address of Bussey's, a boarding house which Prowting Roberts had recommended in the city. "Run by Chartists," Roberts' letter had said.

"Bussey was a loyal supporter of the Charter," John explained. "Yorkshireman... a weaver. I heard him speak once. Wonderful orator, one of the best. I look forward to meeting him again."

They stopped outside a tall, narrow building at 2 Front Street, close to the steamboat dock. There was a drunk slumped in the doorway, and above his head a sign read "Emigrants welcome". Not the most salubrious of neighbourhoods, Catharine thought to herself, and hoped she would have no further need for William's gift.

They rented two small rooms on the third floor, hers facing the river, his looking out on the rear of a run-down tenement block. The partially deaf receptionist informed them, after several attempts at clarification, that Mr Bussey had left to farm in New Jersey and had then gone home to England, but the building was now managed by a Mr Worswick."

"Worswick? Ben Worswick? Makes sense. He and Peter were always close. Can you pass on a message?"

No response. John repeated, twice, eventually shouting, "Can... you... tell... Mr Worswick... we... have... arrived?"

"No need to shout, mister," sniffed the man. "Sure can do. He'll be by later."

***

They headed first for some unfamiliar food from a cheap, slightly grubby street vendor, then headed to the post office on Nassau Street. There was a letter waiting from Mary, written many months before.

"Keep it until we're back out of this cold," Catharine urged. "I can hardly feel my fingers."

"Then that settles our next port of call," John declared. "We need warmer clothing, and you need some decent dresses. You can't wear those in the city, child." And he pointed at her grubby but serviceable travelling skirt and jacket. He noticed her hesitation, and added, "We have funds to cover our stay here – and to purchase some new clothes. Lectures in Chicago and Detroit were completely full; people were generous. It's likely to be the same here too."

***

New York was a cornucopia of surprise. A chaos of noise and smells, its crowded, unpaved streets made life difficult for pedestrians, forcing them regularly into the roads coated with animal faeces. But John was much in admiration of the horse-drawn omnibuses on their sturdy rail tracks which carried passengers up and down Manhattan. They took one to Broadway, where Catharine purchased a copy of *Francis's New Guide to the cities of New York and Brooklyn* with its promise of "what to see and how to see it" and began regaling John with how the recent Crystal Palace Exhibition had led to a much improved public transport.

"They're building a Great Park too," she enthused. "It'll have all sorts in it… oh, here we are!"

They descended in Reade Street, near the front of a stone building which the guidebook called the "Marble Palace". Catharine gasped, confronted unexpectedly by enormous glass plate windows displaying more clothes than she had ever before seen gathered in one venue.

"What is this place?" John asked, frowning. "Is this monstrosity what the future holds for drapers?"

Catharine took his elbow to lead him in. They were about to enter when a tall man in a uniform held out a hand. "Excuse me madam. Only genuine customers welcome here." He was eyeing her dirty skirt and battered bonnet.

John intervened. "We hope to purchase several items today." And he took out his pocketbook as proof. "But if our money does not meet your high standards, we can go elsewhere, of course."

The man touched the brim of his top hat and opened the ornate oak door behind him.

Neither of them had ever seen the like. A cavernous room filled with all manner of things to purchase, the floors in tiers around a central atrium, illuminated by bright chandeliers. Everywhere, the chatter of well-dressed clientele swirling around the displays like bees around a bank of flowers.

"No one seems to need an appointment," John commented. "Some people appear to be just *looking* at objects with no intention to buy… This is indeed very strange."

"There is even a cafeteria upstairs, and rest rooms for the ladies," Catharine added. "A brave new world eh, Father?" she asked, amused at her father's bewilderment.

It had been a long time since she had endured a fitting of this sort, and she despaired at the need for several layers of stiff petticoats and a horsehair crinoline. "Is this absolutely necessary?" she asked the nervous assistant. She had not worn anything like this in many years, and yearned again for the comfort of the clothes she had purchased in a wooden livery store far, far away.

"Madam, they are absolutely essential if you are to enjoy a fashionable circumference… six or seven yards is normal this season."

Catharine had little interest in enjoying a "fashionable" anything, but settled on two dresses, a cloak, a warm shawl and a fur hat and muff against the New York winter ahead. John, muttering how he would prefer the services of a draper and tailor any day, also purchased some warm clothing, at Catharine's insistence.

As her father summoned a carriage outside the store, Catharine, her arms loaded with parcels, could not resist turning back to the doorman to whisper, "You might do well to remember something…"

He was surprised at her forward manner: the ladies usually ignored him whilst their husbands offered a tip. He raised an eyebrow.

"Sometimes, sir, that which is gold does not glitter," she advised, and bade him good day.

When they returned to Bussey's, there was a note from Ben Worswick. He would call on John the next morning and take him to meet other Chartists now in New York. They could then plan the lectures. Pleased that this next stage of his journey was becoming clearer, he sought his room and the letter from home, dated late August.

"My dearest love," he read, his fingers tracing her familiar hand, his memory struggling to hear her voice again.

"I do not know when or if you will receive this, but Mr Roberts suggested New York be the safest place to write. Anne and I are well, and follow closely the regular attempts in Parliament demanding your full pardon and return. We pray that will happen soon… it has been so long, my love, and I miss you still.

"Your letter from San Francisco amused us greatly, and we read with much interest Catharine's news from Chicago. You must find her companionship a real comfort, as Anne's is for me. I have news that will surprise you, my dearest, of another of our children. Your eldest, John, has left Newport and the draper's, and is in America. His last letter came from Pittsburgh, and I hope you and

he will meet, though I confess I do not know how great the distance is between you. It may be that the winter prevents much travel in the new world, as here.

"We have had a warm summer this year, but I dread the cold months ahead, still unable to rid myself of the cough and a general ague. Anne is not gifted in the kitchen, as you know, but there are days when I cannot leave my bed still, and she does her best. I am grateful for her efforts.

"Be sure to take care of yourself, my love, and of Catharine. Write soon,

"Your loving wife, Mary."

"Your brother John is in Pittsburgh." They were eating in a modest restaurant near their boarding house. "I will try to discover where exactly, and why he left Newport."

"Seems your children have a habit of following you, Father!" Catharine said. "Shall we go to Pittsburgh, then?"

"I planned to do so in the spring," he replied. " Mr Roberts said my lecture would attract much interest there. Many Chartists settled in that area… activists and supporters alike. Mines provide work there, and lots of it. Can't see John in a mine, though…"

***

The most striking feature of Mr Ben Worswick was his voice – deep, baritone, compelling. Where he went, people listened. He greeted John warmly, and they travelled in a private carriage past rows of impressive brownstone houses, some still in construction, to a large dwelling on Lower 5th Avenue, unprepossessing in its elegance, with a small garden in the front and stables behind.

Catharine, much to her chagrin, had not been invited.

"Here we are," he said. "This is the home of William Denton. Do you know him, John?"

"We have never met, but I know who he is." John remembered articles from long ago, written by this Bristol weaver and Chartist who had lectured in London. "Didn't he also write on phrenology?"

"That's the man," confirmed Worswick as they approached the front door. "He's made his money here, though, with his lectures on Spiritualism. He's an interesting fellow."

Beyond the grand entrance hall with its sweeping marble staircase was a large, sombre drawing room. Dark drapes ensured even the weak December light had no chance of entry. There was far too much heavy furniture in the room, which smelt of damp. A stuffed fox in a glass case stared at John, who had the sudden sensation he was at a funeral.

"Mr Frost, how wonderful to finally meet you!" William Denton was a lot more welcoming than his home. He crossed the room to a wooden tantalus on the huge oak sideboard and used a little key hanging from his watch chain to open the casing. He poured three generous glasses from the liberated bottle and offered a toast. "To our Chartist friends wherever they have come to rest, and to the finest leader our movement ever had."

"Not sure about that last comment, though I thank you kindly," John replied, slightly embarrassed by the stranger's flattery. "I've been a long while away from political life," he continued. "As I understand it, Feargus O'Connor has been much more active as a leader recently than I."

The other men laughed. "You obviously haven't heard... Mr O'Connor is not the man you might have once known. He was here in New York, you know, some three years ago. We organised a big reception – all the papers were there. Real fanfare... we made sure he wanted for nothing. But the fool disgraced himself. Grabbed a shop girl in a store one day, in public mind you, and made lewd suggestions... He had to leave sharpish back to Britain. Man's lost his wits, I reckon."

John was stunned. O'Connor had always been a hothead, but this was somehow sad to hear.

"There are many here in New York who remember what you did, John, and hold you in great esteem. Your public lectures will be popular, and you will need a reprint of your pamphlets to accompany your talks. May I suggest something?" He poured them a second generous glass. "You might consider a different title. *The Horrors of Convict Life* deserves a broad audience. May I be so bold as to suggest renaming it *A Letter to the people of the United States*?"

John sipped his whisky, considering the unexpected proposal.

"I am expecting other guests this evening," his host continued, "one of whom is William Rider, a Leeds man who used to be a printer's devil. Works now in publishing. He's keen as mustard to meet you. He was active with the Leeds Working Men's Association until he was arrested and imprisoned. He's your man for any printing job, John."

"And I've heard from John Rewcastle," Ben interrupted. "He'll join us this evening, and he'll bring his Irish friend Tom Devyr. You'll like them, John. Devyr's a wild spark, can be unpredictable, but is invariably a passionate Chartist – published *Our Natural Rights* in '42, edited a paper too, the *Williamsburg Democrat*. He'll be sure your lectures get proper coverage here… the man knows everyone."

They were interrupted by the arrival of the other men, and through supper until brandy and cigars, they debated. They argued reasons for the failure of the petitions to Parliament in the '30s and on the many occasions since, discussed John's trial and their own experiences in this new land. They spoke of the patient determination of the moral force Chartists and the danger to the movement presented by physical force Chartists. They worried that with so many of the movement's leaders in exile, Chartism on their home shores would lose momentum and crumble.

The mood, at times nostalgic or angry, shifted to resentful and melancholy. John, by far the eldest, sensed a distance between himself and his companions, but recognised their strength of purpose, their individuality, energy and zeal. Watching, listening, he was gazing down a telescope onto long-past evenings with Francis Place, or with Henry Vincent, or with angry men in Blaina.

"There is much disappointment, John," his host admitted. "I'm sure you've seen that already, in Chicago and Detroit. Desperate men brought their families here believing they could free themselves from poverty, from a servitude to rich masters. Daily we hear of bitter decisions to go home."

"Some had been sold the lie that a day's wage here was three times better than at home." John Rewcastle was quieter than the others, choosing his pertinent comments carefully. "They came with a vague idea of some workers' paradise, and ended like our friend Bussey. Last we saw him, he was peddling three cent trinkets off a cart in Chatham Street."

"No one has campaigned for the end to the abhorrence of slavery more than I," their host continued. "And yet in this city, in this country, we are surrounded by something far broader and more insidious… a wage slavery, a white slavery if you like. A man scarcely surviving by his daily labour is essentially a slave too." He was making sweeping gestures with his whisky glass.

"Take a trip, if you dare, down to Hell's Kitchen or Five Points…" he continued, words slightly slurred. "You'll meet typhoid, cholera, diphtheria… a poverty and a despair far worse than anything Mr Dickens writes of in his London stories. It is why, Mr Frost, I want as many as possible here in America to be encouraged to read your pamphlet. It warns – nay, it rails – against injustice, and tells of the danger of power unchallenged. That applies to far more than convicts, as you well know."

John was convinced. "I agree. We will print with the title you suggest, but I shall add some thoughts about the evils of the British aristocracy too."

Rewcastle spoke again. "There is a class of people in American society, Mr Frost, who would be perfectly at home with British aristocracy," he said quietly. "It should be our mission to ensure the crippling chains of English deference are not transferred to the shoulders of the American working man."

They talked well into the night and parted after agreeing some dates and venues for John's public lectures.

"Come back in a day or two, John, with any alterations for the publication," his host urged. "I'll get them to William for printing. And bring Miss Frost. I shall tell you about my other... interest."

Heading back to his lodgings, John formulated what he wanted to add to his pamphlet and noted it in his journal even before he had removed his coat. After all he had seen and heard in the United States, all the disillusionment he had witnessed, his letter to its people would contain a warning: *The aristocracy of the British Isles is the curse of the world.*

STAPLETON, BRISTOL
1877

"That surely did precious little to advance the case for your pardon!" Anne had told him. She had gone to bed quite cross and had not even said good night.

She woke to heavy rain, and remembered. Blast! Shuffling to the window she pulled back the curtain and saw John's shirts and her petticoats sagging sorrowfully on the garden line where she had forgotten them.

She was surprised to find him downstairs already; this was not their usual routine. Tea was made, and there was a small bunch of flowers from the garden on the table next to the bread and honey. And a large envelope across her plate.

"Happy birthday, lass!" John hugged her awkwardly and brushed his beard across her cheek. She had completely forgotten. It was the first day of July, and she was fifty-one years old. "Go on, open it," he teased, pouring her the weakest tea she had seen in a long time.

Anne stared at the formal wording of the legal document in her hands, not really comprehending. "An agreement is hereby established between Miss Anne Frost..." she read, and looked at her father. "What is this, Father?"

"You will recall the gentleman who came by some days ago, and took tea with me in the parlour?"

Anne swallowed. Chewed her lip. Oh God! What had her father done? A contract with that man... for her hand... like some medieval baron?

"He's George Payne, the son of a printer I used to know well here in Bristol, a Chartist friend, also a George. The son took over the business when his father died. I told him all about your tale of my life, Anne, and he's read some parts... he liked what he saw – the march on Newport, the trial, the *Mandarin*. He's going to publish it as a book, so all you have to do is finish it, and then your job's done. I thought the news would be a suitable gift for your birthday."

She sat staring at the document, her tea untouched. "I… I… don't know what to say." She looked at her father's smile, his grey eyes warm and proud. "Now perhaps you'll believe me when I say you write well. You will soon be a published author, like Miss Austen!"

"I am touched and flattered," she said, her voice catching as she swallowed an uncharacteristic urge to cry. "But the story will always be yours," she said, then added, "and Catharine's, of course, and it's far from finished. Birthday or not, when breakfast is done, we should carry on. Your journal of New York holds helpful detail, and Catharine wrote to us quite regularly, but there are still gaps you need to fill for me, Father."

"But first, some toast and fresh tea…"

"Which *I* shall make," she insisted, placing her hand gently on his shoulder, leaving it just a minute longer than she would normally. "You have already done enough for me today."

The rain stopped, and there was a freshness in the air as Anne opened the windows to let in the day.

"Even the birds are celebrating today," John joked. "Now where were we?"

"You had just met the Chartists in New York," she reminded him, checking what she had last written.

"Well, I reworked that pamphlet and changed the title, as you know. It sold well, following the lectures through December and January around and beyond New York. Everywhere was full to capacity, Anne. Many who came spoke with me, good men who had signed petitions and marched for Chartism, and those conversations left me in no doubt: the working men who had fled Britain were disillusioned, felt betrayed by promises spun back home, and despised what they had found in this new land. In *The horrors of convict life* it seems I had identified a far more general darkness in man, one which lies waiting in many places, not just Van Diemen's Land."

He paused a while, remembering. "It was a blow, Anne. My disappointment with the reality of American 'freedom' was profound. A dream shattered."

"And Catharine? Her letters tell of women she met, and some charity work she did."

"Your sister has the rare ability to make the best of every situation," he said.

Not *every* situation, Anne thought.

Anne found her sister's letters from New York, dated 1855, and had started to make some notes when her father reminded her of something else worthy of inclusion. "And then there were our further encounters with William Denton," he said. "You must write of them. You *must*. I shall be ever indebted to his introducing me to the miracle that is Spiritualism. It has provided an unhoped for solace these last years."

NEW YORK
December 1855 – March 1856

Curiosity had got the better of her, and Catharine wished now she had not come. Her plan had been to visit Barnum's museum that afternoon, much lauded in her guidebook, but the mention of Spiritualism had whetted her appetite. It was the talk of New York… this new idea that the dead were somehow accessible. Her rational mind rejected the notion. And yet…

She was beyond uncomfortable. Her new petticoat was itchy, and the stiff frame which gave her dress that infamous "fashionable volume" made it impossible to move except in slow motion, or indeed to sit, except bolt upright on the edge of a heavy velvet chaise longue in William Denton's study. She felt she was being watched: a bearded patriarch from a bygone world stared down from a sombre oil painting. On her right was a glass case hosting yet another stuffed creature, this time a pheasant, its beady eyes challenging her. To her left, on the desk, sat a large ceramic head, the bald pate covered with strange symbols, the glazed eyes ever open, meeting her own. She got up to examine it more closely.

"Not a very cheerful place, is it?" she mused as they waited for their host. "Do you think this is where he… you know… does whatever he does to speak to the dead?"

"Miss Frost, how good of you to join us!" William Denton was very much of the living, his ruddy complexion and tight waistcoat suggesting a taste for good food and wine. "One of the tools of the trade," he explained, pointing at the china head. "I have long advocated the merits of phrenology. You can tell so much about a person from the shape of the head." Catharine noticed he was staring at hers, and sat back on the velvet seat, trying in vain to push down the hoop beneath her skirt.

A maid brought in a tray with tea and crumpets, and their host asked polite questions about their lodgings, their first impressions of the city, and on the plans for John's lectures.

"May I ask *you* something?" John ventured. "What led you to explore the Spiritualist faith? It seems a long way from lecturing on Chartism."

"I can see how strange you must find it for a former weaver to be living in this way, and it is true that I attract critical voices, John. People say I am making money out of my fellow man's fear and sadness, that I am a fake. But they are wrong. Most things connect in some way. All that we experience of the world starts inside the head, and some of us are more sensitive to currents in the atmosphere around us than others."

Catharine munched her crumpet, wondering what was lurking in the atmosphere of this sombre room. The pheasant continued to stare.

"For me," he went on, "a disappointment with politics and people in *this* life led me to hope the answers lay with folk living in the *next*. When I lecture now, I talk of social reform, yes, but I also tell my audience that there are wise voices from the past ready to assist us in the here and now. Communication with those voices will lead man to a harmonious existence."

Catharine had to work hard to suppress her laughter. Whatever was this nonsense? Surely her father would not fall for this drivel? She managed to lower the teacup across the voluminous skirt to safety on the side table. She just had to say something.

"Whatever makes you think the dead know more than we? Progress lies with the living, surely?"

Her tone was scathing, but her host replied calmly, if a little patronisingly, "The mind does not die with the flesh, Miss Frost. A spirit continues to evolve, increasingly gaining wisdom."

She found it all unconscionably stupid and expected her father to dismiss the ideas outright. But John was deep in thought, listening attentively to his host's words.

"And can you communicate with anyone who has passed?"

She could not believe he was asking the question.

"Last year we held our national convention here in this city," William continued. "It is a growing movement, John, attracting some of the most influential citizens in New York. At a time of disillusionment, I guess it offers some hope. But you must come to one of the private sessions I hold here. There is one such in two days' time."

"Thank you, I shall."

John had accepted before Catharine could even blink. Wild horses would not drag her here. Her father must be deranged.

"To answer your question: yes, I have spoken with the departed," William admitted. "It has taken years of practice and patience to do so, and is never something I do lightly. But it can be a source of great comfort for those left behind. You might like to read this, my friend." He went to his bookshelf and handed John a red leather tome, *The Principles of Nature, Her Divine Revelations and a voice to Mankind.* "It's the best introduction you'll find, by A. Jackson Davis himself. He draws on Mesmer's teachings. Read it, John. Judge for yourself, then come to the meeting… I look forward to hearing your views."

All the way back to their lodgings, she tried to reason with him, appealing to his rational intellect. But John refused to respond, preferring to feign sleep, clutching the dratted book. He could be stubborn at times, and this was one such time.

There was another message waiting at Bussey's, but this one was for Catharine. An expensive envelope and an unfamiliar hand. It was an invitation to "high tea" with a Miss Stanton and a Miss Anthony. Both were friends of Louise Clappe, who had written from San Francisco to alert them to Catharine's arrival in their city.

"How kind!" Catharine said to herself. It would be a welcome distraction from the gloom of Mr Denton and his stuffed pheasant.

They sent a carriage to collect her the next day, and she was driven to a hotel on Broadway. Waiting for her in the elegant tea rooms were two well-dressed women, both clearly delighted to meet her. Catharine felt suddenly nervous and self-conscious in their presence: Elizabeth Cady Stanton had been the force behind the Seneca Falls convention. She had studied law and had compiled the *Declaration of Sentiments* arguing for women's suffrage; Susan Anthony was an activist for women's rights and an abolitionist.

"Miss Anthony… Mrs Stanton, I am deeply honoured…." Catharine's mouth was dry. She felt foolish. "I have so admired your D… D… Declaration…" Dear God, she was actually stuttering.

"It's Elizabeth and Susan," replied the former, her warmth immediately putting Catharine at ease. "I rarely use Stanton, and have long made it clear that I have no desire to be labelled as my husband's property. Dear Louise writes of you with great respect and affection. It seems you are quite the traveller!"

They took tea and talked about the slow progress on either side of the Atlantic towards full enfranchisement. They were keen to hear of her sea voyages, her journey across America and her life in Van Diemen's Land.

"Your independence and courage are most impressive, Catharine, but what will you do here while your father presents his lectures?" Susan asked. "Have you any plans?"

Catharine had been conscious since her arrival that the attractions of the city were finite, that the lure of Barnum's or Vaudeville shows would soon lose their glitter for her. She knew she would need to occupy her time at some point.

"I would be grateful for suggestions," she asked. "I know no one here… apart from my father's contacts, that is."

"And I suspect they are far too occupied with the interests of other *men* to worry about you." Elizabeth was tackling heartily her third slice of fruit cake; Catharine decided she liked this woman.

"I hear your father asks that we weaker mortals absent ourselves from his lectures. To what end, I wonder?" Elizabeth asked through a mouthful of crumbs. "Does he think it will stop us from caring, from campaigning? I asked the same in London fifteen years ago when they stopped me attending the World Antislavery Convention… It is high time men like your father embraced us as equals."

Catharine moved awkwardly in her seat, cursed the stiff underskirts again, and sipped her tea. It would be disloyal to openly agree, but she definitely liked this woman.

Susan changed the subject. "May I invite you to join us in a charitable enterprise recently established?" she asked. "I suspect you have noticed the homeless and runaway children on the streets of our city. Their number grows each week, and their destiny is fixed unless the kindness of strangers can intervene. Two years ago, Elizabeth and I joined other concerned benefactors to found the New York Juvenile Asylum."

"Please, go on," Catharine urged.

Elizabeth called for more tea.

"The idea is to care for these strays, train them, nurture their self-discipline and morality, place them in apprenticeships. Might you be able to help? We are so much in need of volunteers."

"I taught in Hobart," Catharine explained. "So spending my days again with children would bring me great joy."

"Some of them have led quite dissolute lives, you must remember," Elizabeth warned. "You will need to take care."

Catharine smiled. "Then I shall be on familiar ground. Hobart's children were mainly the offspring of convicts, in whose number, you will recall, I could include my own father and brother!"

***

John had spent the day and most of the previous night reading William's book, and was anxious to learn more. He was no stranger to matters of the spirit – his Bible had been a companion for years now – but this possibility of seeking guidance from the deceased intrigued him. He would attend the meeting.

Another turn of the wheel. Another door opening.

Back in the oppressive darkness of the drawing room at William Denton's, John met the other participants seated at the large table in readiness for the evening's séance: two widows, completely attired in black, veils lowered; a hollow-eyed man with bad skin; and a young woman with rouged cheeks whose dress was noticeably cut low at the neck. The room was airless, and lit only by a few strategically placed candles. He watched William place the alphabet cards on his table, his face expressionless, his gaze distant.

John knew from his time in Monmouth Gaol that the mind is a clever magician, that reality can deceive, so was not surprised to feel a coldness creep over his back, nor the hairs on his arms prickle. His heart was racing.

The air became heavier over their table, and William's voice a monotone. What happened next John would never be able to explain, but as the others around the table asked questions – about loved ones, about the future, about the dead – William gave them answers, spelt out by the letter cards. Then suddenly, William turned to John, eyes not quite seeing him.

"Someone wishes to speak with you," he said.

John froze. He had come as an observer, had asked no questions. William began to sing, very softly at first, both his voice and the song familiar to John from somewhere. Then he knew… he had not heard it for many years… it was a favourite Welsh hymn of Henry Hunt's. His beloved son was here.

"Henry?" John whispered. "Henry Hunt? Is that you?"

William started moving a marker towards the letters with ferocious speed. "Yes."

"Are you happy?" John asked. He cursed such a trite question, but he was struggling to comprehend.

"Yes."

"Is your grandmother with you?"

"Yes."

"Will I ever see your mother again?"

He dreaded the answer.

"Yes."

A cold draft across the room blew out some of the candles, causing one of the widows to cry out. The moment was broken, and William collapsed, exhausted, over the table.

As he left, John felt neither fear nor amazement, but rather a strange sense of peace. He knew he would return.

STAPLETON, BRISTOL
1877

There were tears in his old eyes when he spoke of his dead son. Anne did not know what to say, had never heard before of that séance, but she realised for the first time in twenty years what had converted an old man to Spiritualism, and with such strong conviction that he had never wavered since.

She tried to change the focus. "So, tell me about Catharine's new role."

But the question went unheard. "She disapproved... became angry with me. I shouldn't have told her, but I felt so much joy hearing Henry speak again. Your sister said it was all in my imagination, that I had gone to the meeting *wanting* to hear something, and she made me promise not to write to your mother about it... but I know what I heard, Anne. How else could that Englishman sing in perfect Welsh – and in Henry's voice?"

He blew his nose to disguise the tears, then added, sadly, "I went often to William's meetings, saw for myself the comfort he gave to people, but each visit widened the chasm between Catharine and myself... There was a distance I had never felt before. We drifted our separate ways."

This was news indeed to Anne. So the favourite was tarnished a little...

"There were days when I barely saw her," he said. "She never attended any of my lectures in New York, not once, but stayed sometimes in Seneca Falls, or in Boston, or went to meetings of the women's movement. She spoke at some, I know, gave out pamphlets and the like... but did not even bother to argue with me as she had done before. It was a painful time."

He smiled. "But I do know she was happy volunteering at that children's asylum. She is a gifted teacher, Anne, and connects easily with young minds." He became wistful. "I do sometimes wonder if she regrets not having children of her own…"

Some of us have no choice, thought Anne.

NEW YORK
December 1855

He woke to a strange stillness. Lowering his feet onto the cold bare floor, he walked to the window and drew back the thin curtain. Everywhere was white. The streets around Bussey's, normally a cacophony of morning carriages, street vendors and dock workers heading for the Hudson, were silent. He had not seen snow for over twenty years, and it conjured a long-buried memory of two children outside his home in Newport, an eternity ago. Henry Hunt throwing snowballs at a furious Anne as she swept the front steps, Mary reprimanding her son, telling him to bring in some wood instead. Where do these memories lie? he asked himself, and smiled, rubbing the leather band at his wrist.

Catharine was away again with her new friends, so he dressed and ventured out. The cold air hit him like a blow, snatching his breath. He wandered as far as Broadway, stopping only for a warm beverage, and watched in wonder as numerous horse-drawn carriages on sledges carried their squealing passengers up and down the long street. His wanderings took him past the store where they had purchased their new clothes. All the windows displayed the trinkets and finery of Christmas, just a few days away, and John decided he should buy his daughter a gift, a peace offering of sorts. But what?

He still felt a discomfort in the emporium, as if all his senses were under attack, and quickly sought the help of a kind-looking assistant.

"Your daughter will love this," she suggested, and handed him an exquisite silk scarf. "For when the weather improves," she added.

It was only when she was wrapping the gift that he realised the scarf was decorated with bluebells.

Catharine had grudgingly agreed to accompany her father to Ben Worswick's home for Christmas Day, and was arranging her hair when he knocked.

"Happy Christmas, Catharine," he said. He made to embrace her, but she moved her arms to adjust some loose curls. "I have a small gift for you."

It was such a fine silk, slipping like air through her fingers, its colours vibrant. The surprise caught her off guard and she fought back tears.

"I know you have been angry with me, lass," he said. "It pains me after all we have endured together. Let us try to enter the new year as friends again… please."

She hugged him then, this father into whose life her own had been so finely woven, like the flowers into the silk. So far from home, they had need of each other, whatever their differences.

"Who knows what the year ahead might bring?" she said. "I have learnt one thing at least, Father. For as long as I am with you, it will never be dull!"

The dinner with Ben's family was gargantuan, and the day filled with laughter. They sang carols around the piano, and the children, under Catharine's direction, played blind man's bluff. Once again, John was touched by the hospitality of comparative strangers, his regret being that there was no immediate likelihood of his returning the favour in his own home.

They joined the other New York residents on New Year's Eve, crowding into Lower Manhattan to hear Trinity Church's glorious bells, the full octave celebrating a new belfry. Then followed the tradition of "calling" and they went by invitation to William Denton's, with an unspoken promise that there would be no mention of spirits other than those found in a bottle.

So it was that 1856 began on a happy note.

John's lectures continued. Catharine kept busy. Weeks passed.

When spring beckoned in the buds around Madison Gardens, John planned his visit to Pittsburgh. His eldest son had written with an address, and news that he was running a general store, but with no reason given for his rapid departure from Newport. There were Welshmen in Pittsburgh, and many Chartist sympathisers, so John's lectures would be popular, the letter promised.

Prowting Roberts had given John a list of names and addresses, but he chose William Carnegie to arrange the lectures. John had met him often at Francis Place's shop in London, where the Scotsman wrote regularly for *Cobbett's Register*. Catharine wanted to see her older brother again, to visit his new home, so they took the Pittsburgh train together. *Just like it was before,* John thought to himself, as she fussed over his travelling rug and worried about draughts.

Pittsburgh was another Merthyr. Industry was king in this sprawling metropolis with its thousand factories and almost as many chimneys bellowing dark smoke into the heavens. The first words they heard on the platform were in Welsh, the next in German, reminders of the waves of European immigrants now toiling in the coal mines and iron foundries.

John barely recognised his son. He had lost the confidence of youth and was stooped, jaded and sickly, his hair receding and his brow wrinkled. Now in his forties, he looked much older, but the embrace was warm and the reunion tearful.

"It has been so long… so long…" He could barely speak. "And look at you!" He turned to his sister. "Quite the independent miss these days! Your nieces are desperate to see you again."

After supper in their comfortable home next door to the store, after the interminable questions from his granddaughters, now seventeen and sixteen – babies when he was taken away – the women left father and son to talk alone.

"I had to leave Wales in a hurry," the younger man explained. "You do not need to know all the details… let's just say I had a few enemies… so we came where so many Merthyr men had come before. I had a bit put by, and we started the store. Mother wrote with news of your lectures, and there are many here in Pittsburgh who still consider you a hero, are desperate to hear you." He took his father's hands in his own, and said tearfully, "It makes me so proud… being your son."

The working men of Pittsburgh town embraced their celebrated visitor. Packed audiences listened to his accounts of convict life. They cheered his warnings against tyrannical bosses, applauded his pleas for universal franchise, and were generous in their thanks for his efforts years before with the Charter. A Yorkshire miner named John Bates came to relate how he had founded the first miners' union in America – "on Chartist principles" he explained proudly.

An ancient miner shuffled up to the podium, took off his cap and said, "This is the finest day of my life, Mr Frost. I marched with you in Newport and brought this with me when I left home, as a reminder of that time, like. But it belongs to you." Shyly, he opened his hand: in it was the case of a bullet. "From Westgate Square," the man explained quietly, before turning to leave.

That night in his journal John recorded the words of another union activist, Daniel Weaver, who had announced to those at the lecture: "To me there is no East, no West, no North, no South… and I say let there be no English, no Irish, Germans, Scots or Welsh. We are just workers together." The Pittsburgh people reminded John of those who had come in their thousands to listen to him in the valleys of home. It moved him deeply.

STAPLETON, BRISTOL
1877

"I am glad you saw my brother again, before… you know."

"As am I," John agreed. "He must have been quite ill when we in Pittsburgh, but said nothing. Six months later, we heard…"

They sat in silence for a time, watching the sun set.

"A man should not outlive his children, Anne. It has been my curse."

She needed to lift his mood. "I had a note today from the printer," she announced. "He wants to know what my book is to be called. Have you any thoughts, Father?"

"Why, something like *John Frost – a life* will suffice, surely? No need for anything fancy, lass."

She was unconvinced. "I shall give it some thought. But if you are not too tired this evening, I should like us to cover a very important event… You were back in New York when the letter came, I think?"

These last few days Anne had felt an almost visceral urgency to her writing. She could not explain why, but knew she needed to finish her father's story before summer's end. Yet there were times when her eyes would fail her, "one of her heads" would take over, and she would take to her bed. She was becoming her mother.

Not now, though. This part was important to get right.

"I remember that day well," he started. "I had gone again to the post on Nassau Street with a letter for your mother, and the clerk stopped me as I was leaving. 'Two for you today, Mr Frost,' he said. I recognised Henry Vincent's hand on one. The other was formal, postmarked London. It had a grand envelope, my name and postal address in ornate italics.

"There was a small park near the post, so I found a quiet bench and opened the formal letter first."

Anne looked up when he hesitated, saw how his hands trembled, worse than before.

"Oh Anne, lass…" He was whispering, breathless. "I cannot describe what I felt next. Here was my full pardon… after so many years… I could be with you and your mother again… I could go home."

NEW YORK
May 1856

Catharine had spent the morning with her young charges, and had arranged to meet her father for an early birthday treat in Brown's coffee shop on Pearl Street. The restaurant on the ground floor was a favourite of hers, and she loved the edgy atmosphere of travellers, businessmen, politicians. More to her taste than sedate tea rooms.

As he sat at her table, she was studying the menu intently. "They have lamb today, your favourite, so…" She stopped, seeing her father's face. "Whatever is it, Father? You have not been speaking to Mr Denton's ghosts again have you?" They had recently discovered how their differing views might be at least accommodated within the much less contentious cloak of humour.

He passed her the letter and watched her face as she read… *"Her Majesty in her wondrous grace and wisdom has hereby granted Mr John Frost…"* She read to the end in silence. "Is this true? That you are free… You can… We can…"

"Go home." He relished the words, made real now heard aloud.

"But how? I mean, it is wonderful news, but why now?"

He handed her the second letter. "Henry Vincent can explain."

"My dear friend," she read. *"It is my hope that by now you will have received confirmation of the pardon so long deserved, and requested oftentimes in our Parliament. It appears the success of her armies in the Crimea softened Her Majesty's feelings towards political prisoners. Many pardons have been offered, and it lifted my heart to hear yours was one.*

"Our mutual friend Mr Prowting Roberts has received news from Joshua Melville in San Francisco and Matthew Trumbull in Chicago, both extolling the virtues of your lectures. I have no doubt your return to these shores will be the cause of much celebration, and provide an

opportunity to educate the good people of your homeland on the evils to which you were exposed in exile. Should you need assistance in any manner on your return, I remain always at your disposition.

"Please convey my warmest regards to Catharine.

"I wish you both a safe journey, Henry."

It was an unexpected turn of the wheel. A jolt in their steady trajectory.

John wrote immediately to Mary, replied to Henry, and began planning the voyage. His friends in New York were equally pleased for him. He was invited to lunch at William Denton's and arrived to find the others all there. They raised a celebratory glass to their guest.

"We will be saddened when you leave us, John," Ben said. "Your months here and your lectures have reminded us of our common values."

"Of a better world to which we must all continue to strive," Rewcastle added.

"Please accept this as a token of our gratitude." William Denton handed him a large sum of money to cover the trip home.

"With first class cabins this time," Ben insisted. "It is the least you deserve."

"But promise me you'll keep writing," joked William Rider, who had dutifully ensured supportive press coverage during John's stay. "You help ensure we newspaper folk keep our jobs!"

Catharine, however, was not finding the matter quite as simple. She had a difficult decision to make, and tried to hide her uncertainty, not wishing to ruin her father's joy. What should she do? She was happy here in New York, settled even, relatively free and independent. She could earn a living here, as a governess perhaps, and continue to help with the orphans. She could still campaign for women's rights, lead a life of purpose and meaning. What did Bristol hold for her? Domestic routines and lonely spinsterhood with Anne as her constant companion? She shuddered.

She went again to Seneca Falls to talk with her feminist friends. Elizabeth was clear. "You *must* go home with your father. You will of course be sorely missed, Catharine, not least by the institute's children, who love you so dearly, but your family matters more than any campaign. Your mother has not seen you for so long, and is not young. You could bitterly regret a decision to stay... and who knows? Life may yet hold another adventure for you."

"I doubt it," Catharine replied, taken aback by Elizabeth's rather conventional view. "I shall be forty before too long. What can I expect after that? My adventures are behind me, I suspect."

"Then embrace what life might still offer you, my dear, and cherish your many memories. No one can take those from you. Hold fast to your beliefs, and write to us often. Do not ever forget how strong you can be as a woman, believe in yourself, and never, ever allow any man to stifle your dreams or treat you as anything less than his equal."

She tried to fix in her memory the final picture of her two friends waving farewell. Another chapter was closing.

There had been so many final goodbyes recently, each loss almost physical.

But she knew Elizabeth was right, and it was time for home.

***

They were packing again. The battered trunk, open in John's room in Bussey's, was slowly swallowing their familiar possessions. Still at the bottom lay the Chartist flag wrapped around Tom Paine, and John's precious journals. Catharine bought some small gifts from New York for her mother and Anne, and secured them carefully inside her muff, not needed on this summer crossing. She checked her Gladstone for the weapon, hiding it under some books and underwear. Part of a life she could barely believe she had lived.

"We should be spared the storms," John said, placing his Bible in the trunk. He would keep William Denton's book to reread on the journey. "July is usually calm. And we'll be home in ten days or so."

The generosity of his friends had facilitated cabins on the *Atlantic,* pride of the Collins fleet, faster than the rival Cunard line could offer. It had steam heating, running water on board, ventilation in the staterooms. Entering theirs, they stared in disbelief. Catharine whooped like a child, spun and jumped backwards onto the soft bed, boots and all. Next door, John ran his hands over the mahogany fittings, the polished brass, the coats of arms etched on the stateroom window.

"A far cry from the *Mandarin,* Father," Catharine said from his doorway.

"And we won't have to cook, or share a distant privy. Nor will you be organising any deck games!" he laughed.

They left their bags and went on deck to watch New York shrink on the horizon, each lost in memories of what the city had given them.

"It feels strange," she said. "I wondered sometimes if this would ever happen."

John reached out to place his hand over hers, and the leather thread rubbed against her wrist. "Your presence since you joined me in Hobart has tied me to home... has kept me hopeful, and I have been humbled by the efforts of friends and family who for many years never gave up the fight for my full pardon. I owe them so much..."

"But surely you will stay in Stapleton now, Father? At your age, and after this last year, it is rest you need, and time with Mother. Promise me."

" '*Old age hath yet his honour and his toil,* ' lass. Your mother knows that. There is still a battle to win, and I cannot change now... but be assured, I shall see out my days on home soil. After this, I am done with sea travel!"

But this was one final voyage to remember. He recorded in his journal the great saloon, some sixty feet long, the carpeted dining room of rosewood fittings, the silverware on marble table tops, and though she resented her own weakness, Catharine secretly relished the deep seats and quiet calm of a smoke-free ladies' drawing room.

Only once did he succumb to the whisperings of his longtime companion, guilt. He stood alone one evening on deck, after another indulgent dinner, and thought of those travellers in the convict ships, or the Sydney ducks confined to the darkness of steerage. He still had work to do telling their stories. He would continue to be their voice. He owed them that and would not yield.

Not yet.

Home

"Tho' much is taken, much abides; and tho'
We are not now that strength which in old days
Moved earth and heaven, that which we are, we are."

Tennyson, *Ulysses*

STAPLETON, BRISTOL
1877

They were hulling strawberries at the kitchen table, so that Anne could make jam for the winter. She had a poor record with jam: last year's disaster had been inedible. Joe had brought the fruit proudly from his garden, his face as red as his offering as he announced he was to marry in the autumn, the landlord's daughter he had been walking out with for some time. He would move to the inn, and help her father manage it.

"Good luck with that!" John muttered after the lad had left, and swallowed a large strawberry whole from the dish. Anne wondered who would be left to provide help when needed, now that their young neighbour was moving on. Nothing ever stayed the same. Ever.

Her mind wandered to the next section of her father's story, his homecoming.

"Mother was so very angry when you did not come straight home," Anne said. "We had not seen you for seventeen years. She had planned so much…"

"I know, I know," he said, his mouth still full. "But I had no choice. I was summoned to a debate in Parliament. Duncombe arranged everything, and since the man had done so much to secure my release, how could I refuse? There was a letter waiting as we docked in Liverpool… and a ticket to London."

"All we had were the newspaper reports of your reception," Anne said.

"And Catharine," he added. "You had Catharine home. You must have been pleased to see your sister again?"

Anne focused on a particularly tricky strawberry before replying. "Mother was thrilled." She wiped her sticky fingers on her apron, adjusted her spectacles and scanned an old newspaper she had been reading the night before. "The *People's Paper* was particularly effusive, Father. They write how your story was 'uplifting and inspirational', a 'powerful symbol of the potential for moral might'. They call you 'patriarch of politicians', 'a glorious and good man'… even 'a God in the midst of men'."

"Yes, well, those newspaper men are prone to exaggeration."

She continued reading, rapping his hand gently as he reached for another strawberry. "They quote your words here somewhere… Here we are. *'The great men thought to destroy me… but this, instead of weakening me, strengthened me, aroused me to new life and vigour.'*"

"Don't ever remember saying that," he commented. "Vigour is hardly a word I would have used to define myself at three score and ten. But I wasn't in London long: I promised I'd return after two months. I just wanted to be here, Anne. Back home. Now, how may I assist with this jam?"

***

Later, before starting to write of her father's return, she sat organising the journals and newspapers from autumn 1856. Around her, the sweet smell of boiled fruit. She feared she had used too much sugar, not enough lemon. Too late now.

Her thoughts wandered again to a possible title for her father's story. A sudden summer thunderstorm had given her an idea, but she needed to find something first. An hour passed. She was getting cross now, chewing her lip furiously, loose hair hanging in her eyes and her face red. She had last seen the document in the autumn when she was writing about her father's early encounters with Newport authority.

She found John watching the rain, strawberry stains still on his whiskers, a book open, face downwards, across his lap. He had been struggling to read again from that old tome about Spiritualism.

"I need your help," she blurted out. "I think you may have put something back in your trunk which I must check."

He looked up.

"It's that letter to Prothero you had published in 1821," she continued. "Sam Etheridge printed it for you, as I recall."

John took some time finding the thin yellow pamphlet, and handed it shakily to her. "What's brought this on?" he asked.

She flicked through the pamphlet to the last page, and sighed. "Yes! I knew I had read it somewhere. This is perfect."

She saw his puzzled expression and explained. "I've been thinking about titles again. We can't just call the book *John Frost – a life* as you suggest. That just sounds too... well, too *ordinary*. I thought about *A Thread that Binds*, thinking about your leather wristlet, but then I wondered if a potential reader would think the book was about embroidery."

He laughed then.

"I was leaning towards *An Unjust Punishment*," Anne went on, "but that sounds far too... well, too Russian. Then I realised: so many times in your story a storm serves as precursor to a major event."

He was intrigued now. "But what has that to do with Prothero and the letter?" he asked.

"Here," she replied, handing him the pamphlet, still open at the last page. "It's in the postscript written by Sam Etheridge."

John's friend had added, half a century before:

"Is there not
Some hidden thunder in the stores of heaven
Red with uncommon wrath, to blast the men
Who owe their greatness to their neighbours ruin?"

"We have a title, Father." She smiled. "Your book will be called *Some Hidden Thunder*."

STAPLETON, BRISTOL
Late July 1856

Mary had waited at the window all morning. She had swallowed her anger at his delay in London, and just wanted to see him again. Catharine's arrival had somehow filled the house with a new energy and light, her stories taking Anne and her mother out of their quiet domesticity to other worlds they would never know, but it was John she longed for, her wandering hero back in Ithaca.

She had carried an emptiness, familiar like a scar, for so many years. Now one last piece was needed to complete this happy reunion... the cornerstone of her life would be back where he belonged, and she would find peace.

When the carriage from Temple Meads station drew up outside, she could barely breathe. An old man in a velvet coat, with hair completely white, but of a proud and upright demeanour, stepped down and turned to face the house he had never seen but which he would now call home. He walked towards the door which flew open, and she was there, in his arms, his Mary, his love. No words were needed, just familiar kisses, the curls of her hair on his cheek, the warmth of her body, a binding love beyond time and place. Home.

Anne waited inside, holding back a little, shy.

"My child," he said, choking on tears. "I cannot put into words what I feel... I have missed you both so much..."

She stiffened as he embraced her, looking over his shoulder at Catharine, watching them with her perfect smile. "I am glad you are back, Father," Anne said, and went to put the kettle on.

Mary sat next to him on the settle, her hand caressing the frayed and faded leather thread still around his wrist. She noticed the veins now visible there, the knots on his fingers. He noticed her grey hair, lined cheeks and sunken eyes. She did not look well. But it mattered little as they talked – long after the sisters had gone to bed, long after the last pale rays of a July evening had melted to darkness. And about what? Not the politics that had parted them, nor the distances which had separated them, but about that which had always bound them: their children.

He told her about William, Emily and Grace, and they spoke softly again of Agnes. He told her of John making a new life in Pittsburgh. They cried together remembering Henry Hunt, and James. She had news too of Ellen, already on her way to join William. And of Sarah, widowed the year before. Working as a governess, she had met someone and was in love again.

"But she fears you will not approve," Mary added.

"Why ever not? Who has caught her eye this time?"

"Giuseppe is a marquis, John, a Sicilian nobleman. He holds high office. When they marry she will live in Italy, and be a marchioness."

John's first instinct was to laugh. "That will impress Prothero and Phillips! A Chartist daughter with a grand title, eh?"

"Prothero is dead," she informed him. "And Phillips was called to the Bar in London some years ago. He is a QC now." It was the first of such exchanges. In seventeen years, there had been many deaths, many departures.

"Well," he said. "It will matter little what I think of her new husband. She is old enough to make her own mistakes, and I have been an absent father for too many years to expect any deference now. I know that. But I shall not attend the wedding."

"We were unlikely to be invited anyway, John," she replied quietly. She paused, lowered her eyes and whispered, "Shall we to bed?"

They undressed as if on their first night as newlyweds, without a lamp, an awkward silence broken only by the rustling of clothing and a clock ticking in the corner.

"Dewch yma, cariad," he said, holding out his arms.

She was trembling, silent tears on her cheeks. They lay on the bed together, ageing flesh shrouded by the gentle darkness, face to face in the shadows, breath from each warmly caressing the other, every tentative touch exploring the still familiar flesh, a reminder of what they had missed for so long. Then he kissed her with a passion he long ago thought he had lost, recognising in her response the Mary he had made his own amongst the bluebells of Bettws Woods.

***

It was not easy at first, this readjustment. He felt himself a guest visiting someone else's house. Home centres around the small things, the uncharted minutiae of daily routines. But John no longer knew where things were kept, had to learn which doors rattled in the wind unless wedged, how best to coax the fire, how to share a bed. It was like speaking in a language he had not used for a long time.

And as the days passed, he could see Mary was not in good health, which troubled him. She took to her bed often, leaving the housekeeping to Anne. His wife's cough was persistent and she had such headaches she needed the blinds drawn in her room all day, even in the heat of summer. She had planned to be with him in Newport on 11th August for the procession marking his return, but on the day itself, he found her half dressed on the edge of the bed crying. "I can't, John. My head aches so, and my sight is blurred. Perhaps Catharine can go with you? Anne will take care of me."

A thousand or more welcomed John back to his hometown, their cheers heard across the docks as he stepped off the Bristol packet. Followers removed the horses from his carriage, every inch of which was decorated with summer flowers, and pulled him manually through the town. Outside the Westgate they cheered for a full two minutes. He waved and smiled, played his part as the prodigal son, but the cobbles of that square would for ever hold for him the image of a boy dying in a borrowed greatcoat.

From a window of a hotel in Llanarth Street, he addressed them.

"My friends," he began, and they fell silent. He was an old man now, and his voice was weaker. "Your welcome is humbling and I thank you all. The years have taken me to strange places with unfamiliar customs, as you know, but rest assured: he who stands before you today is unchanged. My opinions are identical to, if not stronger than those I held seventeen years ago. I swear before you today that, for as long as I am able, I shall work for a radical reform of Parliament... for in truth, my friends, who could serve us any worse than those we currently have?!"

They laughed and cheered, and he went on: "Few men have seen as much as I, few who are still alive at least, and I believe I have been allowed back to show the good people of this land what sort of rulers they have. The horrors of Van Diemen's Land are well known now, and I thank the Lord no more will be sent to that hell on earth. But though the stories from there may seem far away from your lives, my friends, injustice and cruelty have no nationality. They destroy any man's better judgment, leading him to immediate gratification and a brutality of his own. I saw it in that penal colony, but it happens everywhere. Why does a man commit a crime? From poverty. Why is he poor? From bad governance."

They were listening now, intent, respectful. "Tyranny brings a spiritual unmanning wherever it lurks. And it lurks in the corridors of Westminster too. Fairness must start with a free vote for every man, a lasting political power for the masses." They cheered again. It had been many years since he had felt this level of command. "My desire now is to redress the evils of the convict system, yes, and continue to campaign for universal franchise, but more locally,

I shall seek an end to the injustice of land distribution and power here in Newport."

He was their saviour now.

Like before.

***

Anne was ironing a few days later, her mother sitting wrapped in a blanket despite the August heat, when Catharine burst in carrying a copy of the *Manchester Guardian*. She had been taking a dish of home-made cawl to their neighbour, still recovering from the birth of baby Joseph, a sturdy boy with fine lungs. The baby's father had returned from town with the paper.

"You must see this, Father!" She was breathless, clearly angry. "They have vilified you! The article tells of our reception in Newport. It includes what you said to the crowd there, but it accuses you of ingratitude to a government which has pardoned you and granted your return home."

Mary pulled the blanket closer to her and shook her head. "Could you not refrain from such talk, at least for a while, John?"

His reply did not surprise her. She had always known he would never change.

"It would be a war against my very soul to do so, Mary. You know that."

Catharine threw down the paper in disgust, little realising that the inclusion of her name in that article would shape her destiny in a manner she least expected.

***

By mid-September, John was in London. It was his formal welcome home, and tens of thousands lined the route, applauding and cheering all the way. There were bands and Chartist banners from London Bridge to Finsbury Square. Outside St Paul's they cheered, on the Strand, in Trafalgar Square. In Soho, a banner read *"Es lebe die allgemeine soziale demokratische Republik"* and someone told John that Karl Marx was in the crowd.

It was a hero's return, leading to yet another hostile newspaper report, this time by *The Times*, though it grudgingly admitted how John himself displayed nothing more than a modest and prepossessing appearance for all the accolades and hero worship.

At Primrose Hill, Ernest Jones addressed the crowd, effusive in his praise of the returning Chartist leader. Recently released from prison himself, Jones began by reading from his poem written there:

"I am no less free

Than the serf and the slave who in misery dwell...

For England's a prison fresh modelled from hell."

The crowd roared approval, quietening again when he raised a hand to speak further: "We welcome home today a man who has sacrificed much for our cause. Seventeen years in exile, my friends. Seventeen. His head may now be grey with age, but it has never once bowed to expediency or power. In John Frost we have noble evidence of the Chartist faith, endurance and courage. In the man before us today is the omen of Chartist triumph."

John responded by urging those present to "Stay determined, prudent but fearless." He advised that they "give up no principle, and remain satisfied with nothing less than what is due".

He travelled back to Stapleton a contented man – it seemed that Chartism still inspired in its ideals. There were men, younger than he, willing to carry on the struggle. It may not be in his lifetime, but enfranchisement would come, he felt sure of it. And because his voice was still heard, because people still wanted to listen, he would continue to lecture, would draw on his convict experiences and expose the evil beneath the mask of government.

His time away would not have been in vain.

He longed to tell Mary about the warmth of his reception, but stopped in his tracks at the kitchen door. Sitting on the settle, opposite Catharine, was none other than the Reverend Peter Sinclair.

STAPLETON, BRISTOL
1877

"I remember that time vividly." Anne was filling her inkwell after recording the details of the public reception in London. "You know how Catharine is, father: she had been centre stage since her return, always with a new tale to tell us from her travels, always with an excuse when there were chores to do! Mother seemed besotted. 'Come sit with me and tell me of New York,' she would say while I was left to peel potatoes or wash the steps." She tried not to sound bitter. Stirred her ink.

"When I answered the door on that September day, I was surprised to see a man in clerical dress. We rarely had such visits. He looked nervous, I remember, but he had kind eyes."

"He asked if Miss Frost was at home." Anne laughed. "Silly me. I said, 'I'm Miss Frost'. I'd completely forgotten about Catharine!" She took a large summer apple from the bowl, wiped it on her apron, and continued to describe the visit: "They sat in the kitchen facing each other...I knew there was something odd, an awkwardness if you like. Couldn't quite put my finger on it." She took another bite, munched loudly. "She'd not said a thing about this fellow, not even to Mother."

John finished reading what she had just written about London, and said, "He was a good friend, was Ernest... but I don't think Karl Marx was there, you know, Anne. Never did." He changed focus and said, "I always liked Peter, but we thought he was in Africa."

"Seems he had been, but was back serving in a diocese in Liverpool. He had read that article in the *Manchester Guardian*, and if I remember correctly, he discovered your address from a Chartist supporter in his congregation."

John remembered then, seeing Catharine and her visitor in his kitchen when he returned from London. Catharine's evident embarrassment, but something else too.

She'd appeared pleased to see Peter again, and John had watched her walk with him to the front gate, where they lingered long, heads close.

"He wrote often after that," Anne said, with just a hint of longing. "And they met again, of course, when she went with you to Liverpool for your lecture there."

"Oh yes, I had forgotten about that. One of several in the north," he recalled. "The halls were packed. Thousands came, Anne… folk were even turned away. The pamphlets were all sold, every time." He smiled at the memory. "My old friend Prowting Roberts took the chair in Manchester, and together we relaunched that letter to the American people as a *Letter to the people of Great Britain*. We sent one to every member of Parliament, you know!"

He was still proud of it all, she could tell.

"You were away for months," Anne admonished, unimpressed, her tone harsh. "Mother felt she had lost you again."

John bowed his head then, and she knew he understood, still carried the guilt.

"Then Catharine made her announcement," Anne continued. "…It nearly broke Mother's heart."

Privately, Anne always believed it had.

STAPLETON, BRISTOL
December 1856

His lectures paid handsomely, and John was determined they would spare no expense in celebrating their first Christmas together in many years. He bought a tree and watched with joy as Mary decorated it with her clever homemade decorations. The mantelpiece above the kitchen range was garnered with greens, woven through with red ribbon. Mistletoe hung enticingly above the door. He bought a wooden rocking horse for the neighbours' baby Joe, whose parents had been so kind to Mary and his mother whilst he was away.

Three days before, Catharine and Anne worked together, albeit with some friction, to prepare the suet, breadcrumbs, raisins and spices for the pudding, and the glorious scent of cinnamon consumed their home all day. Carol singers called, and they joined the singing. Their house was all laughter, wassail and warmth.

He had bought each daughter a small trinket box, and was hiding the gifts beneath some nuts in festive stockings by the hearth late that evening when Mary approached behind him, silently in the dark.

"It reminds me of the night when James…" She did not finish.

He turned and held her close. "He is always in our hearts, cariad, and therefore is ever with us," he whispered. "As is Henry Hunt." He had still not told her about the séance.

In London for a lecture, he had purchased a brooch for Mary, and as soon as she had fallen asleep that night, he placed it in its red leather box on the bedside table. An exquisite Limoges ceramic, its surround of pearl and gold, with hand-painted bluebells. When she woke, its beauty made her weep. He took her face in both hands, kissed her tears and whispered, "Nadolig Llawen," into her grey curls.

They went to church and placed some winter blooms on the graves of Henry Hunt and John's mother, then celebrated by the fire with mulled wine.

"Mr Dickens would be proud!" Catharine declared. "No one could accuse you of being Mr Scrooge, Father," she laughed.

Their table had barely a spare inch: after turtle soup, there was stuffed goose, rib of beef, Yorkshire pudding, chestnut stuffing… and then that pudding. Mary had supervised the preparations, guiding Anne, and sometimes Catharine, at every stage, determined to make this day special. There had been too many Christmases apart.

After lunch, they were playing checkers, listening to Catharine as she played the piano, when there was a knock at the door. They heard Anne say, "Merry Christmas! What a surprise! Catharine… there is a visitor for you!"

The music stopped and then the two women entered the kitchen, followed by Peter.

"A glass of Christmas punch, sir?" John was in an excellent mood, the day had gone well, and Mary had some colour. "I'm surprised you have time on this day of all days to visit."

"I've been helping in a Bristol parish," their visitor explained. "The vicar there is indisposed, and I jumped at a chance to be nearer.…" He glanced at Catharine, blushed. "I have a few hours before evensong."

Catharine exchanged a glance with him, which Anne saw. Her sister was planning something. She had seen all this before. "Shall we tell them now, Peter? It seems folly to wait."

"If you wish, my love"

My love. So that was it.

Catharine took a deep breath, held Peter's hand and blurted, "Peter has asked me to marry him, and I have agreed."

There was a minute's silence, which John broke. "But that is excellent news! It has taken a long time, lass, but you have come to your senses at last! Peter, I am delighted." And he took the man's hands in his own. Mary embraced him and Anne held out her hand, a forced smile on her lips.

"There is more news," Catharine had not finished. She was trying to sound excited. "Peter has accepted a post back in Hobart. They need teachers there too, it seems, and I shall offer my services just as soon as we are settled."

Silence. Disbelief. Disappointment.

"You are going back?" John could not believe what he had just heard. "Back there?"

Mary sat in silence, watching the logs crackle in the grate, masking her tears.

Anne went to make some tea. Catharine had done it again, she thought, her sister's selfishness crushing any sense of family duty, as if everyone else lived in the footnotes to her own narrative. She had even managed to ruin Christmas.

Anne had no need of newspapers, pamphlets or journals to recall this next part of her father's life. It was all too vivid still, too painful, the last twenty years gone in a heartbeat. Catharine had breezed around after delivering her unexpected Christmas "gift", busying herself with arrangements for her departure, planned for early February. There was no time for a wedding before they left: it would happen sometime once they were settled.

She had seemed totally unaware of her mother's failing health and profound, consuming sadness, and it had made Anne angry. Her father had been invited to lecture again in London and Birmingham, offers accepted a little too readily, Anne thought. Alone again, she had tried her best to nurse her mother, cajoling her with soups or soft egg dishes, but Mary was fading, slipping out of their lives. Looking back down the years, she asked herself: had she been the only one to see the truth? The only one not blinded by other interests?

Then, just weeks after Catharine's announcement, a letter had arrived from Pittsburgh. Her brother John was dead. All her brothers, now dead. All her sisters might as well have been.

She remembered her father's bent body racked by silent sobs, Catharine's arms around him. It was Anne who had been left to tell her mother. She recalled the slow walk upstairs to where her mother lay staring at the ceiling, a single tear running down her cheek, as if she had known even before the permanence of the words, even before the crushing sadness destroyed her. There would not even be the ritual comfort of a funeral.

Anne remembered now those grey January days of ice and fog, the house cold and bathed constantly in sorrow. Catharine finding the least excuse to absent herself, her father preferring the company of his Chartist friends. He had also found a new distraction, of which Anne had disapproved. A medium in Bristol promised to unite grieving relatives with their dead and, seeking to recreate what had happened in New York, her father had found some comfort there, ignoring Anne's gentle suggestions that there was someone still living who needed him more…

"Are you going to write about John, and about… about…" Her father interrupted her memories. "This would be a chapter best left unwritten perhaps."

"No, I must," she replied. "Of course I must. But those first few months of 1857 held such sadness for us, Father. I need some time is all. It is difficult to find the words, difficult to revisit such pain; writing about it cannot be rushed."

John nodded. He was just not sure how much time he had left.

STAPLETON, BRISTOL
March 1857

On the morning of Catharine's departure, Mary insisted on dressing and coming down to breakfast with her husband and two daughters. They made small talk about train times to London, about the ship's route, about the weather, all the time skirting the rawness of parting, so familiar by now to John. He watched his wife across the table, her eyes fixed lovingly on Catharine, as if Mary needed to etch indelibly every last detail of her daughter's face. When the moment came, she held Catharine's hands in hers so determinedly John had to gently prize her away. Catharine waved once from the carriage which would take her to the station, then was gone, leaving her father a few souvenirs in a box for safekeeping, and a rather fine ink pot for her sister.

Anne's one thought was: why ever did she bother coming back?

Mary stayed in her bed most days after that, eating little, showing no interest when Anne brought up the paper or shared some titbit of gossip from the market. Her mother's cough had become a chesty rattle, and Anne had noticed specks of blood on the lace handkerchiefs she laundered daily. Mary's face was white now, her eyes misty and her skin transparent, her breath strangely sweet.

John tried. He walked up to the ancient Kingswood forest above the village and found the first of the year's bluebells for her room. Mary smiled weakly, and whispered, "Read to me, John." She indicated an old green book at her bedside. The Tennyson. He lay alongside her on the bed, fully dressed, on top of the quilt she had crafted for them so many years before, the poet's words familiar as old friends:

"All times I have enjoyed
Greatly, have suffered greatly. Both with those

That loved me, and alone; on shore, and when
Through scudding drifts the rainy Hyades
Vexed the dim sea."

She was whispering the words as he read, knew the tale of her hero by heart.

"I have something to ask of you, my love," he said suddenly, surprised by his own words. "I have not been the husband you hoped for, Mary, nor the one you deserved... I..." And he traced the outline of her face with his fingers. "Can you ever forgive me?"

She reached out her skeletal fingers to take his hand and, struggling to speak, whispered, "What is there to forgive? I consider myself fortunate to have known great love in my life, John. I want you to remember that, when I am gone."

He chided her then, told her not to speak so. "It is I who have been blessed, my love. No man could have asked for such a loyal and loving wife. I know the burden my absence caused you. I know how lonely you must have been. But the knowledge that you were there, somewhere on the other side of the world, gave me a reason to stay strong..."

"...and not to yield." She smiled. "Just like the poem."

The following day, a letter arrived from Henry Vincent inviting John to a rally in London.

"I shan't go," he told Anne over his porridge. "Your mother needs me here."

"Of course you should go, Father," his daughter replied. "Mother will be fine with me. I can manage without you for a day or two." She was preparing Mary's breakfast tray. "I have coped on my own before."

For many years in fact, she thought.

***

And so he went, unable to admit to himself that he was more comfortable away from the cloying reality of Mary's sickbed. John had not seen Henry since his return, and was struck by the change in the man's appearance. Gone were the dashing good looks and dark curls of youth. He seemed much older than his forty years or so, was balding and had an unkempt white beard. The two men greeted each other warmly.

"This is a moment I have long hoped for," Henry said. "Your return last year was rightly lauded across the land, and your presence at the rally tomorrow will mean so much."

"I can stay but a day or two, my friend. Mary is not at all well."

They raised a glass together at a small tavern, in memory of heady days long past and the youthful vision they once shared. John told his friend about convict life, and of the disillusioned Chartist exiles he had met in America. Henry had tales of a lecture he gave at the Great Exhibition, and of his own disappointments in failing to be elected to Parliament on no fewer than six occasions. "Life has taken us to strange corners," he said.

They continued to drink in silence for a while, then Henry asked, "Do you think it was worth the sacrifice, John? Or were we just foolish young men?"

"I'd say yes to both. We sought a better world and challenged injustice, which is never wrong. But the older I get the more I wonder about the wisdom of a rebellion such as we saw at Newport. Revolutions do not always bear the results hoped for. I saw that in America, and it is as true in France."

Henry was nodding. "Sometimes change needs small steps to be effective, and a wisdom only accrued across time, but that was something we were far too impatient to consider in '39, eh?" He laughed, putting a brotherly arm around his old friend, and they made their unsteady way to Henry's home where John would stay the night

***

John knew something had changed the moment he opened his front door. The air felt different. His axis had shifted.

"Anne!" he called, but he knew. He ran up the stairs, and saw beyond the drooping bluebells that the curtains were drawn in his bedroom. Anne was in black, sitting at her mother's bedside in the gloom, but Mary was not in their world now.

He spent the night lying beside her, holding her close for one final time.

***

Anne took great care preparing her mother for burial, insisting she alone would carry out this final act. She spent quiet time bathing the cold face and hands, then pinning Mary's new bluebell brooch to the lace collar of her favourite dress, a blue silk decorated with velvet scalloped edging, tying carefully the fine laces of her mother's best boots. One last kiss, her duty fulfilled.

They buried her in Holy Trinity, Horfield alongside Henry Hunt. A harsh March wind kept chiding the cemetery's daffodils to bow their heads in reverence as the bluebells were doing, those Mary had planted for her son.

After the organist was paid and the neighbours had gone, after the teacups were cleared away, when the busy-ness of death was done, John allowed himself to cry, placing one gnarled and trembling hand around the other wrist, where he still wore her leather thread. He picked up her tortoiseshell hairbrush and removed the finest of grey hairs, now all that remained. "Mary, my Mary..." he sighed, and a breeze moved the closed curtain for the briefest of moments. "...How will I live without my lodestone?" He was sitting on their empty bed, holding her favourite shawl to his face, burying his sorrow in her scent, breathing in what remained of her self. "Who will steer my course now? Who will call me home?" He lowered his head slowly onto the pillow and wept.

Anne stood on the landing, her back pressed against the wall, running her fingers back and forth across the cold, floral wallpaper her mother had so loved, as if she might still connect somehow. She was listening to his pain, her own grief a crippling, silent ache in her throat and chest, a vision of the future unfolding before her. Each of them needed the other now: there was no one else. Whatever the years ahead might bring, they would live out their lives together. And to their ordinary, humdrum daily rhythms she would do all in her power to bring a dignity and grace.

STAPLETON, BRISTOL
July 1877

It had taken Anne over a week to write about her mother's death. She had rewritten and rewritten the scene, knowing she would never perfectly capture that time. Eventually, she handed the pages to her father, who had read them in silence, simply nodding when he had finished.

"Diolch," he said softly, touched her shoulder briefly, and went to fetch his pipe.

"Everything changed after that," she said. "At least that's how I see it. There are no more journals after '57. There were no more lectures."

"I had nothing left to say," he replied. "My words had been the root of all her pain, after all, selfish outpourings fuelled by my stupid pride... even after I came home. Fame is addictive, Anne, and makes you feel alive, then silently traps you, like opium, till there is no way out. Dear God, it shames me now to admit how good it felt to be important again, to see how easily I could still draw a crowd. But what really mattered, that deep, unquestioning love so rare and so precious in life, was here all the time, waiting patiently for me, and I let it slip away..."

Minutes passed before she spoke again. "I have a few of your newspaper articles from later years, Father, one or two letters, but nothing much," she admitted. "It is almost as if your life ended there, twenty years ago."

"And I was content for it to be so, lass. The interest in convict life was waning anyway, and it would only have been a matter of time before people stopped coming to hear me speak. Besides, I found it tiresome travelling so much. I did not enjoy the exigencies of those modern trains."

"But you have had your... faith." She hesitated to call it that.

John looked out of the window and said, "Walk with me in the garden a while, will you, lass? I want to smell the summer flowers."

They sat in the arbour as a linnet sang, and he tried to explain. "I cannot accept this is all there is, that a man's life is finite. It comforts me to believe that the spirit endures, and can even offer us guidance as we stumble blindly along, seeking answers."

Anne remained unconvinced. She had heard all this before. "And over the years, have you spoken with... you know, Henry Hunt... John... Mother?"

John nodded, and she gasped.

"They are at peace," he reassured her, though she wondered if he was in reality referring to himself. "And I spoke once with Feargus O'Connor, who told me he had been at my lectures."

She thought that a very odd conversation to have had with someone from the hereafter, but said nothing. The whole charade had undoubtedly helped her father deal with his grief twenty years ago, and regularly across the decades since. Who was she to question the value of that?

***

Their daily lives had been sculpted and smoothed into familiar routines. Until his eyes were too weak, he would pass the hours reading and writing at his desk while Anne busied herself with the home. He watched Joe grow from a surly schoolboy to a gangly teenager into a cheerful young man who helped them often, and John mourned the years he had missed seeing his own sons grow to adulthood.

He made his will as he entered his tenth decade, tidying up his life, leaving all to his surviving daughters. Seasons came and went, carrying memories of other shores and other times. Birthdays came and went... 75, 80, 85, 90... death was toying with him, taking others he knew well, far younger than he. He saw fewer and fewer people until a point came when he rarely left the house.

All that remained was an overwhelming desire to record his life before the end. Too late for him to tackle that now, he told himself; he struggled to write legibly even in broad daylight. Catharine might have done it, he thought, but she would not return now. She never did marry Peter, and had offered no explanation, just the news that he had left Hobart but that she was staying, living near William. Her letters grew shorter, and arrived with decreasing frequency until now he barely heard from her.

Then last year he had found Anne scribbling. Anne, his companion and solace through the long years of decline, determined at the end to tell his tale. Relentlessly, she had persevered, squirrelling away the details, digging determinedly at long-buried memories, so that the completed manuscript was bound now and ready for George Payne to collect. This was the second daughter who had travelled with him across oceans and continents, laughing and crying along the way, but there was a difference: Anne's journey had been completely selfless, and he was humbled by her efforts. *Some Hidden Thunder* was her gift of love to him. He could not have asked for more.

STAPLETON, BRISTOL
Late July – August 1877

A glorious morning. Birdsong and sunlight. Anne had been in the garden and had her arms full of roses. A sudden summer storm the night before had broken their beauty, and there were petals strewn across the path as if waiting for a bride. She and John had listened to the thunder in the distance somewhere over Bristol docks until dusk had descended on the damp streets of Stapleton.

"I have saved some that the storm missed..." she began, then stopped.

He was slumped sideways in the high-backed wooden armchair with the curved arms, facing an empty fireplace. From behind, she could see his spectacles were on the floor, just below his wrist, which dangled loosely down towards them, the leather thread almost slipping over his fingers.

"Father, you have dropped your..." Then she knew.

Her father was at peace, his journey done.

In defiance of his failing sight till the end, he had beside him on the side table a battered copy of *The Rights of Man*. On his lap, the volume of Tennyson, open to Mary's favourite, its metre the heartbeat of their love.

Joe came to help her move John to his bed until the undertaker could call. She removed her father's shoes tenderly, and ran her fingers over the faint scars he still bore around the ankles. She brushed his hair and folded his hands across his chest. Only later, alone, burial arrangements in place, sitting in the dark silence, did she realise she had not yet cried.

The young apprentice undertaker, in shiny black shoes and a coat a size too big, which he had clearly inherited from someone much taller, had tried to remove a shabby, fragile leather thread wound around the dead man's wrist, but Anne stopped him in time.

"That brought him home," she scolded.

Puzzled, the young man just nodded. He was beginning to learn the strangeness of grief.

***

Before they nailed down the lid, Anne folded the Chartist flag carefully and laid it over her father's heart. By his side, she nestled the two books, and in his pockets the remainder of the lavender she had sewn into scraps of her mother's petticoat, a pharaoh's treasure for the afterlife. She kissed his cold forehead, knowing he was not there, but said the words anyway.

"Rest now, Father, your story has reached its end. Be at peace."

He had been clear in his will: he would lie with Mary, his odyssey complete. Joe came to Holy Trinity with his parents and sweetheart, one or two local people and a few Anne did not recognise, strangers from the Spiritualist meetings John frequented. They filled just two pews in the ancient church, a sad reminder of how few knew he was still alive, this once nationally revered hero of the working man.

"It was a life that merited more than this," she whispered to Joe as he led her to her seat. "He said it himself: few live their lives such as he."

Anne had asked George Payne to print the service sheets. She chose her father's photograph for the front, and smiled remembering how he had joked with the intense young man who came with his "magic box" to preserve her father's memory for all time. The image on the albumen paper had captured John's still plentiful white hair, his enigmatic smile, and eyes which had seen so much. Beneath the photograph she chose the last line of the

Tennyson: *To strive, to seek, to find, and not to yield.* Inside was the psalm Iolo had read to the lost souls of Impression Bay, her father's favourite. Then, after the hymns and readings, she had the printer include the words her father had written to her mother from the *Mandarin*, almost four decades before:

"The value of life depends on the use we can be to others: if we cannot use it for the good of family or society then it is hardly worth having."

***

The long days and weeks that followed were draped in silence. Anne could not bear the tedium of condolences, so saw no one except Joe, who called occasionally, bringing strawberries or fresh baked bread to tempt her back to life.

Behind the closed curtains of the grieving house, in the oppressive August heat, Anne tried to sort through John's possessions, knowing her father would want anything of use to be sent to the workhouse. But with each attempt she failed, returning to retrieve from the box this shirt, that pipe, those boots, whatever, because she could not bear to part with what little remained.

She found her father's Bible on his bedside table, all the time directing her gaze away from the bed where the mattress still bore his familiar profile like a footprint in sand, soon to be erased by the tide. Anne ran her finger down the family names her father had entered years ago in fine italic print inside its front cover. Trembling, she took her pen and recorded 27th July 1877, the last words of a story, the last filial duty.

There was sadness in every corner of the home, memories in every cup. If she closed her eyes, Anne could hear her grandmother calling from her bed, or her mother reading the latest letter from Van Diemen's Land, or Catharine at the piano, and clearest of all, John's familiar voice spinning the tapestry of his life as she struggled to give it shape.

It was all too much. After one particularly difficult day, she walked around the empty home, heavy with silences, and out into the garden. She sat in the arbour and for the briefest of moments, Anne could smell the familiar pipe smoke. With sudden clarity, she decided: she could no longer stay; it was time now to start a new story of her own. There were distant cousins in Dorset needing a companion housekeeper, and she would end her days there. She had fulfilled her pledge, and her book would soon be ready for strangers to share her father's story. Others could now judge if his had indeed been a life worth having.

Postscript

Anne died in Middlesex in 1909. In 1884, she published *A Plea for innocent people Convicted and Imprisoned* in which she claimed her father was the victim of a conspiracy to entrap him, that "he stood by men he taught to think, to consider rights, but never by him trained to fight".

Catharine returned from Australia in 1884, when records reveal her to have been in dispute with one of the solicitors who drafted John's will. She died in 1900.

John Frost lay in an unmarked grave in Horfield Cemetery until 1986, when its location was identified by a local historian, Richard Frame. He had searched the graveyard for hours to no avail before the vicar found a reference in an old book to a memorial for one Henry Hunt Frost. In the area referenced, they found a piece of a headstone almost buried, the surname on it eroded by the years, but bearing clearly the name Henry Hunt.

A new headstone was duly commissioned in Welsh slate and unveiled by Neil Kinnock, the then leader of the Labour party. It bears Frost's words:

"The outward mark of respect paid to men merely because they are rich and powerful... hath no communication with the heart."

Author's Notes

I have wanted to write this book for a long time. The idea took root when I found myself living in Monmouth Gaol, by then a private residence, but still with its portcullis and two original cell doors. Someone told me it had once held within its walls John Frost, about whom at that point, and to my shame, I knew little. But my interest grew, particularly when I realised many of his followers on that march to Newport came from the impoverished valley villages where my ancestors once lived. In 2000, whilst visiting Sydney library, I was granted access to documents Frost had signed, and, in requisite white gloves such as Anne wears in my story, I handled other memorabilia including a Chartist flag. I wondered at the time who might have brought it so far.

There are outstanding scholarly texts available on the rise and fall of Chartism, and on Frost's role therein. Of particular note are the works of David Williams and David D.V. Jones. Additionally, John Humphries has researched extensively the lives of Jack the Fifer and Zephaniah Williams. To all three I owe an immense debt. Opinions still differ as to why the Newport uprising ended so violently, or indeed why it took place at all, and I have tried to reflect the confusion. Undoubtedly, the cold Welsh rain did not help.

Robert Hughes compiled the definitive account of convict life, including the terrors of the sea journey and the savagery of those who controlled the convicts sent to Van Diemen's Land. Ray Boston offered details of exiled Chartists in America and his insights regarding their disaffection were invaluable.

Many characters who appear in the tale were real: I have endeavoured to treat them fairly, and apologise if I have inadvertently offended. But this is principally a work of fiction based on the available documentation, some of which may of course be inaccurate or biased. Anne calls memory a "fickle mistress", and she might just as well have been describing much that we call "history".

Some things we know are true: Frost did indeed spend his final decades in Stapleton with his spinster daughter, Anne, and did express a deep desire to write his memoirs. In my story she does that for him, and he gives her permission to add a little colour where his memory might fail him. I too have "added colour", taking liberties at times to create what I hope is a plausible reality.

In many ways, writing is at the heart of John's story: books shape his childhood, his own inflammatory publications lead to his clashes with the authorities over the years, his journals and letters provide source material for Anne. And there is her own writing, her confidence growing as she maps her father's journey, a labour of love culminating in the manuscript's publication.

Writing a story around the lives of real people demands humility and respect from an author. Frost suffered horribly in Van Diemen's Land, of that there is no doubt. But it puzzled me that a former draper and mayor, not used to heavy physical endeavours in his life, should survive what was a brutally hard labour and appear in relatively good health when a journalist from *Fraser's Magazine* visited him in Impression Bay. Hence my invention of Iolo, the gentle giant. A Welshman and Chartist sympathiser, he protects John as best he can during that time.

As I was getting to know John and his wife Mary, I kept thinking of Tennyson's stubborn hero Ulysses and his long-suffering wife, the poem always a favourite of mine. Lines kept coming to mind as I wrote, so I decided early in the tale to weave the verse through the text. I confess I have exercised a little creative liberty with dates: written in 1833, the poem was not published until 1842, after John had left Britain, so I offer my apologies to the purists. I rather suspect the poet would not mind. He mentions a Chartist flag in "Walking to the mail" (1842). The lines

"These two parties still divide the world
Of those that want, and those that have: and still
The same old sore breaks out from age to age
With much the same result."

could have come directly from one of John Frost's lectures. Imagine my delight, then, to discover by happenstance that Sir John Franklin, later of the *Terror* but in 1840 commander in Hobart, someone John would almost certainly have met, was in reality the uncle of Tennyson's wife!

That John Frost travelled with Catharine to San Francisco after being granted a conditional pardon is a fact, as is their delay in Callao. That a lecture tour was arranged by William Prowting Roberts is also true. That he was in New York a year later when his full pardon was granted is also factual. But there is no record, at least none I could find, of the route the two travellers took across what at that time was still a wild and lawless land. Transport was primitive; danger lurked everywhere. The railroad had yet to make an impact. Anne and I both needed to research John's possible route, albeit from different sources.

I considered it likely that he would have visited at least some of the Chartist exiles listed in Mr Boston's book, many of whom he would have known before 1839, and that he would have given the lectures in what were then new centres of mining or industry such as Kansas, St Louis and Pittsburgh. One of the Chartist exiles listed as living in New York at the time was a keen Spiritualist. It seemed possible that he was the source of Frost's interest during those final decades.

Writing does not happen in a void, and I am indebted to the support of many people, not least my husband. (The gun was entirely his idea.) Thanks also to my son for his encouragement, for the visit to Monmouth courthouse and holding cells, and for sharing his knowledge (and books) of American history. His lovely family made it easy to imagine William's.

I must also mention Dr Katherine Stansfield, whose enthusiastic online classes on the writing of historical fiction provided the necessary fuel when I was in danger of grinding to a halt. She will smile at the inclusion of a tantalus in my tale. Thanks also go to Linda and Ian, my first readers, for their encouragement and helpful comments.

My thanks go to all my friends for their unwavering interest in this project, and especially to the Willows group – you know who you are. Finally, my deepest gratitude to all at Rowanvale, and especially Ellie, Alice, Cat and Cody without whose extraordinary skills and exemplary assistance this book would most definitely not exist.

And finally there is John, the story's hero. I hope I have been faithful to the courageous spirit of a man driven by a passionate desire to change this world for the better. His own claim that "Few men have seen as much as I" is as true now as it was in the 19th century: to leave the Colonies at seventy after fifteen punitive years, then undertake a five-month sea journey to San Francisco before crossing America as far as New York took strength of character and remarkable fortitude. Flawed but fearless, a charismatic leader plagued by self-doubt, John Frost was willing to challenge tyrants and hypocrites whether they hid in Westminster, Newport or Port Arthur. His life story deserves to be told: today's world with its continuing litany of injustice would benefit from such heroic spirit.

I salute you, John: an ordinary man who lived a truly extraordinary life.

Bibliography

Though by no means an exhaustive list, I found the following books of enormous help, grateful for their meticulous scholarship:

- Ray Boston, *British Chartists in America*
- Alexander Cordell, *Requiem for a Patriot*
- Richard D. Heffner, *A Documentary History of the United States*
- Robert Hughes, *The Fatal Shore*
- John Humphries, *The Man from the Alamo*
- David J.V. Jones, *The Last Rising: The Newport Insurrection of 1839*
- Maldwyn A. Jones, *The Limits of Liberty: American History 1607–1992*
- Edward Rutherford, *New York*
- David Williams, *John Frost: A Study in Chartism*
- Howard Zinn, *A People's History of the United States*

Of particular interest online were:

- Sarah Richards, "Descendants of John Frost" (*eMagazine* 2019)
- E. Hope Varney, "An overland journey from San Francisco to New York 1865" (*Genealogy Trails*)

Author Profile

Brenda Despontin grew up in Wales, where she also spent most of her working life. For some years, she lived in the Old Gaol, Monmouth, now a private residence, and discovered that it had once housed as a condemned prisoner the Chartist leader John Frost. She began to research this radical leader and realised that those who marched to Newport with Frost in 1839 were from the valley villages where her ancestors had lived and worked. What followed was a determination to fulfil Frost's own wish to record his life, albeit as a piece of historical fiction with Frost's daughter Anne as the scribe.

Brenda lives on the Welsh coast with her husband and dog.

***

What Did You Think of
Some Hidden Thunder?

A big thank you for purchasing this book. It means a lot that you chose this book specifically from such a wide range on offer. I do hope you enjoyed it.

Book reviews are incredibly important for an author. All feedback helps them improve their writing for future projects and for developing this edition. If you are able to spare a few minutes to post a review on Amazon, that would be much appreciated.

Publisher Information

**rowanvale
books**

Rowanvale Books provides publishing services to independent authors, writers and poets all over the globe. We deliver a personal, honest and efficient service that allows authors to see their work published, while remaining in control of the process and retaining their creativity. By making publishing services available to authors in a cost-effective and ethical way, we at Rowanvale Books hope to ensure that the local, national and international community benefits from a steady stream of good quality literature.

For more information about us, our authors or our publications, please get in touch.

www.rowanvalebooks.com
info@rowanvalebooks.com

John Frost

www.ingramcontent.com/pod-product-compliance
Lightning Source LLC
Chambersburg PA
CBHW021133090426
42740CB00008B/775